ABCTE

Elementary Education/ Multiple Subject Exam Part 1 of 2

SECRETS

Study Guide

Your Key to Exam Success

ABCTE Test Review for the American Board for Certification of Teacher Excellence Exam

Dear Future Exam Success Story:

First of all, **THANK YOU** for purchasing Mometrix study materials!

Second, congratulations! You are one of the few determined test-takers who are committed to doing whatever it takes to excel on your exam. **You have come to the right place.** We developed these study materials with one goal in mind: to deliver you the information you need in a format that's concise and easy to use.

In addition to optimizing your guide for the content of the test, we've outlined our recommended steps for breaking down the preparation process into small, attainable goals so you can make sure you stay on track.

We've also analyzed the entire test-taking process, identifying the most common pitfalls and showing how you can overcome them and be ready for any curveball the test throws you.

Standardized testing is one of the biggest obstacles on your road to success, which only increases the importance of doing well in the high-pressure, high-stakes environment of test day. Your results on this test could have a significant impact on your future, and this guide provides the information and practical advice to help you achieve your full potential on test day.

Your success is our success

We would love to hear from you! If you would like to share the story of your exam success or if you have any questions or comments in regard to our products, please contact us at **800-673-8175** or **support@mometrix.com**.

Thanks again for your business and we wish you continued success!

Sincerely,
The Mometrix Test Preparation Team

Need more help? Check out our flashcards at: http://MometrixFlashcards.com/ABCTE

Written and edited by the Mometrix Exam Secrets Test Prep Team
Printed in the United States of America

TABLE OF CONTENTS

Introduction

Thank you for purchasing this resource! You have made the choice to prepare yourself for a test that could have a huge impact on your future, and this guide is designed to help you be fully ready for test day. Obviously, it's important to have a solid understanding of the test material, but you also need to be prepared for the unique environment and stressors of the test, so that you can perform to the best of your abilities.

For this purpose, the first section that appears in this guide is the **Secret Keys**. We've devoted countless hours to meticulously researching what works and what doesn't, and we've boiled down our findings to the five most impactful steps you can take to improve your performance on the test. We start at the beginning with study planning and move through the preparation process, all the way to the testing strategies that will help you get the most out of what you know when you're finally sitting in front of the test.

We recommend that you start preparing for your test as far in advance as possible. However, if you've bought this guide as a last-minute study resource and only have a few days before your test, we recommend that you skip over the first two Secret Keys since they address a long-term study plan.

If you struggle with **test anxiety**, we strongly encourage you to check out our recommendations for how you can overcome it. Test anxiety is a formidable foe, but it can be beaten, and we want to make sure you have the tools you need to defeat it.

Secret Key #1 – Plan Big, Study Small

There's a lot riding on your performance. If you want to ace this test, you're going to need to keep your skills sharp and the material fresh in your mind. You need a plan that lets you review everything you need to know while still fitting in your schedule. We'll break this strategy down into three categories.

Information Organization

Start with the information you already have: the official test outline. From this, you can make a complete list of all the concepts you need to cover before the test. Organize these concepts into groups that can be studied together, and create a list of any related vocabulary you need to learn so you can brush up on any difficult terms. You'll want to keep this vocabulary list handy once you actually start studying since you may need to add to it along the way.

Time Management

Once you have your set of study concepts, decide how to spread them out over the time you have left before the test. Break your study plan into small, clear goals so you have a manageable task for each day and know exactly what you're doing. Then just focus on one small step at a time. When you manage your time this way, you don't need to spend hours at a time studying. Studying a small block of content for a short period each day helps you retain information better and avoid stressing over how much you have left to do. You can relax knowing that you have a plan to cover everything in time. In order for this strategy to be effective though, you have to start studying early and stick to your schedule. Avoid the exhaustion and futility that comes from last-minute cramming!

Study Environment

The environment you study in has a big impact on your learning. Studying in a coffee shop, while probably more enjoyable, is not likely to be as fruitful as studying in a quiet room. It's important to keep distractions to a minimum. You're only planning to study for a short block of time, so make the most of it. Don't pause to check your phone or get up to find a snack. It's also important to **avoid multitasking**. Research has consistently shown that multitasking will make your studying dramatically less effective. Your study area should also be comfortable and well-lit so you don't have the distraction of straining your eyes or sitting on an uncomfortable chair.

The time of day you study is also important. You want to be rested and alert. Don't wait until just before bedtime. Study when you'll be most likely to comprehend and remember. Even better, if you know what time of day your test will be, set that time aside for study. That way your brain will be used to working on that subject at that specific time and you'll have a better chance of recalling information.

Finally, it can be helpful to team up with others who are studying for the same test. Your actual studying should be done in as isolated an environment as possible, but the work of organizing the information and setting up the study plan can be divided up. In between study sessions, you can discuss with your teammates the concepts that you're all studying and quiz each other on the details. Just be sure that your teammates are as serious about the test as you are. If you find that your study time is being replaced with social time, you might need to find a new team.

Secret Key #2 – Make Your Studying Count

You're devoting a lot of time and effort to preparing for this test, so you want to be absolutely certain it will pay off. This means doing more than just reading the content and hoping you can remember it on test day. It's important to make every minute of study count. There are two main areas you can focus on to make your studying count:

Retention

It doesn't matter how much time you study if you can't remember the material. You need to make sure you are retaining the concepts. To check your retention of the information you're learning, try recalling it at later times with minimal prompting. Try carrying around flashcards and glance at one or two from time to time or ask a friend who's also studying for the test to quiz you.

To enhance your retention, look for ways to put the information into practice so that you can apply it rather than simply recalling it. If you're using the information in practical ways, it will be much easier to remember. Similarly, it helps to solidify a concept in your mind if you're not only reading it to yourself but also explaining it to someone else. Ask a friend to let you teach them about a concept you're a little shaky on (or speak aloud to an imaginary audience if necessary). As you try to summarize, define, give examples, and answer your friend's questions, you'll understand the concepts better and they will stay with you longer. Finally, step back for a big picture view and ask yourself how each piece of information fits with the whole subject. When you link the different concepts together and see them working together as a whole, it's easier to remember the individual components.

Finally, practice showing your work on any multi-step problems, even if you're just studying. Writing out each step you take to solve a problem will help solidify the process in your mind, and you'll be more likely to remember it during the test.

Modality

Modality simply refers to the means or method by which you study. Choosing a study modality that fits your own individual learning style is crucial. No two people learn best in exactly the same way, so it's important to know your strengths and use them to your advantage.

For example, if you learn best by visualization, focus on visualizing a concept in your mind and draw an image or a diagram. Try color-coding your notes, illustrating them, or creating symbols that will trigger your mind to recall a learned concept. If you learn best by hearing or discussing information, find a study partner who learns the same way or read aloud to yourself. Think about how to put the information in your own words. Imagine that you are giving a lecture on the topic and record yourself so you can listen to it later.

For any learning style, flashcards can be helpful. Organize the information so you can take advantage of spare moments to review. Underline key words or phrases. Use different colors for different categories. Mnemonic devices (such as creating a short list in which every item starts with the same letter) can also help with retention. Find what works best for you and use it to store the information in your mind most effectively and easily.

Secret Key #3 – Practice the Right Way

Your success on test day depends not only on how many hours you put into preparing, but also on whether you prepared the right way. It's good to check along the way to see if your studying is paying off. One of the most effective ways to do this is by taking practice tests to evaluate your progress. Practice tests are useful because they show exactly where you need to improve. Every time you take a practice test, pay special attention to these three groups of questions:

- The questions you got wrong
- The questions you had to guess on, even if you guessed right
- The questions you found difficult or slow to work through

This will show you exactly what your weak areas are, and where you need to devote more study time. Ask yourself why each of these questions gave you trouble. Was it because you didn't understand the material? Was it because you didn't remember the vocabulary? Do you need more repetitions on this type of question to build speed and confidence? Dig into those questions and figure out how you can strengthen your weak areas as you go back to review the material.

Additionally, many practice tests have a section explaining the answer choices. It can be tempting to read the explanation and think that you now have a good understanding of the concept. However, an explanation likely only covers part of the question's broader context. Even if the explanation makes sense, **go back and investigate** every concept related to the question until you're positive you have a thorough understanding.

As you go along, keep in mind that the practice test is just that: practice. Memorizing these questions and answers will not be very helpful on the actual test because it is unlikely to have any of the same exact questions. If you only know the right answers to the sample questions, you won't be prepared for the real thing. **Study the concepts** until you understand them fully, and then you'll be able to answer any question that shows up on the test.

It's important to wait on the practice tests until you're ready. If you take a test on your first day of study, you may be overwhelmed by the amount of material covered and how much you need to learn. Work up to it gradually.

On test day, you'll need to be prepared for answering questions, managing your time, and using the test-taking strategies you've learned. It's a lot to balance, like a mental marathon that will have a big impact on your future. Like training for a marathon, you'll need to start slowly and work your way up. When test day arrives, you'll be ready.

Start with the strategies you've read in the first two Secret Keys—plan your course and study in the way that works best for you. If you have time, consider using multiple study resources to get different approaches to the same concepts. It can be helpful to see difficult concepts from more than one angle. Then find a good source for practice tests. Many times, the test website will suggest potential study resources or provide sample tests.

Practice Test Strategy

When you're ready to start taking practice tests, follow this strategy:

Untimed and Open-Book Practice

Take the first test with no time constraints and with your notes and study guide handy. Take your time and focus on applying the strategies you've learned.

Timed and Open-Book Practice

Take the second practice test open-book as well, but set a timer and practice pacing yourself to finish in time.

Timed and Closed-Book Practice

Take any other practice tests as if it were test day. Set a timer and put away your study materials. Sit at a table or desk in a quiet room, imagine yourself at the testing center, and answer questions as quickly and accurately as possible.

Keep repeating timed and closed-book tests on a regular basis until you run out of practice tests or it's time for the actual test. Your mind will be ready for the schedule and stress of test day, and you'll be able to focus on recalling the material you've learned.

Secret Key #4 – Pace Yourself

Once you're fully prepared for the material on the test, your biggest challenge on test day will be managing your time. Just knowing that the clock is ticking can make you panic even if you have plenty of time left. Work on pacing yourself so you can build confidence against the time constraints of the exam. Pacing is a difficult skill to master, especially in a high-pressure environment, so **practice is vital**.

Set time expectations for your pace based on how much time is available. For example, if a section has 60 questions and the time limit is 30 minutes, you know you have to average 30 seconds or less per question in order to answer them all. Although 30 seconds is the hard limit, set 25 seconds per question as your goal, so you reserve extra time to spend on harder questions. When you budget extra time for the harder questions, you no longer have any reason to stress when those questions take longer to answer.

Don't let this time expectation distract you from working through the test at a calm, steady pace, but keep it in mind so you don't spend too much time on any one question. Recognize that taking extra time on one question you don't understand may keep you from answering two that you do understand later in the test. If your time limit for a question is up and you're still not sure of the answer, mark it and move on, and come back to it later if the time and the test format allow. If the testing format doesn't allow you to return to earlier questions, just make an educated guess; then put it out of your mind and move on.

On the easier questions, be careful not to rush. It may seem wise to hurry through them so you have more time for the challenging ones, but it's not worth missing one if you know the concept and just didn't take the time to read the question fully. Work efficiently but make sure you understand the question and have looked at all of the answer choices, since more than one may seem right at first.

Even if you're paying attention to the time, you may find yourself a little behind at some point. You should speed up to get back on track, but do so wisely. Don't panic; just take a few seconds less on each question until you're caught up. Don't guess without thinking, but do look through the answer choices and eliminate any you know are wrong. If you can get down to two choices, it is often worthwhile to guess from those. Once you've chosen an answer, move on and don't dwell on any that you skipped or had to hurry through. If a question was taking too long, chances are it was one of the harder ones, so you weren't as likely to get it right anyway.

On the other hand, if you find yourself getting ahead of schedule, it may be beneficial to slow down a little. The more quickly you work, the more likely you are to make a careless mistake that will affect your score. You've budgeted time for each question, so don't be afraid to spend that time. Practice an efficient but careful pace to get the most out of the time you have.

Secret Key #5 – Have a Plan for Guessing

When you're taking the test, you may find yourself stuck on a question. Some of the answer choices seem better than others, but you don't see the one answer choice that is obviously correct. What do you do?

The scenario described above is very common, yet most test takers have not effectively prepared for it. Developing and practicing a plan for guessing may be one of the single most effective uses of your time as you get ready for the exam.

In developing your plan for guessing, there are three questions to address:

- When should you start the guessing process?
- How should you narrow down the choices?
- Which answer should you choose?

When to Start the Guessing Process

Unless your plan for guessing is to select C every time (which, despite its merits, is not what we recommend), you need to leave yourself enough time to apply your answer elimination strategies. Since you have a limited amount of time for each question, that means that if you're going to give yourself the best shot at guessing correctly, you have to decide quickly whether or not you will guess.

Of course, the best-case scenario is that you don't have to guess at all, so first, see if you can answer the question based on your knowledge of the subject and basic reasoning skills. Focus on the key words in the question and try to jog your memory of related topics. Give yourself a chance to bring the knowledge to mind, but once you realize that you don't have (or you can't access) the knowledge you need to answer the question, it's time to start the guessing process.

It's almost always better to start the guessing process too early than too late. It only takes a few seconds to remember something and answer the question from knowledge. Carefully eliminating wrong answer choices takes longer. Plus, going through the process of eliminating answer choices can actually help jog your memory.

Summary: Start the guessing process as soon as you decide that you can't answer the question based on your knowledge.

How to Narrow Down the Choices

The next chapter in this book (**Test-Taking Strategies**) includes a wide range of strategies for how to approach questions and how to look for answer choices to eliminate. You will definitely want to read those carefully, practice them, and figure out which ones work best for you. Here though, we're going to address a mindset rather than a particular strategy.

Your chances of guessing an answer correctly depend on how many options you are choosing from.

How many choices you have	How likely you are to guess correctly
5	20%
4	25%
3	33%
2	50%
1	100%

You can see from this chart just how valuable it is to be able to eliminate incorrect answers and make an educated guess, but there are two things that many test takers do that cause them to miss out on the benefits of guessing:

- Accidentally eliminating the correct answer
- Selecting an answer based on an impression

We'll look at the first one here, and the second one in the next section.

To avoid accidentally eliminating the correct answer, we recommend a thought exercise called **the $5 challenge**. In this challenge, you only eliminate an answer choice from contention if you are willing to bet $5 on it being wrong. Why $5? Five dollars is a small but not insignificant amount of money. It's an amount you could afford to lose but wouldn't want to throw away. And while losing $5 once might not hurt too much, doing it twenty times will set you back $100. In the same way, each small decision you make—eliminating a choice here, guessing on a question there—won't by itself impact your score very much, but when you put them all together, they can make a big difference. By holding each answer choice elimination decision to a higher standard, you can reduce the risk of accidentally eliminating the correct answer.

The $5 challenge can also be applied in a positive sense: If you are willing to bet $5 that an answer choice *is* correct, go ahead and mark it as correct.

Summary: Only eliminate an answer choice if you are willing to bet $5 that it is wrong.

Which Answer to Choose

You're taking the test. You've run into a hard question and decided you'll have to guess. You've eliminated all the answer choices you're willing to bet $5 on. Now you have to pick an answer. Why do we even need to talk about this? Why can't you just pick whichever one you feel like when the time comes?

The answer to these questions is that if you don't come into the test with a plan, you'll rely on your impression to select an answer choice, and if you do that, you risk falling into a trap. The test writers know that everyone who takes their test will be guessing on some of the questions, so they intentionally write wrong answer choices to seem plausible. You still have to pick an answer though, and if the wrong answer choices are designed to look right, how can you ever be sure that you're not falling for their trap? The best solution we've found to this dilemma is to take the decision out of your hands entirely. Here is the process we recommend:

Once you've eliminated any choices that you are confident (willing to bet $5) are wrong, select the first remaining choice as your answer.

Whether you choose to select the first remaining choice, the second, or the last, the important thing is that you use some preselected standard. Using this approach guarantees that you will not be enticed into selecting an answer choice that looks right, because you are not basing your decision on how the answer choices look.

This is not meant to make you question your knowledge. Instead, it is to help you recognize the difference between your knowledge and your impressions. There's a huge difference between thinking an answer is right because of what you know, and thinking an answer is right because it looks or sounds like it should be right.

Summary: To ensure that your selection is appropriately random, make a predetermined selection from among all answer choices you have not eliminated.

Test-Taking Strategies

This section contains a list of test-taking strategies that you may find helpful as you work through the test. By taking what you know and applying logical thought, you can maximize your chances of answering any question correctly!

It is very important to realize that every question is different and every person is different: no single strategy will work on every question, and no single strategy will work for every person. That's why we've included all of them here, so you can try them out and determine which ones work best for different types of questions and which ones work best for you.

Question Strategies

Read Carefully

Read the question and answer choices carefully. Don't miss the question because you misread the terms. You have plenty of time to read each question thoroughly and make sure you understand what is being asked. Yet a happy medium must be attained, so don't waste too much time. You must read carefully, but efficiently.

Contextual Clues

Look for contextual clues. If the question includes a word you are not familiar with, look at the immediate context for some indication of what the word might mean. Contextual clues can often give you all the information you need to decipher the meaning of an unfamiliar word. Even if you can't determine the meaning, you may be able to narrow down the possibilities enough to make a solid guess at the answer to the question.

Prefixes

If you're having trouble with a word in the question or answer choices, try dissecting it. Take advantage of every clue that the word might include. Prefixes and suffixes can be a huge help. Usually they allow you to determine a basic meaning. Pre- means before, post- means after, pro - is positive, de- is negative. From prefixes and suffixes, you can get an idea of the general meaning of the word and try to put it into context.

Hedge Words

Watch out for critical hedge words, such as *likely, may, can, sometimes, often, almost, mostly, usually, generally, rarely,* and *sometimes.* Question writers insert these hedge phrases to cover every possibility. Often an answer choice will be wrong simply because it leaves no room for exception. Be on guard for answer choices that have definitive words such as *exactly* and *always.*

Switchback Words

Stay alert for *switchbacks.* These are the words and phrases frequently used to alert you to shifts in thought. The most common switchback words are *but, although,* and *however.* Others include *nevertheless, on the other hand, even though, while, in spite of, despite, regardless of.* Switchback words are important to catch because they can change the direction of the question or an answer choice.

Face Value

When in doubt, use common sense. Accept the situation in the problem at face value. Don't read too much into it. These problems will not require you to make wild assumptions. If you have to go beyond creativity and warp time or space in order to have an answer choice fit the question, then you should move on and consider the other answer choices. These are normal problems rooted in reality. The applicable relationship or explanation may not be readily apparent, but it is there for you to figure out. Use your common sense to interpret anything that isn't clear.

Answer Choice Strategies

Answer Selection

The most thorough way to pick an answer choice is to identify and eliminate wrong answers until only one is left, then confirm it is the correct answer. Sometimes an answer choice may immediately seem right, but be careful. The test writers will usually put more than one reasonable answer choice on each question, so take a second to read all of them and make sure that the other choices are not equally obvious. As long as you have time left, it is better to read every answer choice than to pick the first one that looks right without checking the others.

Answer Choice Families

An answer choice family consists of two (in rare cases, three) answer choices that are very similar in construction and cannot all be true at the same time. If you see two answer choices that are direct opposites or parallels, one of them is usually the correct answer. For instance, if one answer choice says that quantity x increases and another either says that quantity x decreases (opposite) or says that quantity y increases (parallel), then those answer choices would fall into the same family. An answer choice that doesn't match the construction of the answer choice family is more likely to be incorrect. Most questions will not have answer choice families, but when they do appear, you should be prepared to recognize them.

Eliminate Answers

Eliminate answer choices as soon as you realize they are wrong, but make sure you consider all possibilities. If you are eliminating answer choices and realize that the last one you are left with is also wrong, don't panic. Start over and consider each choice again. There may be something you missed the first time that you will realize on the second pass.

Avoid Fact Traps

Don't be distracted by an answer choice that is factually true but doesn't answer the question. You are looking for the choice that answers the question. Stay focused on what the question is asking for so you don't accidentally pick an answer that is true but incorrect. Always go back to the question and make sure the answer choice you've selected actually answers the question and is not merely a true statement.

Extreme Statements

In general, you should avoid answers that put forth extreme actions as standard practice or proclaim controversial ideas as established fact. An answer choice that states the "process should be used in certain situations, if..." is much more likely to be correct than one that states the "process should be discontinued completely." The first is a calm rational statement and doesn't even make a definitive, uncompromising stance, using a hedge word *if* to provide wiggle room, whereas the second choice is a radical idea and far more extreme.

Benchmark

As you read through the answer choices and you come across one that seems to answer the question well, mentally select that answer choice. This is not your final answer, but it's the one that will help you evaluate the other answer choices. The one that you selected is your benchmark or standard for judging each of the other answer choices. Every other answer choice must be compared to your benchmark. That choice is correct until proven otherwise by another answer choice beating it. If you find a better answer, then that one becomes your new benchmark. Once you've decided that no other choice answers the question as well as your benchmark, you have your final answer.

Predict the Answer

Before you even start looking at the answer choices, it is often best to try to predict the answer. When you come up with the answer on your own, it is easier to avoid distractions and traps because you will know exactly what to look for. The right answer choice is unlikely to be word-for-word what you came up with, but it should be a close match. Even if you are confident that you have the right answer, you should still take the time to read each option before moving on.

General Strategies

Tough Questions

If you are stumped on a problem or it appears too hard or too difficult, don't waste time. Move on! Remember though, if you can quickly check for obviously incorrect answer choices, your chances of guessing correctly are greatly improved. Before you completely give up, at least try to knock out a couple of possible answers. Eliminate what you can and then guess at the remaining answer choices before moving on.

Check Your Work

Since you will probably not know every term listed and the answer to every question, it is important that you get credit for the ones that you do know. Don't miss any questions through careless mistakes. If at all possible, try to take a second to look back over your answer selection and make sure you've selected the correct answer choice and haven't made a costly careless mistake (such as marking an answer choice that you didn't mean to mark). This quick double check should more than pay for itself in caught mistakes for the time it costs.

Pace Yourself

It's easy to be overwhelmed when you're looking at a page full of questions; your mind is confused and full of random thoughts, and the clock is ticking down faster than you would like. Calm down and maintain the pace that you have set for yourself. Especially as you get down to the last few minutes of the test, don't let the small numbers on the clock make you panic. As long as you are on track by monitoring your pace, you are guaranteed to have time for each question.

Don't Rush

It is very easy to make errors when you are in a hurry. Maintaining a fast pace in answering questions is pointless if it makes you miss questions that you would have gotten right otherwise. Test writers like to include distracting information and wrong answers that seem right. Taking a little extra time to avoid careless mistakes can make all the difference in your test score. Find a pace that allows you to be confident in the answers that you select.

Keep Moving

Panicking will not help you pass the test, so do your best to stay calm and keep moving. Taking deep breaths and going through the answer elimination steps you practiced can help to break through a stress barrier and keep your pace.

Final Notes

The combination of a solid foundation of content knowledge and the confidence that comes from practicing your plan for applying that knowledge is the key to maximizing your performance on test day. As your foundation of content knowledge is built up and strengthened, you'll find that the strategies included in this chapter become more and more effective in helping you quickly sift through the distractions and traps of the test to isolate the correct answer.

Now it's time to move on to the test content chapters of this book, but be sure to keep your goal in mind. As you read, think about how you will be able to apply this information on the test. If you've already seen sample questions for the test and you have an idea of the question format and style, try to come up with questions of your own that you can answer based on what you're reading. This will give you valuable practice applying your knowledge in the same ways you can expect to on test day.

Good luck and good studying!

Reading and English Language Arts

Literacy

Literacy is commonly understood to refer to the *ability to read and write*. UNESCO has further defined literacy as the "ability to identify, understand, interpret, create, communicate, compute, and use printed and written materials associated with varying contexts." Under the UNESCO definition, understanding cultural, political, and historical contexts of communities falls under the definition of literacy. While **reading literacy** may be gauged simply by the ability to read a newspaper, **writing literacy** includes spelling, grammar, and sentence structure. To be literate in a foreign language, one would also need to have the ability to understand a language by listening and to speak the language. Some argue that visual representation and numeracy should be included in the requirements one must meet to be considered literate. Computer literacy refers to one's ability to utilize the basic functions of computers and other technologies. Subsets of reading literacy include phonological awareness, decoding, comprehension, and vocabulary.

Phonological Awareness

A subskill of literacy, **phonological awareness** is the ability to perceive sound structures in a spoken word, such as syllables and the individual phonemes within syllables. **Phonemes** are the sounds represented by the letters in the alphabet. The ability to separate, blend, and manipulate sounds is critical to developing reading and spelling skills. Phonological awareness is concerned with not only syllables, but also **onset sounds** (the sounds at the beginning of words) and **rime** (the same thing as rhyme, but spelled differently to distinguish syllable rime from poetic rhyme). Phonological awareness is an auditory skill that does not necessarily involve print. It should be developed before the student has learned letter to sound correspondences. A student's phonological awareness is an indicator of future reading success.

Activities That Teach Phonological Awareness

Classroom activities that teach **phonological awareness** include language play and exposure to a variety of sounds and contexts of sounds. Activities that teach phonological awareness include:

- Clapping to the sounds of individual words, names, or all words in a sentence
- Practicing saying blended phonemes
- Singing songs that involve phoneme replacement (e.g., The Name Game)
- Reading poems, songs, and nursery rhymes out loud
- Reading patterned and predictable texts out loud
- Listening to environmental sounds or following verbal directions
- Playing games with rhyming chants or fingerplays
- Reading alliterative texts out loud
- Grouping objects by beginning sounds
- Reordering words in a well-known sentence or making silly phrases by deleting words from a well-known sentence (perhaps from a favorite storybook)

Alphabetic Principle and Alphabet Writing Systems

The **alphabetic principle** refers to the use of letters and combinations of letters to represent speech sounds. The way letters are combined and pronounced is guided by a system of rules that establishes relationships between written and spoken words and their letter symbols. Alphabet writing systems are common around the world. Some are **phonological** in that each letter stands for an individual sound and words are spelled just as they sound. However, there are other writing systems as well, such as the Chinese **logographic** system and the Japanese **syllabic** system.

Development of Language Skills

Children learn language through interacting with others, by experiencing language in daily and relevant context, and through understanding that speaking and listening are necessary for effective communication. Teachers can promote **language development** by intensifying the opportunities a child has to experience and understand language.

Teachers can assist language development by:

- Modeling enriched vocabulary and teaching new words
- Using questions and examples to extend a child's descriptive language skills
- Providing ample response time to encourage children to practice speech
- Asking for clarification to provide students with the opportunity to develop communication skills
- Promoting conversations among children
- Providing feedback to let children know they have been heard and understood, and providing further explanation when needed

Relationship Between Oral and Written Language Development

Oral and written language develops simultaneously. The acquisition of skills in one area supports the acquisition of skills in the other. However, oral language is not a prerequisite to written language. An immature form of oral language development is babbling, and an immature form of written language development is scribbling. **Oral language development** does not occur naturally, but does occur in a social context. This means it is best to include children in conversations rather than simply talk at them. **Written language development** can occur without direct instruction. In fact, reading and writing do not necessarily need to be taught through formal lessons if the child is exposed to a print-rich environment. A teacher can assist a child's language development by building on what the child already knows, discussing relevant and meaningful events and experiences, teaching vocabulary and literacy skills, and providing opportunities to acquire more complex language.

Print-Rich Environment

A teacher can provide a **print-rich environment** in the classroom in a number of ways. These include:

- **Displaying** the following in the classroom:
    - Children's names in print or cursive
    - Children's written work
    - Newspapers and magazines
    - Instructional charts
    - Written schedules
    - Signs and labels
    - Printed songs, poems, and rhymes
- Using **graphic organizers** such as KWL charts or story road maps to:
    - Remind students about what was read and discussed

    - Expand on the lesson topic or theme
    - Show the relationships among books, ideas, and words
- Using **big books** to:
    - Point out features of print, such as specific letters and punctuation
    - Track print from right to left
    - Emphasize the concept of words and the fact that they are used to communicate

Benefits of Print and Book Awareness

Print and book awareness helps a child understand:

- That there is a **connection** between print and messages contained on signs, labels, and other print forms in the child's environment
- That reading and writing are ways to obtain information and communicate ideas
- That **print** runs from left to right and from top to bottom
- That a book has **parts**, such as a title, a cover, a title page, and a table of contents
- That a book has an **author** and contains a **story**
- That **illustrations** can carry meaning
- That **letters and words** are different
- That **words and sentences** are separated by spaces and punctuation
- That different **text forms** are used for different functions
- That print represents **spoken language**
- How to **hold** a book.

Facts Children Should Know About Letters

To be appropriately prepared to learn to read and write, a child should learn:

- That each letter is **distinct** in appearance
- What **direction and shape** must be used to make each letter
- That each letter has a **name**, which can be associated with the shape of a letter
- That there are **26** letters in the English alphabet, and letters are grouped in a certain order
- That letters represent **sounds of speech**
- That **words** are composed of letters and have meaning
- That one must be able to **correspond** letters and sounds to read

Decoding

Decoding is the method or strategy used to make sense of printed words and figure out how to correctly pronounce them. In order to decode, a student needs to know the relationships between letters and sounds, including letter patterns; that words are constructed from phonemes and phoneme blends; and that a printed word represents a word that can be spoken. This knowledge will help the student recognize familiar words and make informed guesses about the pronunciation of unfamiliar words. Decoding is not the same as **comprehension**. It does not require an understanding of the meaning of a word, only a knowledge of how to recognize and pronounce it. Decoding can also refer to the skills a student uses to determine the meaning of a **sentence**. These skills include applying knowledge of vocabulary, sentence structure, and context.

Teaching of Reading Through Phonics

Phonics is the process of learning to read by learning how spoken language is represented by letters. Students learn to read phonetically by sounding out the **phonemes** in words and then blending them together to produce the correct sounds in words. In other words, the student connects speech sounds with letters or groups of letters and blends the sounds together to determine the pronunciation of an unknown word. Phonics is a commonly used method to teach **decoding and reading**, but has been challenged by other methods, such as the whole language approach. Despite the complexity of pronunciation and combined sounds in the English language, research shows that phonics is a highly effective way to teach reading. Being able to read or pronounce a word does not mean the student comprehends the meaning of the word, but context aids comprehension. When phonics is used as a foundation for decoding, children eventually learn to recognize words automatically and advance to decoding multisyllable words with practice.

Role of Fluency in Literacy Development

Fluency is the goal of literacy development. It is the ability to read accurately and quickly. Evidence of fluency includes the ability to recognize words automatically and group words for comprehension. At this point, the student no longer needs to decode words except for complex, unfamiliar ones. He or she is able to move to the next level and understand the **meaning** of a text. The student should be able to self-check for comprehension and should feel comfortable expressing ideas in writing. Teachers can help students build fluency by continuing to provide: reading experiences and discussions about text, gradually increasing the level of difficulty; reading practice, both silently and out loud; word analysis practice; instruction on reading comprehension strategies; and opportunities to express responses to readings through writing.

Role of Vocabulary in Literacy Development

When students do not know the meaning of words in a text, their comprehension is limited. As a result, the text becomes boring or confusing. The larger a student's **vocabulary** is, the better their reading comprehension will be. A larger vocabulary is also associated with an enhanced ability to **communicate** in speech and writing. It is the teacher's role to help students develop a good working vocabulary. Students learn most of the words they use and understand from listening to the world around them (adults, other students, media, etc.) They also learn from their reading experiences, which include being read to and reading independently. Carefully designed activities can also stimulate vocabulary growth, and should emphasize useful words that students see frequently, important words necessary for understanding text, and difficult words such as idioms or words with more than one meaning.

Teaching Techniques Promoting Vocabulary Development

A student's **vocabulary** can be developed by:

- Calling upon a student's **prior knowledge** and making comparisons to that knowledge
- **Defining** a word and providing multiple examples of the use of the word in context
- Showing a student how to use **context clues** to discover the meaning of a word
- Providing instruction on **prefixes, roots, and suffixes** to help students break a word into its parts and decipher its meaning
- Showing students how to use a **dictionary and a thesaurus**
- Asking students to **practice** new vocabulary by using the words in their own writing

- Providing a **print-rich environment** with a word wall
- Studying a group of words related to a **single subject**, such as farm words, transportation words, etc. so that concept development is enhanced.

Affixes, Prefixes, and Root Words

Affixes are syllables attached to the beginning or end of a word to make a derivative or inflectional form of a word. Both prefixes and suffixes are affixes. A **prefix** is a syllable that appears at the beginning of a word that, in combination with the root or base word, creates a specific meaning. For example, the prefix "mis" means "wrong." When combined with the root word "spelling," the word "misspelling" is created, which means the "wrong spelling." A **root word** is the base of a word to which affixes can be added. For example, the prefix "in" or "pre" can be added to the root word "vent" to create "invent" or "prevent," respectively. The suffix "er" can be added to the root word "work" to create "worker," which means "one who works." The suffix "able," meaning "capable of," can be added to "work" to create "workable," which means "capable of working."

Suffixes

A suffix is a syllable that appears at the end of a word that, in combination with the root or base word, creates a specific meaning. There are three types of suffixes:

- **Noun suffixes** – There are two types of noun suffixes. One denotes the act of, state of, or quality of. For example, "-ment" added to "argue" becomes "argument," which is defined as "the act of arguing." The other denotes the doer, or one who acts. For example, "-eer" added to "auction" becomes "auctioneer," meaning "one who auctions." Other examples include "-hood," "-ness," "-tion," "-ship," and "-ism."
- **Verb suffixes** – These denote "to make" or "to perform the act of." For example, "-en" added to "soft" makes "soften," which means "to make soft." Other verb suffixes are "-ate" (perpetuate), "-fy" (dignify), and "-ize" (sterilize).
- **Adjectival suffixes** – These include suffixes such as "-ful," which means "full of." When added to "care," the word "careful" is formed, which means "full of care." Other examples are "-ish," "-less," and "-able."

Strategies to Improve Reading Comprehension

Teachers can model in a read-aloud the strategies students can use on their own to better comprehend a text. First, the teacher should do a walk-through of the story **illustrations** and ask, "What's happening here?" Based on what they have seen, the teacher should then ask students to **predict** what the story will be about. As the book is read, the teacher should ask open-ended questions such as, "Why do you think the character did this?" and "How do you think the character feels?" The teacher should also ask students if they can **relate** to the story or have background knowledge of something similar. After the reading, the teacher should ask the students to **retell** the story in their own words to check for comprehension. This retelling can take the form of a puppet show or summarizing the story to a partner.

Role of Prior Knowledge in Determining Appropriate Literacy Education

Even preschool children have some literacy skills, and the extent and type of these skills have implications for instructional approaches. Comprehension results from relating two or more pieces of information. One piece comes from the text, and another piece might come from **prior knowledge** (something from a student's long-term memory). For a child, that prior knowledge comes from being read to at home; taking part in other literacy experiences, such as playing computer or word games; being exposed to a print-rich environment at home; and observing examples of parents' reading habits. Children who have had **extensive literacy experience** are better prepared to further develop their literacy skills in school than children who have not been read to, have few books or magazines in their homes, are seldom exposed to high-level oral or written language activities, and seldom witness adults engaged in reading and writing. Children with a scant literacy background are at a disadvantage. The teacher must not make any assumptions about their prior knowledge, and should use intense, targeted instruction. Otherwise, reading comprehension will be limited.

Using Puppetry in the Classroom

Using puppets in the classroom puts students at ease and allows them to enjoy a learning experience as if it were play. The purpose of using puppetry is to generate ideas, encourage imagination, and foster language development. Using a puppet helps a child "become" the character and therefore experience a different **outlook**. **Language development** is enhanced through the student interpreting a story that has been read in class and practicing new words from that story in the puppet show. Children will also have the opportunity to practice using descriptive adjectives for the characters and the scene, which will help them learn the function of adjectives. **Descriptive adjectives and verbs** can also be learned by practicing facial expressions and movements with puppets. The teacher can model happy, sad, eating, sleeping, and similar words with a puppet, and then ask students to do the same with their puppets. This is an especially effective vocabulary activity for ESL children.

Using Drama or Story Theater in the Classroom

Drama activities are fun learning experiences that capture a child's attention, engage the imagination, and motivate vocabulary expansion. For example, after reading a story, the teacher could ask children to act it out as the teacher repeats the story. This activity, which works best with very young learners, will help children work on listening skills and their ability to pretend. The best stories to use for this passive improvisation are ones that have lots of simple actions that children will be able to understand and perform easily. Older children can create their own improvisational skits and possibly write scripts. **Visualization** also calls upon the imagination and encourages concentration and bodily awareness. Children can be given a prompt for the visualization and then asked to draw what they see in their mind's eye. **Charades** is another way to act out words and improve vocabulary skills. This activity can be especially helpful to encourage ESL students to express thoughts and ideas in English. These students should be given easier words to act out to promote confidence.

Classroom Practices Benefiting Second Language Acquisition

Since some students may have limited understanding of English, a teacher should employ the following practices to promote second language acquisition:

- Make all instruction as **understandable** as possible and use simple and repeated terms.
- Relate instruction to the **cultures** of ESL children.
- Increase **interactive activities** and use gestures or non-verbal actions when modeling.
- Provide language and literacy development instruction in **all curriculum areas**.
- Establish **consistent routines** that help children connect words and events.
- Use a **schedule** so children know what will happen next and will not feel lost.
- Integrate ESL children into **group activities** with non-ESL children.
- Appoint bilingual students to act as **student translators**.

- Explain actions as activities happen so that a **word to action relationship** is established.
- Initiate opportunities for ESL children to **experiment** with and practice new language.
- Employ multisensory learning.

Theories of Language Development

Four theories of language development are:

- **Learning approach** – This theory assumes that language is first learned by imitating the speech of adults. It is then solidified in school through drills about the rules of language structures.
- **Linguistic approach** – Championed by Noam Chomsky in the 1950s, this theory proposes that the ability to use a language is innate. This is a biological approach rather than one based on cognition or social patterning.
- **Cognitive approach** – Developed in the 1970s and based on the work of Piaget, this theory states that children must develop appropriate cognitive skills before they can acquire language.
- **Sociocognitive approach** – In the 1970s, some researchers proposed that language development is a complex interaction of linguistic, social, and cognitive influences. This theory best explains the lack of language skills among children who are neglected, have uneducated parents, or lives in poverty.

Teaching Strategies to Promote Listening Skills of ESL Students

Listening is a critical skill when learning a new language. Students spend a great deal more time listening than they do speaking, and far less time reading and writing than speaking. Two ways to encourage ESL students to listen are to:

- Talk about topics that are of **interest** to the ESL learner. Otherwise, students may tune out the speaker because they don't want to put in that much effort to learn about a topic they find boring.
- Talk about content or give examples that are **easy** to understand or are **related** to a topic that is familiar to ESL students. Culturally relevant materials will be more interesting to ESL students, will make them feel more comfortable, and will contain vocabulary that they may already be familiar with.

Considerations Relevant to ESL Students Related to Learning by Listening

Listening is not a passive skill, but an **active** one. Therefore, a teacher needs to make the listening experience as rewarding as possible and provide as many auditory and visual clues as possible. Three ways that the teacher can make the listening experience rewarding for ESL students are:

- Avoid **colloquialisms** and **abbreviated or slang terms** that may be confusing to the ESL listener, unless there is enough time to define them and explain their use.
- Make the spoken English understandable by stopping to **clarify** points, **repeating** new or difficult words, and **defining** words that may not be known.
- Support the spoken word with as many **visuals** as possible. Pictures, diagrams, gestures, facial expressions, and body language can help the ESL learner correctly interpret the spoken language more easily and also leaves an image impression that helps them remember the words.

Top-Down and Bottom-Up Processing

ESL students need to be given opportunities to practice both top-down and bottom-up processing. If they are old enough to understand these concepts, they should be made aware that these are two processes that affect their listening comprehension. In **top-down processing**, the listener refers to **background and global knowledge** to figure out the meaning of a message. For example, when asking an ESL student to perform a task, the steps of the task should be explained and accompanied by a review of the vocabulary terms the student already understands so that the student feels comfortable tackling new steps and new words. The teacher should also allow students to ask questions to verify comprehension. In **bottom-up processing**, the listener figures out the meaning of a message by using "**data**" obtained from what is said. This data includes sounds (stress, rhythm, and intonation), words, and grammatical relationships. All data can be used to make conclusions or interpretations. For example, the listener can develop bottom-up skills by learning how to detect differences in intonation between statements and questions.

Listening Lessons

All students, but especially ESL students, can be taught **listening** through specific training. During listening lessons, the teacher should guide students through three steps:

- **Pre-listening activity** – This establishes the purpose of the lesson and engages students' background knowledge. This activity should ask students to think about and discuss something they already know about the topic. Alternatively, the teacher can provide background information.
- **The listening activity** – This requires the listener to obtain information and then immediately do something with that information. For example, the teacher can review the schedule for the day or the week. The students are being given information about a routine they already know, but need to be able to identify names, tasks, and times.
- **Post-listening activity** – This is an evaluation process that allows students to judge how well they did with the listening task. Other language skills can be included in the activity. For example, this activity could involve asking questions about who will do what according to the classroom schedule (Who is the lunch monitor today?) and could also involve asking students to produce whole sentence replies.

Helping ESL Students Understand Subject Matter

<u>Speaking</u>

To help ESL students better understand subject matter, the following teaching strategies using spoken English can be used:

- **Read aloud** from a textbook, and then ask ESL students to **verbally summarize** what was read. The teacher should assist by providing new words as needed to give students the opportunity to practice vocabulary and speaking skills. The teacher should then read the passage again to students to verify accuracy and details.
- The teacher could ask ESL students to explain why the subject matter is important to them and where they see it fitting into their lives. This verbalization gives them speaking practice and helps them relate to the subject.
- Whenever small group activities are being conducted, ESL students can be placed with **English-speaking students**. It is best to keep the groups to two or three students so that the ESL student will be motivated by the need to be involved. English-speaking students should be encouraged to include ESL students in the group work.

Reading

There are supplemental printed materials that can be used to help ESL students understand subject matter. The following strategies can be used to help ESL students develop English reading skills.

- Make sure all ESL students have a **bilingual dictionary** to use. A thesaurus would also be helpful.
- Try to keep **content area books** written in the ESL students' native languages in the classroom. Students can use them side-by-side with English texts. Textbooks in other languages can be ordered from the school library or obtained from the classroom textbook publisher.
- If a student lacks confidence in his/her ability to read the textbook, the teacher can read a passage to the student and have him or her **verbally summarize** the passage. The teacher should take notes on what the student says and then read them back. These notes can be a substitute, short-form, in-their-own-words textbook that the student can understand.

General Teaching Strategies to Help ESL Students

Some strategies can help students develop more than one important skill. They may involve a combination of speaking, listening, and/or viewing. Others are mainly classroom management aids. General teaching strategies for ESL students include:

- **Partner** English-speaking students with ESL students as study buddies and ask the English-speaking students to share notes.
- Encourage ESL students to ask **questions** whenever they don't understand something. They should be aware that they don't have to be able to interpret every word of text to understand the concept.
- Dictate **key sentences** related to the content area being taught and ask ESL students to write them down. This gives them practice in listening and writing, and also helps them identify what is important.
- **Alternate** difficult and easy tasks so that ESL students can experience academic success.
- Ask ESL students to **label** objects associated with content areas, such as maps, diagrams, parts of a leaf, or parts of a sentence. This gives students writing and reading experience and helps them remember key vocabulary.

Impact of Reading Skills on Student Success

The ability to read is not simply one academic area; it is a basic skill set underlying all academic activity and determines whether students fail or succeed in school. Research shows that of first-graders with poor **reading skills**, 88% still read poorly in fourth grade. By this time, most information that students require is provided in text form. For this reason, the focus shifts from *learning to read* in the earlier grades, to *reading to learn* by fourth grade. Consequently, students with poor reading skills can find it harder to access and interact with the content in their schools' curricula. Moreover, reading abilities that are delayed or disordered usually are identified in higher elementary grades. Yet research finds remediation attempts then could be too late, because children acquire language and have literacy experiences from birth. Phonemic awareness, the alphabetic principle, and print awareness normally develop in early childhood. Children missing such early experiences will fall behind peers without extra instruction. This means elementary school teachers must give these children **literacy-rich environments**.

Reading Comprehension

The whole point of reading is to **comprehend** what someone else is trying to say through writing. Without comprehension, a student is just reading the words without understanding them or increasing knowledge of a topic. Comprehension results when the student has the vocabulary and reading skills necessary to make sense of the **whole picture**, not just individual words. Students can self-monitor because they know when they are comprehending the material and when they are not. Teachers can help students solve problems with comprehension by teaching them strategies such as pre-reading titles, sidebars, and follow-up questions; looking at illustrations; predicting what's going to happen in the story; asking questions to check understanding while reading; connecting to background knowledge; and relating to the experiences or feelings of the characters.

Review Video: Predicting What Will Happen in a Story
Visit mometrix.com/academy and enter code: 288778

Review Video: Predictions
Visit mometrix.com/academy and enter code: 437248

Review Video: Reading Comprehension Tips
Visit mometrix.com/academy and enter code: 280215

Skills Needed to Develop Literacy

According to studies by the National Reading Panel, for children to develop **literacy**, they must have developed skills in phonemic awareness, phonics, vocabulary, comprehension, and fluency. A prerequisite to developing these five skill areas is having an understanding of how literacy works, what it does, and how it is used. While young children exposed to spoken and printed language interactions from birth often develop this understanding of the functions and applications of literacy in a natural way, children with language and learning disabilities may not. A **literacy-rich environment** is defined as one that provides students having disabilities with stimulation to take part in activities involving language and literacy during their everyday life routines. Stimulating such participation in and integration of language and literacy into daily living is an effective way to help disabled students begin to develop understanding of how spoken and printed language function and are used. Teaching strategies to establish literacy-rich environments can not only remediate language and literacy deficits, but also benefit all elementary-level students.

Literacy-Rich Environment in Elementary School Classrooms

An elementary classroom constituting a **literacy-rich setting** would engage all students in various literacy activities, some working individually and others in groups. Students would explore different *genres* of books, not only during reading periods or in the library, but during math, social studies, and science periods or lessons. The teacher might read aloud to students from a book about math during math period, and lead class discussions of the book's content, and have students explore eyewitness science books during science time to learn about scientific concepts. These activities help students experience literacy across all curriculum subject content areas. Students also use books on tapes and CD-ROMs. The classroom includes adapted materials to motivate disabled students to read and help them interact with text. Students write in notebooks and journals, write reports in all subjects, and compose books. A literacy-rich classroom environment features *information resources* for students including dictionaries, encyclopedias, books in varied genres, word walls, and computers, as well as teachers and peers.

Vocabulary Instruction

There are a number of factors to consider when developing **vocabulary**, academic language, and background knowledge. To begin with, not all words should be given equal emphasis. Some words occur much more frequently and should therefore be of greater importance in instruction. This is yet another reason why the context of vocabulary and academic language is so important. It is a bad idea to find a list of difficult words and proceed through it alphabetically, because the students will have very little context for the words they are learning. Instead, teachers should approach vocabulary *thematically*. For instance, a teacher might spend one week teaching vocabulary words related to government, and the next teaching words related to legislation. It is a good idea to link new vocabulary to the lesson being covered in other content areas. The most important thing is to ensure that students have a context for new words, so that they will be able to incorporate them in their speaking and writing as soon as possible.

Word Analysis

Semantic and Syntactic Approaches

Word analysis instruction should be balanced and comprehensive. It is a good idea to let students approach unfamiliar words from both the semantic and syntactic perspectives. A **semantic approach** emphasizes the meaning of words. A child is using the semantic approach when he thinks about context and about what type of word would make sense in a given sentence. A teacher can guide the student towards an appreciation of semantics by asking questions about the meaning of the sentence and the likely meaning of an unfamiliar word. The **syntactic approach**, on the other hand, emphasizes the order of the words in a sentence. English has fairly regular syntax, so the reader can often predict what type of word (e.g., noun, verb) will appear next in a sentence. A teacher can stimulate students to think about syntax by asking the student to read a sentence and determine whether it makes sense. A teacher can ask the student whether the words in a sentence appear to be in the right order.

Differentiation of Word Analysis Instruction

Word analysis can be a challenge for many students, and so there is likely to be a great range of performance in the same class. Teachers must be able to address the strong and weak students in the class. In particular, teachers need to provide differentiated instruction for students who are struggling or have reading difficulties or disabilities. For instance, a teacher needs to be able to go back and focus on key skills and knowledge, like syllable patterns and morphemes that occur frequently. Some students need to have the same material approached from different perspectives before they fully master it. The teacher should be able to outline a number of real-world examples for an abstract concept. The use of songs and poems to illustrate syllabification is one helpful way to bring struggling students up to speed. Finally, a teacher should be able to provide differentiated practice situations for the skills that have been taught.

Review Video: Defining a Word
Visit mometrix.com/academy and enter code: 648080

Review Video: Denotation and Connotation
Visit mometrix.com/academy and enter code: 310092

Literal and Critical Comprehension

Literal comprehension refers to the skills a reader uses to deal with the actual words in a text. It involves skills such as identifying the topic sentence, main idea, important facts, and supporting details; using context clues to determine the meaning of a word; and sequencing events.

Critical comprehension involves prior knowledge and an understanding that written material, especially in nonfiction, is the author's version of the subject and not necessarily anybody else's. Critical comprehension involves analysis of meaning, evaluation, validation, questioning, and the reasoning skills a reader uses to recognize:

- Inferences and conclusions
- Purpose, tone, point of view, and themes
- The organizational pattern of a work
- Explicit and implicit relationships among words, phrases, and sentences
- Biased language, persuasive tactics, valid arguments, and the difference between fact and opinion

Review Video: Author's Main Point or Purpose
Visit mometrix.com/academy and enter code: 734339

Review Video: Author's Position
Visit mometrix.com/academy and enter code: 827954

Review Video: Inference
Visit mometrix.com/academy and enter code: 379203

Metacognition

Metacognition is thinking about thinking. For the student, this involves taking control of their own learning process, self-monitoring progress, evaluating the effectiveness of strategies, and making adjustments to strategies and learning behaviors as needed. Students who develop good metacognitive skills become more independent and confident about learning. They develop a sense of ownership about their education and realize that information is readily available to them.

Metacognitive skills can be grouped into three categories:

- **Awareness** – This involves identifying prior knowledge; defining learning goals; inventorying resources such as textbooks, libraries, computers, and study time; identifying task requirements and evaluation standards; and recognizing motivation and anxiety levels.
- **Planning** – This involves doing time estimates for tasks, prioritizing, scheduling study time, making checklists of tasks, gathering needed materials, and choosing strategies for problem solving or task comprehension.
- **Self-monitoring and reflection** – This involves identifying which strategies or techniques work best, questioning throughout the process, considering feedback, and maintaining focus and motivation.

Role of Metacognitive Skills in Literacy Development

In terms of literacy development, **metacognitive skills** include taking an active role in reading, recognizing reading behaviors and changing them to employ the behaviors that are most effective, relating information to prior knowledge, and being aware of text structures. For example, if there is a problem with comprehension, the student can try to form a mental image of what is described, read the text again, adjust the rate of reading, or employ other reading strategies such as identifying unknown vocabulary and predicting meaning. Being aware of **text structures** is critical to being able to follow the author's ideas and relationships among ideas. Being aware of difficulties with text structure allows the student to employ strategies such as hierarchical summaries, thematic organizers, or concept maps to remedy the problem.

Critical Thinking Tools

It is important to teach students to use critical thinking skills when reading. Three of the **critical thinking tools** that engage the reader are:

- **Summarization** – The student reviews the main point(s) of the reading selection and identifies important details. For nonfiction, a good summary will briefly describe the main arguments and the examples that support those arguments. For fiction, a good summary will identify the main characters and events of the story.
- **Question generation** – A good reader will constantly ask questions while reading about comprehension, vocabulary, connections to personal knowledge or experience, predictions, etc.
- **Textual marking** – This skill engages the reader by having him or her interact with the text. The student should mark the text with questions or comments that are generated by the text using underlining, highlighting, or shorthand marks such as "?," "!," and "*" that indicate lack of understanding, importance, or key points, for example.

Context Clues

Context clues are words or phrases that help the reader figure out the meaning of an unknown word. They are built into a sentence or paragraph by the writer to help the reader develop a clear understanding of the writer's message. Context clues can be used to make **intelligent guesses** about the meaning of a word instead of relying on a dictionary. Context clues are the reason most vocabulary is learned through reading. There are four types of commonly used context clues:

- **Synonyms** – A word with the same meaning as the unknown word is placed close by for comparison.
- **Antonyms** – A word with the opposite meaning as the unknown word is placed close by for contrast.
- **Explanations** – An obvious explanation is given close to the unknown word.
- **Examples** – Examples of what the word means are given to help the reader define the term.

Review Video: Synonyms and Antonyms
Visit mometrix.com/academy and enter code: 105612

Review Video: Multiple Meaning Words
Visit mometrix.com/academy and enter code: 371666

Topic Sentence

The **topic sentence** of a paragraph states the paragraph's subject. It presents the **main idea**. The rest of the paragraph should be related to the topic sentence, which should be explained and supported with facts, details, proofs, and examples. The topic sentence is more general than the **body sentences**, and should cover all the ideas in the body of the paragraph. It may contain words such as "many," "most," or "several." The topic sentence is usually the first sentence in a paragraph, but it can appear after an introductory or background sentence, can be the last sentence in a paragraph, or may simply be implied, meaning a topic sentence is not present. **Supporting sentences** can often be identified by their use of transition terms such as "for example" or "that is." Supporting sentences may also be presented in numbered sequence. The topic sentence provides **unity** to a paragraph because it ties together the supporting details into a coherent whole.

Review Video: Topics and Main Ideas
Visit mometrix.com/academy and enter code: 407801

Review Video: Supporting Details
Visit mometrix.com/academy and enter code: 396297

Theme

Theme is the central idea of a work. It is the thread that ties all the elements of a story together and gives them purpose. The theme is not the subject of a work, but what a work says about a subject. A theme must be **universal**, which means it must apply to everyone, not just the characters in a story. Therefore, a theme is a comment about the nature of humanity, society, the relationship of humankind to the world, or moral responsibility. There may be more than one theme in a work, and the determination of the theme is affected by the viewpoint of the reader. Therefore, there is not always necessarily a definite, irrefutable theme. The theme can be implied or stated directly.

Review Video: Theme
Visit mometrix.com/academy and enter code: 732074

Types of Definition Paragraphs or Essays

A **definition paragraph** or essay describes what a word or term means. There are three ways the explanation can be presented:

- **Definition by synonym** – The term is defined by comparing it to a more familiar term that the reader can more easily understand (A phantom is a ghost or spirit that appears and disappears mysteriously and creates dread).
- **Definition by class** – Most commonly used in exams, papers, and reports, the class definition first puts the term in a larger category or class (The Hereford is a breed of cattle), and then describes the distinguishing characteristics or details of the term that differentiate it from other members of the class (The Hereford is a breed of cattle distinguished by a white face, reddish-brown hide, and short horns).
- **Definition by negation** – The term is defined by stating what it is not and then saying what it is (Courage is not the absence of fear, but the willingness to act in spite of fear).

Types of Paragraphs and Essays

Illustrative — An illustrative paragraph or essay explains a general statement through the use of specific examples. The writer starts with a topic sentence that is followed by one or more examples that clearly relate to and support the topic.

Narrative — A narrative tells a story. Like a news report, it tells the who, what, when, where, why, and how of an event. A narrative is usually presented in chronological order.

Descriptive — This type of writing appeals to the five senses to describe a person, place, or thing so that the readers can see the subject in their imaginations. Space order is most often used in descriptive writing to indicate place or position.

Process — There are two kinds of process papers: the "how-to" that gives step-by-step directions on how to do something and the explanation paper that tells how an event occurred or how something works.

Review Video: Reading Essays
Visit mometrix.com/academy and enter code: 169166

Cause and Effect

Causes are reasons for actions or events. **Effects** are the results of a cause or causes. There may be multiple causes for one effect (evolutionary extinction, climate changes, and a massive comet caused the demise of the dinosaurs, for example) or multiple effects from one cause (the break-up of the Soviet Union has had multiple effects on the world stage, for instance). Sometimes, one thing leads to another and the effect of one action becomes the cause for another (breaking an arm leads to not driving, which leads to reading more while staying home, for example). The ability to identify causes and effects is part of critical thinking, and enables the reader to follow the course of events, make connections among events, and identify the instigators and receivers of actions. This ability improves comprehension.

Review Video: Cause and Effect
Visit mometrix.com/academy and enter code: 428037

Review Video: Rhetorical Strategy of Cause-and-Effect Analysis
Visit mometrix.com/academy and enter code: 725944

Distinguishing Between Facts and Opinions

Facts are statements that can be verified through research. Facts answer the questions of who, what, when, and where, and evidence can be provided to prove factual statements. For example, it is a fact that water turns into ice when the temperature drops below 32 degrees Fahrenheit. This fact has been proven repeatedly. Water never becomes ice at a higher temperature. **Opinions** are personal views, but facts may be used to support opinions. For example, it may be one person's opinion that Jack is a great athlete, but the fact that he has made many achievements related to sports supports that opinion. It is important for a reader to be able to distinguish between fact and opinion to determine the validity of an argument. Readers need to understand that some unethical writers will try to pass off an opinion as a fact. Readers with good critical thinking skills will not be deceived by this tactic.

Review Video: Fact or Opinion
Visit mometrix.com/academy and enter code: 870899

Review Video: Text Evidence
Visit mometrix.com/academy and enter code: 486236

Inductive and Deductive Reasoning

Inductive reasoning is using particulars to draw a general conclusion. The inductive reasoning process starts with **data**. For example, if every apple taken out of the top of a barrel is rotten, it can be inferred without investigating further that all the apples are probably rotten. Unless all data is examined, conclusions are based on probabilities. Inductive reasoning is also used to make inferences about the universe. The entire universe cannot be examined, but inferences can be made based on observations about what can be seen. These inferences may be proven false when more data is available, but they are valid at the time they are made if observable data is used. **Deductive reasoning** is the opposite of inductive reasoning. It involves using general facts or premises to come to a specific conclusion. For example, if Susan is a sophomore in high school, and all sophomores take geometry, it can be inferred that Susan takes geometry. The word "all" does not allow for exceptions. If all sophomores take geometry, assuming Susan does too is a logical conclusion. It is important for a reader to recognize inductive and deductive reasoning so he or she can follow the line of an argument and determine if the inference or conclusion is **valid**.

Style, Tone, and Point of View

Style is the manner in which a writer uses language in prose or poetry. Style is affected by:

- Diction or word choices
- Sentence structure and syntax
- Types and extent of use of figurative language
- Patterns of rhythm or sound
- Conventional or creative use of punctuation

Tone is the attitude of the writer or narrator towards the theme of, subject of, or characters in a work. Sometimes the attitude is stated, but it is most often implied through word choices. Examples of tone are serious, humorous, satiric, stoic, cynical, flippant, and surprised.

Point of view is the angle from which a story is told. It is the perspective of the narrator, established by the author. Common points of view are:

- *Third person* – Third person points of view include omniscient (knows everything) and limited (confined to what is known by a single character or a limited number of characters). When the third person is used, characters are referred to as he, she, or they.
- *First person* – When this point of view is used, the narrator refers to himself or herself as "I."

Review Video: Style, Tone, and Mood
Visit mometrix.com/academy and enter code: 416961

Review Video: Point of View
Visit mometrix.com/academy and enter code: 383336

Types of Figurative Language

A **simile** is a comparison between two unlike things using the words "like" or "as." Examples are Robert Burn's sentence "O my love's like a red, red, rose" or the common expression "as pretty as a picture."

A **metaphor** is a direct comparison between two unlike things without the use of "like" or "as." One thing is identified as the other instead of simply compared to it. An example is D. H. Lawrence's sentence "My soul is a dark forest."

Personification is the giving of human characteristics to a non-human thing or idea. An example is "The hurricane howled its frightful rage."

Synecdoche is the use of a part of something to signify the whole. For example, "boots on the ground" could be used to describe soldiers in a field.

Metonymy is the use of one term that is closely associated with another to mean the other. An example is referring to the "crown" to refer to the monarchy.

Alliteration, Assonance, and Onomatopoeia

Alliteration is the repetition of the first sounds or stressed syllables (usually consonants) in words in close proximity. An example is: "Chirp, chirp," said the chickadee.

Assonance is the repetition of identical or similar vowel sounds, particularly in stressed syllables, in words in close proximity. Assonance is considered to be a form of near rhyme. An example is: the quiet bride cried.

Onomatopoeia refers to words that imitate sounds. It is sometimes called echoism. Examples are hiss, buzz, burp, rattle, and pop. It may also refer to words that correspond symbolically to what they describe, with high tones suggesting light and low tones suggesting darkness. An example is the *gloom* of night versus the *gleam* of the stars.

Parallelism, Euphemism, Hyperbole, and Climax

Parallelism — Subjects, objects, verbs, modifiers, phrases, and clauses can be structured in sentences to balance one with another through a similar grammatical pattern. Parallelism helps to highlight ideas while showing their relationship and giving style to writing.

Examples are:

- **Parallel words** - The killer behaved coldly, cruelly, and inexplicably.
- **Parallel phrases** - Praised by comrades, honored by commanders, the soldier came home a hero.
- **Parallel clauses** - "We shall fight on the beaches, we shall fight on the landing grounds, we shall fight in the hills." (Winston Churchill)

Euphemism — This is a "cover-up" word that avoids the explicit meaning of an offensive or unpleasant term by substituting a vaguer image. An example is using "expired" instead of "dead."

Hyperbole — This is an example or phrase that exaggerates for effect. An example is the extravagant overstatement "I thought I would die!" Hyperbole is also used in tall tales, such as those describing Paul Bunyan's feats.

Climax — This refers to the process of building up to a dramatic highpoint through a series of phrases or sentences. It can also refer to the highpoint or most intense event in a story.

Bathos, Oxymoron, Irony, and Malapropism

Bathos — This is an attempt to evoke pity, sorrow, or nobility that goes overboard and becomes ridiculous. It is an insincere pathos and a letdown. It is also sometimes called an anticlimax, although an anticlimax might be intentionally included for comic or satiric effect.

Oxymoron — This refers to two terms that are used together for contradictory effect, usually in the form of an adjective that doesn't fit the noun. An example is: a "new classic."

Irony — This refers to a difference between what is and what ought to be, or between what is said and what is meant. Irony can be an unexpected result in literature, such as a twist of fate. For example, it is ironic that the tortoise beat the hare.

Malapropism — This is confusing one word with another, similar-sounding word. For example, saying a movie was a cliff dweller instead of a cliffhanger is a malapropism.

Invalid Arguments

There are a number of **invalid or false arguments** that are used unethically to gain an advantage, such as:

- The "**ad hominem**" or "against the person" argument – This type attacks the character or behavior of a person taking a stand on an issue rather than the issue itself. The statement "That fat slob wants higher taxes" is an example of this type of argument.
- **Hasty generalizations** – These are condemnations of a group based on the behavior of one person or part. An example of this type of argument is someone saying that all McDonald's restaurants are lousy because he or she had a bad experience at one location.
- **Faulty causation** – This is assigning the wrong cause to an event. An example is blaming a flat tire on losing a lucky penny rather than on driving over a bunch of nails.
- **Bandwagon effect** – This is the argument that if everybody else is doing something, it must be a good thing to do. The absurdity of this type of argument is highlighted by the question: "If everybody else is jumping off a cliff, should you jump, too?"

It is important for a reader to be able to identify various types of invalid arguments to prevent being deceived and making faulty conclusions.

Fiction and Nonfiction

Fiction is a literary work usually presented in prose form that is not true. It is the product of the writer's imagination. Examples of fiction are novels, short stories, television scripts, and screenplays. **Nonfiction** is a literary work that is based on facts. In other words, the material is true. The purposeful inclusion of false information is considered dishonest, but the expression of opinions or suppositions is acceptable. Libraries divide their collections into works of fiction and nonfiction. Examples of nonfiction include historical materials, scientific reports, memoirs, biographies, most essays, journals, textbooks, documentaries, user manuals, and news reports.

Review Video: Reading Fiction
Visit mometrix.com/academy and enter code: 391411

Review Video: Historical Context
Visit mometrix.com/academy and enter code: 169770

Review Video: Interpretation of Expository or Literary Text
Visit mometrix.com/academy and enter code: 860442

Prose and Poetry

Prose is language as it is ordinarily spoken as opposed to verse or language with metric patterns. Prose is used for everyday communication, and is found in textbooks, memos, reports, articles, short stories, and novels. Distinguishing characteristics of prose include:

- It may have some sort of rhythm, but there is **no formal arrangement**.
- The common unit of organization is the **sentence**.
- It may include literary devices of repetition and balance.
- It must have more coherent relationships among sentences than a list would.

Poetry, or verse, is the manipulation of language with respect to meaning, meter, sound, and rhythm. A line of poetry can be any length and may or may not rhyme. Related groups of lines are called **stanzas**, and may also be any length. Some poems are as short as a few lines, and some are as long as a book. Poetry is a more ancient form of literature than prose.

Role of Emotions in Poetry

Poetry is designed to appeal to the physical and emotional senses. Using appeals to the **physical senses** through words that evoke sight, sound, taste, smell, and touch also causes the imagination to respond **emotionally**. Poetry appeals to the soul and memories with language that can be intriguingly novel and profoundly emotional in connotation. Poetry can focus on any topic, but the feelings associated with the topic are magnified by the ordered presentation found in poetry. Verse, however, is merely a matter of structure. The thing that turns words into poetry is the feeling packed into those words. People write poetry to express their feelings and people read poetry to try to experience those same feelings. Poetry interprets the human condition with understanding and insight. Children respond well to poetry because it has an inviting, entertaining sound that they are eager to mimic.

Short Story

A **short story** is prose fiction that has the same elements as a novel, such as plot, characters, and point of view. Edgar Allan Poe defined the short story as a **narrative** that can be read in **one sitting** (one-half to two hours), and is limited to a **single effect**. In a short story, there is no time for extensive character development, large numbers of characters, in-depth analysis, complicated plot lines, or detailed backgrounds. Historically, the short story is related to the fable, the exemplum, and the folktale. Short stories have become mainly an American art form. Famous short story writers include William Faulkner, Katherine Anne Porter, Eudora Welty, Flannery O'Connor, O. Henry, and J. D. Salinger.

Character Types

Readers need to be able to differentiate between **major and minor characters**. The difference can usually be determined based on whether the characters are round, flat, dynamic, or static. **Round characters** have complex personalities, just like real people. They are more commonly found in longer works such as novels or full-length plays. **Flat characters** display only a few personality traits and are based on stereotypes. Examples include the bigoted redneck, the lazy bum, or the absent-minded professor. **Dynamic characters** are those that change or grow during the course of the narrative. They may learn important lessons, fall in love, or take new paths. **Static characters** remain the same throughout a story. Usually, round characters are dynamic and flat characters are static, but this is not always the case. Falstaff, the loyal and comical character in Shakespeare's plays about Henry IV, is a round character in terms of his complexity. However, he never changes, which makes him a reliable figure in the story.

Line Structure in Poems

A **line of poetry** can be any length and can have any metrical pattern. A line is determined by the physical position of words on a page. A line is simply a group of words on a single line. Consider the following example:

> When I consider how my light is spent,
>
> E're half my days, in this dark world and wide,

These are two lines of poetry written by John Milton. Lines may or may not have punctuation at the end, depending, of course, on the need for punctuation. If these two lines were written out in a paragraph, they would be written with a **slash line** and a **space** in between the lines: "When I consider how my light is spent, / E're half my days, in this dark world and wide."

Blank Verse and Free Verse

Blank verse is unrhymed verse that consists of lines of iambic pentameter, which is five feet (sets) of unstressed and stressed syllables. The rhythm that results is the closest to natural human speech. It is the most commonly used type of verse because of its versatility. Well-known examples of blank verse are Shakespearean plays, Milton's epic poems, and T. S. Eliot's *The Waste Land*. **Free verse** lacks regular patterns of poetic feet, but has more controlled rhythm than prose in terms of pace and pauses. Free verse has no rhyme and is usually written in short lines of irregular length. Well-known examples of free verse are the King James translation of the Psalms, Walt Whitman's *Leaves of Grass*, and the poetry of Ezra Pound and William Carlos Williams.

Review Video: Forms of Poetry
Visit mometrix.com/academy and enter code: 451705

Stanza Structure in Poems

A **stanza** is a group of lines. The grouping denotes a relationship among the lines. A stanza can be any length, but the separation of lines into different stanzas indicates an intentional *pattern* created by the poet. The breaks between stanzas indicate a change of subject or thought. As a group of lines, the stanza is a melodic unit that can be analyzed for *metrical and rhyme patterns*. Various common rhyme patterns have been named. The Spenserian stanza, which has a rhyme pattern of a b a b b c b c c, is an example. Stanzas of a certain length also have names. Examples include the **couplet**, which has two lines; the **tercet**, which has three lines; and the **quatrain**, which has four lines.

Meter

A recurring pattern of stressed and unstressed syllables in language creates a rhythm when spoken. When the pattern is regular, it is called **meter**. When meter is used in a composition, it is called **verse**. The most common types of meter are:

- **Iambic** – An unstressed syllable followed by a stressed syllable
- **Anapestic** – Two unstressed syllables followed by a stressed syllable
- **Trochaic** – One stressed syllable followed by an unstressed syllable
- **Dactylic** – A stressed syllable followed by two unstressed syllables
- **Spondaic** – Two consecutive syllables that are stressed almost equally
- **Pyrrhic** – Two consecutive syllables that are equally unstressed

Types of Children's Literature

A **fairy tale** is a fictional story involving humans, magical events, and usually animals. Characters such as fairies, elves, giants, and talking animals are taken from folklore. The plot often involves impossible events (as in "Jack and the Beanstalk") and/or an enchantment (as in "Sleeping Beauty"). Other examples of fairy tales include "Cinderella," "Little Red Riding Hood," and "Rumpelstiltskin." A **fable** is a tale in which animals, plants, and forces of nature act like humans. A fable also teaches a moral lesson. Examples are "The Tortoise and the Hare," *The Lion King*, and *Animal Farm*. A **tall tale** exaggerates human abilities or describes unbelievable events as if the story were true. Often, the narrator seems to have witnessed the event described. Examples are fish stories, Paul Bunyan and Pecos Bill stories, and hyperboles about real people such as Davy Crockett, Mike Fink, and Calamity Jane.

Preadolescent and Adolescent Literature

Preadolescent literature is mostly concerned with the "tween" issues of changing lives, relationships, and bodies. **Adolescents** seeking escape from their sometimes difficult lives enjoy fantasy and science fiction. For both groups, books about modern, real people are more interesting than those about historical figures or legends. Boys especially enjoy nonfiction. Reading interests as well as reading levels for this group vary. Reading levels will usually range from 6.0 to 8.9. Examples of popular literature for this age group and reading level include:

- Series – Sweet Valley High, Bluford High, Nancy Drew, Hardy Boys, and Little House on the Prairie
- Juvenile fiction authors – Judy Blume and S. E. Hinton
- Fantasy and horror authors – Ursula LeGuin and Stephen King
- Science fiction authors – Isaac Asimov, Ray Bradbury, and H. G. Wells
- Classic books: Lilies of the Field, Charlie and the Chocolate Factory, Pippi Longstocking, National Velvet, Call of the Wild, Anne of Green Gables, The Hobbit, The Member of the Wedding, and Tom Sawyer

Grammatical Terms

The definitions for grammatical terms are as follows:

Adjective – This is a word that modifies or describes a noun or pronoun. Examples are a *green* apple or *every* computer.

Adverb – This is a word that modifies a verb (*instantly* reviewed), an adjective (*relatively* odd), or another adverb (*rather* suspiciously).

Conjunctions: There are three types of conjunctions:

- **Coordinating conjunctions** are used to link words, phrases, and clauses. Examples are and, or, nor, for, but, yet, and so.
- **Correlative conjunctions** are paired terms used to link clauses. Examples are either/or, neither/nor, and if/then.
- **Subordinating conjunctions** relate subordinate or dependent clauses to independent ones. Examples are although, because, if, since, before, after, when, even though, in order that, and while.

Gerund – This is a verb form used as a noun. Most end in "ing." An example is: *Walking* is good exercise.

Infinitive – This is a verbal form comprised of the word "to" followed by the root form of a verb. An infinitive may be used as a noun, adjective, adverb, or absolute. Examples include:

- *To hold* a baby is a joy. (noun)
- Jenna had many files *to reorganize.* (adjective)
- Andrew tried *to remember* the dates. (adverb)
- *To be honest,* your hair looks awful. (absolute)

Noun – This is a word that names a person, place, thing, idea, or quality. A noun can be used as a subject, object, complement, appositive, or modifier.

Object – This is a word or phrase that receives the action of a verb.

- A direct object states *to* whom/what an action was committed. It answers the question "to what?" An example is: Joan served *the meal.*
- An indirect object states *for* whom/what an action was committed. An example is: Joan served *us* the meal.

Preposition – This is a word that links a noun or pronoun to other parts of a sentence. Examples include above, by, for, in, out, through, and to.

Prepositional phrase – This is a combination of a preposition and a noun or pronoun. Examples include across the bridge, against the grain, below the horizon, and toward the sunset.

Pronoun – This is a word that represents a specific noun in a generic way. A pronoun functions like a noun in a sentence. Examples include I, she, he, it, myself, they, these, what, all, and anybody.

Sentence – This is a group of words that expresses a thought or conveys information as an independent unit of speech. A **complete sentence** must contain a noun and a verb (I ran). However, all the other parts of speech can also be represented in a sentence.

Verb – This is a word or phrase in a sentence that expresses action (Mary played) or a state of being (Mary is).

Review Video: Parts of Speech
Visit mometrix.com/academy and enter code: 899611

Capitalization and Punctuation

Capitalization refers to the use of capital letters. Capital letters should be placed at the beginning of:

- **Proper names** (Ralph Waldo Emerson, Australia)
- **Places** (Mount Rushmore, Chicago)
- Historical periods and holidays (Renaissance, Christmas)
- **Religious terms** (Bible, Koran)
- **Titles** (Empress Victoria, General Smith)
- All main words in **literary, art, or music titles** (Grapes of Wrath, Sonata in C Major)

Punctuation consists of:

Periods – A period is placed at the end of a sentence.

Commas – A comma is used to separate:

- Two adjectives modifying the same word (long, hot summer)
- Three or more words or phrases in a list (Winken, Blinken, and Nod; life, liberty, and the pursuit of happiness)
- Phrases that are not needed to complete a sentence (The teacher, not the students, will distribute the supplies.)

Colons and Semicolons

Colons – A colon is used to:

- Set up a **list** (We will need these items: a pencil, paper, and an eraser.)
- Direct readers to **examples or explanations** (We have one chore left: clean out the garage.)
- Introduce **quotations or dialogue** (The Labor Department reported on unemployment: "There was a 3.67% increase in unemployment in 2010."; Scarlett exclaimed: "What shall I do?")

Review Video: Colons
Visit mometrix.com/academy and enter code: 868673

Semicolons – A semicolon is used to:

- Join **related independent clauses** (There were five major hurricanes this year; two of them hit Florida.)
- Join **independent clauses connected by conjunctive adverbs** (Popular books are often made into movies; however, it is a rare screenplay that is as good as the book.)
- Separate items in a **series** if commas would be confusing (The characters include: Robin Hood, who robs from the rich to give to the poor; Maid Marian, his true love; and Little John, Robin Hood's comrade-in-arms.)

Review Video: Semicolon Usage
Visit mometrix.com/academy and enter code: 370605

Subject-Verb Agreement

A verb must **agree** in number with its subject. Therefore, a verb changes form depending on whether the subject is singular or plural. Examples include "I do," "he does," "the ball is," and "the balls are." If two subjects are joined by "and," the **plural** form of a verb is usually used. For example: *Jack and Jill want* to get some water (Jack wants, Jill wants, but together they want). If the compound subjects are preceded by each or every, they take the **singular** form of a verb. For example: *Each man and each woman brings* a special talent to the world (each brings, not bring). If one noun in a compound subject is plural and the other is singular, the verb takes the form of the subject **nearest** to it. For example: Neither the *students* nor their *teacher was* ready for the fire drill. **Collective nouns** that name a group are considered singular if they refer to the group acting as a unit. For example: The *choir is going* on a concert tour.

Review Video: Subject Verb Agreement
Visit mometrix.com/academy and enter code: 479190

Syntax

Syntax refers to the rules related to how to properly **structure** sentences and phrases. Syntax is not the same as grammar. For example, "I does" is syntactically correct because the subject and verb are in proper order, but it is grammatically incorrect because the subject and verb don't agree.

There are three types of sentence structures:

- **Simple** – This type is composed of a single independent clause with one subject and one predicate (verb or verb form).
- **Compound** – This type is composed of two independent clauses joined by a conjunction (Amy flew, but Brenda took the train), a correlative conjunction (Either Tom goes with me or I stay here), or a semicolon (My grandfather stays in shape; he plays tennis nearly every day).
- **Complex** – This type is composed of one independent clause and one or more dependent clauses joined by a subordinating conjunction (Before we set the table, we should replace the tablecloth).

Types of Paragraphs or Essays

A **comparison and contrast essay** examines the similarities and differences between two things. In a paragraph, the writer presents all the points about subject A and then all the points about subject B. In an essay, the writer might present one point at a time, comparing subject A and subject B side by side.

A **classification paper** sorts information. It opens with a topic sentence that identifies the group to be classified, and then breaks that group into categories. For example, a group might be baseball players, while a category might be positions they play.

A **cause and effect paper** discusses the causes or reasons for an event or the effects of a cause or causes. Topics discussed in this type of essay might include the causes of a war or the effects of global warming.

A **persuasive essay** is one in which the writer tries to convince the audience to agree with a certain opinion or point of view. The argument must be supported with facts, examples, anecdotes, expert testimony, or statistics, and must anticipate and answer the questions of those who hold an opposing view. It may also predict consequences.

Role of Purpose and Audience in Writing a Paper

Early in the writing process, the writer needs to definitively determine the **purpose** of the paper and then keep that purpose in mind throughout the writing process. The writer needs to ask: "Is the purpose to explain something, to tell a story, to entertain, to inform, to argue a point, or some combination of these purposes?" Also at the beginning of the writing process, the writer needs to determine the **audience** of the paper by asking questions such as: "Who will read this paper?" "For whom is this paper intended?" "What does the audience already know about this topic?" "How much does the audience need to know?" and "Is the audience likely to agree or disagree with my point of view?" The answers to these questions will determine the content of the paper, the tone, and the style.

Writing Processes

Drafting is creating an early version of a paper. A draft is a prototype or sketch of the finished product. A draft is a rough version of the final paper, and it is expected that there will be multiple drafts.

Revising is the process of making major changes to a draft in regards to clarity of purpose, focus (thesis), audience, organization, and content.

Editing is the process of making changes in style, word choice, tone, examples, and arrangement. These are more minor than the changes made during revision. Editing can be thought of as fine tuning. The writer makes the language more precise, checks for varying paragraph lengths, and makes sure that the title, introduction, and conclusion fit well with the body of the paper.

Proofreading is performing a final check and correcting errors in punctuation, spelling, grammar, and usage. It also involves looking for parts of the paper that may be omitted.

Review Video: Recursive Writing Process
Visit mometrix.com/academy and enter code: 951611

Title and Conclusion of an Essay

The **title** is centered on the page and the main words are capitalized. The title is not surrounded by quotation marks, nor is it underlined or italicized. The title is rarely more than four or five words, and is very rarely a whole sentence. A good title suggests the subject of the paper and catches the reader's interest. The **conclusion** should flow logically from the body of the essay, should tie back to the introduction, and may provide a summary or a final thought on the subject. New material should never be introduced in the conclusion. The conclusion is a wrap-up that may contain a call to action, something the writer wants the audience to do in response to the paper. The conclusion might end with a question to give the reader something to think about.

Review Video: Drafting Conclusions
Visit mometrix.com/academy and enter code: 209408

Introduction of an Essay

The **introduction** contains the **thesis statement**, which is usually the first or last sentence of the opening paragraph. It needs to be interesting enough to make the reader want to continue reading.

- Possible openings for an introduction include:
- The thesis statement
- A general idea that gives background or sets the scene
- An illustration that will make the thesis more concrete and easy to picture
- A surprising fact or idea to arouse curiosity
- A contradiction to popular belief that attracts interest
- A quotation that leads into the thesis

Review Video: Introduction
Visit mometrix.com/academy and enter code: 961328

Review Video: Introduction II
Visit mometrix.com/academy and enter code: 254411

Sentence Types

A **declarative sentence** makes a statement and is punctuated by a period at the end. An example is: The new school will be built at the south end of Main Street.

An **interrogative sentence** asks a question and is punctuated by a question mark at the end. An example is: Why will the new school be built so far out?

An **exclamatory sentence** shows strong emotion and is punctuated by an exclamation mark at the end. An example is: The new school has the most amazing state-of-the-art technology!

An **imperative sentence** gives a direction or command and may be punctuated by an exclamation mark or a period. Sometimes, the subject of an imperative sentence is you, which is understood instead of directly stated. An example is: Come to the open house at the new school next Sunday.

Transitional Words and Phrases

Transitional words are used to signal a relationship. They are used to link thoughts and sentences. Some types of transitional words and phrases are:

- **Addition** – Also, in addition, furthermore, moreover, and then, another
- **Admitting a point** – Granted, although, while it is true that
- **Cause and effect** – Since, so, consequently, as a result, therefore, thus
- **Comparison** – Similarly, just as, in like manner, likewise
- **Contrast** – On the other hand, yet, nevertheless, despite, but, still
- **Emphasis** – Indeed, in fact, without a doubt, certainly, to be sure
- **Illustration** – For example, for instance, in particular, specifically
- **Purpose** – In order to, for this purpose, for this to occur
- **Spatial arrangement** – Beside, above, below, around, across, inside, near, far, to the left
- **Summary or clarification** – In summary, in conclusion, that is, in other words
- **Time sequence** – Before, after, later, soon, next, meanwhile, suddenly, finally

Pre-Writing Techniques

Pre-writing techniques that help a writer find, explore, and organize a topic include:

- **Brainstorming** – This involves letting thoughts make every connection to the topic possible, and then spinning off ideas and making notes of them as they are generated. This is a process of using imagination, uninhibited creativity, and instincts to discover a variety of possibilities.
- **Freewriting** – This involves choosing items from the brainstorming list and writing about them nonstop for a short period. This unedited, uncensored process allows one thing to lead to another and permits the writer to think of additional concepts and themes.
- **Clustering/mapping** – This involves writing a general word or phrase related to the topic in the middle of a paper and circling it, and then quickly jotting down related words or phrases. These are circled and lines are drawn to link words and phrases to others on the page. Clustering is a visual representation of brainstorming that reveals patterns and connections.
- **Listing** – Similar to brainstorming, listing is writing down as many descriptive words and phrases (not whole sentences) as possible that relate to the subject. Correct spelling and grouping of these descriptive terms can come later if needed. This list is merely intended to stimulate creativity and provide a vibrant vocabulary for the description of the subject once the actual writing process begins.
- **Charting** – This prewriting technique works well for comparison/contrast purposes or for the examination of advantages and disadvantages (pros and cons). Any kind of chart will work, even a simple two-column list. The purpose is to draw out points and examples that can be used in the paper.

Purpose of Writing

Writing always has a purpose. The five reasons to write are:

- **To tell a story** – The story does not necessarily need to be fictional. The purposes are to explain what happened, to narrate events, and to explain how things were accomplished. The story will need to make a point, and plenty of details will need to be provided to help the reader imagine the event or process.
- **To express oneself** – This type of writing is commonly found in journals, diaries, or blogs. This kind of writing is an exercise in reflection that allows writers to learn something about themselves and what they have observed, and to work out their thoughts and feelings on paper.
- **To convey information** – Reports are written for this purpose. Information needs to be as clearly organized and accurate as possible. Charts, graphs, tables, and other illustrations can help make the information more understandable.
- **To make an argument** – This type of writing also makes a point, but adds opinion to the facts presented. Argumentative, or persuasive, writing is one of the most common and important types of writing. It should follow rules of logic and ethics.
- **To explore ideas** – This is speculative writing that is quite similar to reflective writing. This type of writing explores possibilities and asks questions without necessarily expecting an answer. The purpose is to stimulate readers to further consider and reflect on the topic.

Review Video: Author's Main Point or Purpose
Visit mometrix.com/academy and enter code: 734339

Arranging Information Strategically

The order of the elements in a writing project can be organized in the following ways:

- **Logical order** – There is a coherent pattern in the presentation of information, such as inductive or deductive reasoning or a division of a topic into its parts.
- **Hierarchical order** – There is a ranking of material from most to least important or least to most important, depending on whether the writer needs a strong start or a sweeping finish. It can also involve breaking down a topic from a general form into specifics.
- **Chronological order** – This is an order that follows a sequence. In a narrative, the sequence will follow the time order of beginning to middle to end. In a "how to," the sequence will be step 1, step 2, step 3, and so on.
- **Order defined by genre** – This is a pre-determined order structured according to precedent or professional guidelines, such as the order required for a specific type of research or lab report, a resume, or an application form.
- **Order of importance** – This method of organization relies on a ranking determined by priorities. For example, in a persuasive paper, the writer usually puts the strongest argument in the last body paragraph so that readers will remember it. In a news report, the most important information comes first.
- **Order of interest** – This order is dependent on the level of interest the audience has in the subject. If the writer anticipates that reader knowledge and interest in the subject will be low, normal order choices need to be changed. The piece should begin with something very appealing. This will hook the reader and make for a strong opening.

Beginning Stages of Learning to Write

The following are the beginning stages of learning to write:

- **Drawing pictures** is the first written attempt to express thoughts and feelings. Even when the picture is unrecognizable to the adult, it means something to the child.
- The **scribble stage** begins when the child attempts to draw shapes. He or she may also try to imitate writing. The child may have a story or explanation to go with the shapes.
- Children have the most interest in learning to **write their own names**, so writing lessons usually start with that. Children will soon recognize that there are other letters too.
- Children are learning the **alphabet** and how to associate a **sound with each letter**. Reversing letters is still common, but instruction begins with teaching children to write from left to right.
- Written words may not be complete, but will likely have the correct **beginning and end sounds/letters**.
- Children will make some attempt to use **vowels** in writing.
- Children will write with more ease, although spelling will still be phonetic and only some punctuation will be used.

Journal Writing

Writing in a **journal** gives students practice in writing, which makes them more comfortable with the writing process. Journal writing also gives students the opportunity to sort out their thoughts, solve problems, examine relationships and values, and see their personal and academic growth when they revisit old entries. The advantages for the teacher are that the students become more experienced with and accustomed to writing. Through reading student journals, the teacher can also gain **insight** into the students' problems and attitudes, which can help the teacher tailor his or her lesson plans. A journal can be kept in a **notebook** or in a **computer file**. It shouldn't be just a record of daily events, but an expression of thoughts and feelings about everything and anything. Grammar and punctuation don't matter since journaling is a form of private communication. Teachers who review journals need to keep in mind that they should not grade journals and that comments should be encouraging and polite.

Revising a Paper

Revising a paper involves rethinking the choices that were made while constructing the paper and then rewriting it, making any necessary changes or additions to word choices or arrangement of points. Questions to keep in mind include:

- Is the thesis clear?
- Do the body paragraphs logically flow and provide details to support the thesis?
- Is anything unnecessarily repeated?
- Is there anything not related to the topic?
- Is the language understandable?
- Does anything need to be defined?
- Is the material interesting?

Another consideration when revising is **peer feedback**. It is helpful during the revision process to have someone who is knowledgeable enough to be helpful and will be willing to give an honest critique read the paper.

Review Video: General Revision and Proofreading
Visit mometrix.com/academy and enter code: 385882

Paragraph Coherence

Paragraph coherence can be achieved by linking sentences by using the following strategies:

- **Repetition of key words** – It helps the reader follow the progression of thought from one sentence to another if key words (which should be defined) are repeated to assure the reader that the writer is still on topic and the discussion still relates to the key word.
- **Substitution of pronouns** – This doesn't just refer to using single word pronouns such as I, they, us, etc., but also alternate descriptions of the subject. For example, if someone was writing about Benjamin Franklin, it gets boring to keep saying Franklin or he. Other terms that describe him, such as that notable American statesman, this printer, the inventor, and so forth can also be used.
- **Substitution of synonyms** – This is similar to substitution of pronouns, but refers to using similar terms for any repeated noun or adjective, not just the subject. For example, instead of constantly using the word great, adjectives such as terrific, really cool, awesome, and so on can also be used.

Verbs

In order to understand the role of a verb and be able to identify the verb that is necessary to make a sentence, it helps to know the different types of verbs. These are:

- **Action verbs** – These are verbs that express an action being performed by the subject. An example is: The outfielder caught the ball (outfielder = subject and caught = action).
- **Linking verbs** – These are verbs that link the subject to words that describe or identify the subject. An example is: Mary is an excellent teacher (Mary = subject and "is" links Mary to her description as an excellent teacher). Common linking verbs are all forms of the verb "to be," appear, feel, look, become, and seem.
- **Helping verbs** – When a single verb cannot do the job by itself because of tense issues, a second, helping verb is added. Examples include: should have gone ("gone" is the main verb, while "should" and "have" are helping verbs), and was playing ("playing" is the main verb, while "was" is the helping verb).

Coordinating Conjunctions and Subordinating Conjunctions

There are different ways to connect two clauses and show their relationship:

- A **coordinating conjunction** is one that can join two independent clauses by placing a comma and a coordinating conjunction between them. The most common coordinating conjunctions are and, but, or, nor, yet, for, and so. Examples include: "It was warm, so I left my jacket at home" and "It was warm, and I left my jacket at home."
- A **subordinating conjunction** is one that joins a subordinate clause and an independent clause and establishes the relationship between them. An example is: "We can play a game after Steve finishes his homework." The dependent clause is "after Steve finishes his homework" because the reader immediately asks, "After Steve finishes, then what?" The independent clause is "We can play a game." The concern is not the ability to play a game, but "when?" The answer to this question is dependent on when Steve finishes his homework.

Review Video: Conjunctions
Visit mometrix.com/academy and enter code: 904603

Run-On Sentences and Comma Splices

A **run-on sentence** is one that tries to connect two independent clauses without the needed conjunction or punctuation and makes it hard for the reader to figure out where one sentence ends and the other starts. An example is: "Meagan is three years old she goes to pre-school." Two possible ways to fix the run-on would be: "Meagan is three years old, and she goes to pre-school" or "Meagan is three years old; however, she goes to pre-school." A **comma splice** occurs when a comma is used to join two independent clauses without a proper conjunction. The comma should be replaced by a period or one of the methods for coordination or subordination should be used. An example of a comma splice is: "Meagan is three years old, she goes to pre-school."

Fragments

A **fragment** is an incomplete sentence, which is one that does not have a subject to go with the verb, or vice versa. The following are types of fragments:

- **Dependent clause fragments** – These usually start with a subordinating conjunction. An example is: "Before you can graduate." "You can graduate" is a sentence, but the subordinating conjunction "before" makes the clause dependent, which means it needs an independent clause to go with it. An example is: "Before you can graduate, you have to meet all the course requirements."
- **Relative clause fragments** – These often start with who, whose, which, or that. An example is: "Who is always available to the students." This is a fragment because the "who" is not identified. A complete sentence would be: "Mr. Jones is a principal who is always available to the students."
- **The "-ing" fragment** lacks a subject. The "-ing" form of a verb has to have a helping verb. An example is: "Walking only three blocks to his job." A corrected sentence would be: "Walking only three blocks to his job, Taylor has no need for a car."
- **Prepositional phrase fragments** are ones that begin with a preposition and are only a phrase, not a complete thought. An example is: "By the time we arrived." "We arrived" by itself would be a complete sentence, but the "by" makes the clause dependent and the reader asks, "By the time you arrived, what happened?" A corrected sentence would be: "By the time we arrived, all the food was gone."
- **Infinitive phrase fragments** have the same problem as prepositional phrase ones. An example is: "To plant the seed." A corrected sentence would be: "To plant the seed, Isaac used a trowel."

Review Video: Fragments and Run-on Sentences
Visit mometrix.com/academy and enter code: 541989

Primary and Secondary Research Information

Primary research material is material that comes from the "horse's mouth." It is a document or object that was created by the person under study or during the time period under study. Examples of primary sources are original documents such as manuscripts, diaries, interviews, autobiographies, government records, letters, news videos, and artifacts (such as Native American pottery or wall writings in Egyptian tombs). **Secondary research material** is anything that is not primary. Secondary sources are those things that are written or otherwise recorded about the main subject. Examples include a critical analysis of a literary work (a poem by William Blake is primary, but the analysis of the poem by T. S. Eliot is secondary), a magazine article about a person (a direct quote would be primary, but the report is secondary), histories, commentaries, and encyclopedias.

Primary sources are the raw material of research. This can include results of experiments, notes, and surveys or interviews done by the researcher. Other primary sources are books, letters, diaries, eyewitness accounts, and performances attended by the researcher. **Secondary sources** consist of oral and written accounts prepared by others. This includes reports, summaries, critical reviews, and other sources not developed by the researcher. Most research writing uses both primary and secondary sources: primary sources from first-hand accounts and secondary sources for background and supporting documentation. The research process calls for active reading and writing throughout. As research yields information, it often calls for more reading and research, and the cycle continues.

Drafting Research Essays

Introduction

The **introduction** to a research essay is particularly important, as it sets the *context* for the essay. It needs to draw the reader into the subject and provide necessary background to understand the subject. It is sometimes helpful to open with the research question and explain how the question will be answered. The major points of the essay may be forecast or previewed to prepare readers for the coming arguments. In a research essay, it is a good idea to establish the writer's credibility by reviewing credentials and experience with the subject. Another useful opening involves quoting several sources that support the points of the essay, again to establish credibility. The tone should be appropriate to the audience and subject, maintaining a sense of careful authority while building the arguments. *Jargon* should be kept to a minimum, and language should be carefully chosen to reflect the appropriate tone.

Conclusion

The **conclusion** to a research essay helps readers summarize what they have learned. Conclusions are not meant to convince, as this has been done in the body of the essay. It can be useful to leave the reader with a memorable phrase or example that supports the argument. Conclusions should be both memorable and logical restatements of the arguments in the body of the essay. A *specific-to-general pattern* can be helpful, opening with the thesis statement and expanding to more general observations. A good idea is to restate the main points in the body of the essay, leading to the conclusion. An ending that evokes a vivid image or asks a provocative question makes the essay memorable. The same effect can be achieved by a call for action, or a warning. Conclusions may be tailored to the audience's background, in terms of language, tone, and style.

Reviewing the Draft

Checklist for Reviewing a Draft of a Research Essay

1. **Introduction**: Is the reader's attention gained and held by the introduction?
2. **Thesis**: Does the essay fulfill the promise of the thesis? Is it strong enough?
3. **Main points**: Are the main points listed and ranked in order of importance?
4. **Organization**: What is the organizing principle of the essay? Does it work?
5. **Supporting information**: Is the thesis adequately supported? Is the thesis convincing?
6. **Source material**: Are there adequate sources and are they smoothly integrated into the essay?
7. **Conclusion**: Does the conclusion have sufficient power? Does it summarize the essay well?
8. **Paragraphs, sentences, words**: Are these elements effective in promoting the thesis?
9. **Overall review**: Evaluate the essay's strengths and weaknesses. What revisions are needed?

Modern Language Association Style

The **Modern Language Association style** is widely used in literature and languages as well as other fields. The MLA style calls for noting brief references to sources in parentheses in the text of an essay and adding an alphabetical list of sources, called "Works Cited," at the end. Specific recommendations of the MLA include the following:

1. "**Works Cited**": Include in this section only works actually cited. List on a separate page the author's name, title, and publication information, which must include the location of the publisher, the publisher's name, and the date of publication.

2. **Parenthetical citations**: MLA style uses parenthetical citations following each quotation, reference, paraphrase, or summary to a source. Each citation is made up of the author's last name and page reference, keyed to a reference in Works Cited.
3. **Explanatory notes**: Explanatory notes are numbered consecutively and identified by superscript numbers in the text. The full notes may appear as endnotes or as footnotes at the bottom of the page.

Media Literacy

Media literacy is the ability to access, read, and interpret information from various parts of the media. Parts of the media can include the Internet, artifacts, printed materials, primary source documents, and visual media. A student who has achieved media literacy can effectively navigate the Internet (and other facets of media) without losing focus or accessing information deemed inappropriate or unsafe. Students with media literacy also develop the ability to question the validity of the information they are accessing by questioning the source and accuracy of the information being presented. In addition, students with media literacy can identify the key components of what they are accessing without becoming overwhelmed by the amount of information available.

Key Points Related to Speaking

The following are key points to remember about volume, pace, pronunciation, body language, word choice, and visual aids as they relate to speaking:

- **Volume** – Voice volume should be appropriate to the room and adjusted according to whether or not a microphone is used. The speaker should not shout at the audience, mumble, or speak so softly that his or her voice is inaudible.
- **Pace and pronunciation** – The speaker shouldn't talk so fast that his or her speech is unintelligible, nor should the speaker speak so slowly as to be boring. The speaker should enunciate words clearly.
- **Body language and gestures** – Body language can add to or distract from the message, so annoying, repetitive gestures such as waving hands about, flipping hair, or staring at one spot should be avoided. Good posture is critical.
- **Word choice** – The speaker should use a vocabulary level that fits the age and interest level of the audience. Vocabulary may be casual or formal depending on the audience.
- **Visual aids** – The speaker should use whatever aids will enhance the presentation, such as props, models, media, etc., but should not use anything that will be distracting or unmanageable.

Communicating Emotions

The majority of communications taking place in academic and business settings involve **factual information**. Unfortunately, individuals who are adept at communicating facts may struggle when attempting to communicate **personal feelings** in a relationship. Personal relationships, which are basic to happiness, can develop only when feelings are openly and honestly shared. In order to do this, people should work on asking straight-forward questions and honestly answering questions about themselves. Being a good listener, asking the right questions, and respecting the other person's answers are necessary parts of establishing good emotional communication. Sometimes, though, this may mean putting aside your own opinions so that you can fully engage with another person and come to understand the other's point of view.

Nonverbal Communication

Even though we normally think of communication as something we do through spoken or written language, we are constantly sending messages to one another with our **bodies** and **tone of voice**. Often, physical messages are sent and interpreted without either party being aware. Some of the signals that are used are consistent across cultures, whereas others are unique to a particular culture. For instance, slumped shoulders generally mean passivity and submission in every society. Alternatively, some cultures interpret eye contact as a sign of respect, and others see it as a sign of hostility. One should try to be aware of the messages one is sending with one's posture and gestures to avoid sending messages that are insulting or self-defeating.

Self-Concept in Interpersonal Communication

During **interpersonal communication**, all the participating parties filter information through their own **self-concept**. Everyone naturally applies new information to his or her own self-concept. Often, however, self-interested concerns can make it difficult for a listener to get a true sense of what the other person is saying. As much as possible, listeners should strive to understand and take into account their own self-image, so they can be as objective as possible when evaluating an incoming message. Although a slight degree of egotism or self-centeredness is natural, these traits can hinder accurate and insightful listening. Therefore, the goal of speech communication education is to mitigate these distorting factors.

Images of Self and Others Existing During Two-Person Conversations

When two individuals have a conversation, their **self-images** and the **images they hold of each other** exert a great influence on the course of the conversation. For instance, imagine you are talking to your teacher. You have a self-image and an image of the teacher. You also have an image of how you hope your teacher sees you. Finally, you have an image of how you think your teacher actually sees you. Similarly, your teacher holds his or her own set of four images in mind. Obviously, then, even carrying on a simple conversation becomes a complicated event. Speech communication theorists assert that conversations tend to go better when there is less discrepancy between these various images. For instance, if your self-image is similar to the image you imagine your teacher has of you, you are less likely to have trouble coming up with appropriate things to say. Similarly, if your impression of what the teacher thinks of you is similar to what you *hope* the teacher would think of you, you are less likely to make outlandish claims or try to justify yourself.

Self-Disclosure

According to speech communication theorists, conversations work best when both parties are as honest and forthcoming about themselves as possible. In other words, when engaged in conversation, a person should strive to be as accurate as possible in revealing his or her self-image. This process is known as **self-disclosure**. To the degree that we hide information about ourselves, we prevent others from truly understanding us. There are a number of reasons why a person might not engage in total self-disclosure. Propriety, pride, and fear are probably the most common reasons for hiding information about oneself. Difficulty can also arise when one individual in a conversation has information about the other without the other party being aware of it. This kind of asymmetrical knowledge can create underlying but unexpressed tension in a conversation. Ideally, people should attempt to continually increase their level of self-disclosure while encouraging their interlocutor to do the same.

Encoding Meaning

When one person speaks to another, he or she is "**encoding**" the verbal message with supplemental nonverbal forms of communication. The precise "**code**" the speaker uses is the particular set of words, with their agreed-upon meaning, as well as syntax and grammar. To the degree that the speaker has a command of vocabulary and a strong sense of meaning, he or she will be able to construct a subtle and effective code. The process of encoding meaning is also influenced by individual bias, desire, and perception. People encode meaning differently based on the personal "agenda" they bring to any conversation. Two people speaking to one another should be able to increase the complexity and accuracy of their message encoding as the conversation progresses because they will be acquiring more and better information about one another's intentions, knowledge, and character.

Interpreting Meaning

When we listen to another person speak in conversation, we are attempting to **decode** their meaning through the **filter** of our own prejudices and perceptions. Speech communication theorists assert that listeners tend to emphasize the components of a message that are associated with their own pre-existing knowledge or interests. In particular, we all tend to emphasize the importance of those aspects of a message that directly pertain to us. Starting out, we are more likely to make mistakes in the interpretation of what a speaker is saying. As we acquire more information and become more familiar with the other person's speaking style, however, we tend to make beneficial adjustments to our interpretation. The more time we spend with another person, the better we are able to correctly interpret the meanings of their communications.

Communication Appropriate to Cooperating on Tasks

For people to **cooperate** effectively on a task, they all need good **communication skills**. This is especially true in the adult professional world. Without effective communication among those involved, success will be more difficult to achieve, but many people do not learn to work effectively with others until late childhood. For the most part, any job-related task is most easily accomplished when all parties know enough about the task-related tools, ideas, and skills to communicate effectively among themselves. In some cases, two individuals working together on a task may have unequal power, such as in the case of an employer and employee collaborating on a work-related project. Such unequal distribution of power also has a strong effect on communication.

Classroom Materials That Support Literacy Across the Curriculum

In a classroom that supports literacy, the teacher should provide **labels** combining words and pictures on all objects. This continually stimulates students to associate written language with the objects and concepts it represents. Especially to support disabled students, teachers should use their particular interests and needs as a guide for labeling things. Printed directions, signs, calendars, and schedules are materials that students should use regularly in the classroom. These help students realize how language is used in everyday life. When the class is studying a certain topic, theme, or book, the teacher and students can work together to redesign the classroom using printed/written materials that reflect that topic, theme, or book. This enables students to experience fully and "live" the lesson rather than just observing it. All of the materials must be adapted for any students' special needs. For instance, in a class including blind/visually impaired students, labels, signs and other print materials can incorporate Braille words and textured surfaces.

Addressing Diverse Student Abilities and Needs

Teachers must consider the **diversity** among the skills and needs of their students as they design their classroom learning environments. The teachers should **individualize** the setting and their instruction so that these represent every student. Individualization and instructional differentiation should not only address disabled students' needs; they should also regularly provide suitable opportunities for these students to participate on an ongoing basis in activities that involve literacy and integrate it into all content areas. According to research, a salient need of students with diverse literacy backgrounds is that they often have trouble connecting new information to their existing knowledge. This ability is a critical component of learning. When teachers plan and organize their classrooms to offer literacy activities that are accessible to disabled students—and that immerse them in literacy experiences and give them opportunities to connect both new with old information, and spoken with printed language—these students can then access the general education curriculum.

Activities for Students with Disabilities to Develop Literacy Skills and Participate in General Curriculum

To participate in the general curriculum, students with disabilities need to understand the **alphabetic principle**, i.e. that printed language represents spoken language; connect print with speech; and be able to relate new information to their prior knowledge. Teachers can support these developments by designing classrooms as literacy-rich settings, immersing special-needs and other students in **accessible literacy activities** across all content areas. For example, students can interact with alphabet-letter magnets, cookie-cutters, and stamps: concrete manipulatives allow students not developmentally ready for exclusively abstract thought to understand concepts using real objects. Discussing daily schedules requires students to read and comprehend printed language, and then use spoken language to demonstrate and apply their understanding. Playing letter/word games like Bingo, Pictionary, Boggle, and Scrabble gives practice with creating and manipulating language, enhancing recognition and cognitive flexibility. Providing photos of peers, teachers, staff, and classroom activities and having students label them helps students connect written language with familiar, meaningful images. Daily communication notebooks help students further integrate literacy into their school days.

Implications of Cultural and Linguistic Differences Regarding Literacy Development

Educational research shows that the **cultural values** of families and/or communities influence children's literacy development, and also that culture is a significant factor to understanding children's home literacy environments. Researchers have also found that cultural purposes, perspectives, and contexts affect how students with disabilities in particular interact with the literacy environments they encounter. They say children's preparation levels entering formal education reflect their families'/communities' values and beliefs about literacy. Cultural attitudes about literacy then influence how schools deliver instruction and literacy experiences. Teachers must assess culturally diverse students' interactions with the environment, and design literacy-rich classrooms, with students' diverse backgrounds in mind. Students learning English (ELL/ESL) enter school either not knowing English or just learning it, lacking exposure to specific vocabulary and literature. Literacy-rich classrooms help them participate in regular curriculum. Teacher should read aloud often to these students; include print in their native language in classrooms; permit mistakes during student attempts to use English; encourage students to reread books repeatedly; and plan activities entailing language use.

Drawbacks of Whole-Class and Small-Group Reading, and Flexible Grouping Model

A major disadvantage of **whole-class reading** is that students who read above the average class level go unchallenged and can become bored, while students reading below average level are lost. Yet the **small-group method** intended to remedy this also has the drawback that, as traditionally implemented, most time is used for skill instruction, leaving far too little time for students actually to read the text. One solution is a **flexible grouping model**, e.g., Grouping Without Tracking (Paratore, 1990). This model uses a "sandwich" structure: teachers give students shared-reading processes at the beginning and end of the lesson, but provide differentiated instruction to two groups in the middle as they read the text. Teachers give indirect guidance to students who can read more independently, and more direct support to struggling readers. Teachers reunite the groups to lead them in a final discussion. Students with reading difficulties gain reading proficiency and comprehension from direct teacher support, enabling them to contribute better to the whole-class discussion, so all share this experience equally.

Jigsaw Approach to Shared Reading

Students reading below grade level may be able to access and comprehend some texts or portions of them, but have difficulty with harder parts/texts—for example, informational texts with more challenging subject matter and specialized vocabulary. When a text intended for the whole class contains such challenging material, one solution the teacher can use is a **jigsaw approach**. The teacher selects various portions of the text that are less difficult and assigns them to students reading below grade level. Whereas such texts overall might present struggles for these students, they find the easier portions more manageable when they tackle only these parts, as selected and assigned by the teacher, in small groups of students with comparable reading levels. The teacher makes each small student group responsible for comprehension of their assigned portion of text. Then the teacher brings the class back together, having each group report what they read, understood, and learned. The whole class then collaborates to help each other make connections among the learning each group reported.

Using Themes to Connect Texts

Any inclusive classroom will contain students who read at various age/grade levels. As a result, some books used as core texts are going to present difficulties for some of the students, who read below grade level and/or lack background knowledge and vocabulary of the subject. One way a teacher can facilitate all students' comprehension of such texts is to provide **supplementary texts** that allow readers at different levels easier access—texts on the same subject or theme as the more difficult core text. Teachers have students read these more accessible texts independently during small-group reading periods. This makes it easier for students with less reading proficiency to learn the core vocabulary and build their background knowledge. Thus, they are more prepared to tackle the more difficult core text during whole-class shared reading periods. With such preparation, less proficient readers are more likely to become engaged and active participants in the shared reading of a difficult text in the whole-group setting.

Assigning Students to Small Groups for Guided Reading Exercises

Expert educators and researchers recommend that when teachers divide classes into small student groups for **guided reading**, they should not be overly concerned with assigning students to exact reading levels. Rather, though they will want to group students whose literacy development is similar and who read around a similar level, they should give more attention to organizing groups according to the students' *areas of need*. For example, a teacher might identify students who share in common a need for help with noticing changes in setting; other students who share difficulties with recognizing and differentiating characters; some students who demonstrate problems with following and/or reproducing events they read in a text in the correct chronological sequence; some students who have trouble identifying and/or articulating the main idea in a text portion, etc. The teacher can create a group of students sharing one of these challenges; announce to the class what this group's focus is; and then invite other students to join this group by choice if they experience the same need.

Helping Teachers Provide More Equitable Learning Opportunities Using Word Counts

Books designed for lower reading levels typically contain fewer words, both per page and overall. Yet students who are reading below their grade levels require not fewer reading opportunities, but more, to practice and improve their reading skills. For example, within one class of second-grade students, the teacher might have one group using a text with over 80 words on just the first page, while another group uses a text with a total of 80 words in the entire book. This difference shows that the teacher will need to use several texts within certain groups to give them equal amounts of reading material and practice as readers of denser/longer texts during group reading times. Teachers can look at the backs of the books they assign during guided reading sessions, and maintain simple logs of their **word counts**. Comparing these word counts among groups can help teachers to equalize the numbers of words that each student group actually works with during small-group guided reading periods.

Connecting Text Sets for Small-Group Guided Reading Across Different Reading Difficulty Levels

When teachers select textbooks to teach a unit/lesson on a certain topic, they often compile **text sets**—groups of books all related to the same topic/theme. Because classes usually include students reading at different levels, teachers also often gather books at different reading levels for text sets. When collecting books representing multiple reading levels, the teacher can also intentionally organize the text set so all books are connected. For example, the books might share similar content; similar language, style, and vocabulary words; or similar layouts. Selecting books sharing such a commonality at different reading levels makes it easier for students to draw useful connections between easier and harder texts. It also facilitates students' flexibility in working across multiple reading levels, which builds their skills and confidence for faster progress. Additionally, to prepare some students to read books that teachers felt would prove too difficult otherwise, they can use easier texts with similar themes/language/formats to establish contexts for the harder ones.

Enhancing Students' Independent Reading Through the Reading Material Provided

In addition to whole-class and small-group reading exercises, students need some time reading **texts of their own choice**, which they can easily read with little/no support, to attain comfort, fluency, and confidence. To ensure more opportunities for practice, with equal time for all students, teachers should provide text sets at multiple reading levels for each content area. Experts suggest 70% of books should be easily accessible; and, in addition to classroom libraries, using rolling carts lets book collections travel among classrooms. Multiple reading levels let more advanced readers peruse a harder text, while less advanced readers read several easier texts; this equalizes the time and words they have for practicing. Because critics find some leveled readers lack variety in gender/race/class/other sociocultural aspects of characters, teachers should build diverse book collections representing all students. Teachers can inform their selections via student interest surveys; and familiarity with students' individual identities, personalities, and special interests. Knowing individual students can help match them to texts as effectively as leveled book lists.

Engaging Students in Reading

Experts find excessive attention to **leveling** as a way of matching texts to students can be restrictive, undermining high-quality instruction that balances the needs of the reader with the demands of the text. Teachers must consider that assigning certain texts will cause students to disengage from reading and avoid it rather than engage in it. In the real world, people read many different kinds of materials. Therefore, a teacher has better chances of finding texts that engage students, and that motivate them to read and allow them to perceive themselves as readers, by mindfully selecting **varied text genres** with **varied difficulty**. In classrooms incorporating various student reading levels, this can be the best method to procure classroom acceptability of accessible texts. Teachers can also use **individualized instructional formats**, such as Readers Workshop (Atwell, 1998), which balance issues of difficulty, choice, and engagement; develop reader communities affording more reading experiences with authenticity, meaning, and enjoyment; and stronger positive teacher-student relationships via individualized consultations. Teachers should also incorporate **accessible alternative texts** for independent activities.

Alternative Reading and Writing Forms to Help Students Attain Greater Progress in Reading

When students read and write outside of school, they choose many alternative forms of reading and writing. To engage these students while they are in school, teachers should think about adding such **alternative materials** to their own instructional programs. For example, teachers might incorporate such media as graphic novels, magazines, newspapers, plays, anthologies of poetry, e-books and other digital/online content, and text that students have written themselves. Educational experts advise that just because it can be harder to determine the reading levels of such alternative text formats, teachers should not shy away from using them. Because they represent examples of text that people (including students) read in real life, they provide not only excellent practice for students' present and future reading of real-world materials, but also motivation to read and meaningful experiences in reading. Another boon of using these authentic, alternative texts is that they frequently incorporate multiple reading levels, so that nearly every student can read some portions of them.

Viewing Skills

Viewing skills can be sharpened by having students look at a single image, such as a work of art or a cartoon, and simply asking students what they **see**. The teacher can ask what is happening in the image, and then elicit the details that clue the students in to what is happening. Of course, there may be more than one thing happening. The teacher should also question the students about the message of the image, its purpose, its point of view, and its intended audience. The teacher should ask for first impressions, and then provide some background or additional information to see if it changes the way students look at or interpret the image. The conclusion of the lesson should include questions about what students learned from the exercise about the topic, themselves, and others.

<u>Benefits</u>

Students are exposed to multiple **images** every day. It is important for them to be able to effectively **interpret** these images. They should be able to make sense of the images and the spoken and print language that often accompany them. Learning can be enhanced with images because they allow for quicker connections to prior knowledge than verbal information. Visuals in the classroom can also be motivational, can support verbal information, and can express main points, sometimes resulting in instant recognition.

Some of the common types of images that students see every day include: bulletin boards, computer graphics, diagrams, drawings, illustrations, maps, photographs, posters, book covers, advertisements, Internet sites, multimedia presentations, puppet shows, television, videos, print cartoons, models, paintings, animation, drama or dance performances, films, and online newscasts and magazines.

Activities to Strengthen Skills

Activities at school that can be used to strengthen the **viewing skills** of students of varying ages include:

- **Picture book discussions** – Students can develop an appreciation of visual text and the language that goes with it through guided discussions of picture books that focus on the style and color of the images and other details that might capture a child's attention.
- **Gallery walks** – Students can walk around a room or hallway viewing the posted works of other students and hear presentations about the works. They can also view a display prepared by the teacher. Students are expected to take notes as they walk around, have discussions, and perhaps do a follow-up report.
- **Puppet theater and drama presentations** – Students can learn about plots, dialogue, situations, characters, and the craft of performance from viewing puppet or drama presentations, which also stimulate oral communication and strengthen listening skills. Discussions or written responses should follow performances to check for detail acquisition.

Classroom Viewing Center

A **classroom viewing center** should contain magazines, CD-ROMs, books, videos, and individual pictures (photographs or drawings). Students should have a **viewing guide** that explains expectations related to the viewing center (before, during, and after using the center). For younger students, the teacher can ask questions that guide them through the viewing rather than expecting them to read the guidelines and write responses.

- **Before** viewing, students should think about what they already know about the subject and what they want to learn from the viewing.
- **During** the viewing, students should make notes about whatever interests them or is new to them.
- **After** viewing, students could discuss or individually write down what they found to be the most interesting idea or striking image and explain why it caught their attention.

Types of Questions to Ask If Viewing Is a Narrative

A teacher should make students responsible for gaining information or insight from the **viewing**. Setting expectations increases student attention and critical thinking. As with any viewing, the students should consider what they already know about the topic and what they hope to gain by watching the narrative before viewing it. During the viewing, the students should take notes (perhaps to answer questions provided by the teacher).

After the viewing, students should be able to answer the following questions:

- What was the time period and setting of the story?
- Who were the main characters?
- How effective was the acting?
- What was the problem or goal in the story?
- How was the problem solved or the goal achieved?
- How would you summarize the story?
- What did you learn from the story?
- What did you like or dislike about the story or its presentation?
- Would you recommend this viewing to others?
- How would you rate it?

Difficulties Related to Learning by Listening

It is difficult to learn just by listening because the instruction is presented only in spoken form. Therefore, unless students take notes, there is nothing for them to review. However, an active listener will anticipate finding a **message** in an oral presentation and will listen for it, **interpreting** tone and gestures as the presentation progresses. In group discussions, students are often too busy figuring out what they will say when it is their turn to talk to concentrate on what others are saying. Therefore, they don't learn from others, but instead come away knowing only what they already knew. Students should be required to respond directly to the previous speaker before launching into their own comments. This practice will force students to listen to each other and learn that their own responses will be better because of what can be added by listening to others.

Graphic Organizers

The purpose of **graphic organizers** is to help students classify ideas and communicate more efficiently and effectively. Graphic organizers are visual outlines or templates that help students grasp key concepts and master subject matter by simplifying them down to basic points. They also help guide students through processes related to any subject area or task. Examples of processes include brainstorming, problem solving, decision making, research and project planning, and studying. Examples of graphic organizers include:

- **Reading** – These can include beginning, middle, and end graphs or event maps.
- **Science** – These can include charts that show what animals need or how to classify living things.
- **Math** – These can include horizontal bar graphs or time lines.
- **Language arts** – These can include alphabet organizers or charts showing the components of the five-paragraph essay.
- **General** – These can include KWL charts or weekly planners.

Speaking Skills Children in Elementary/Intermediate School Should Have

Children of elementary/intermediate school age should be able to:

- Speak at an appropriate volume, tone, and pace that is understandable and appropriate to the audience
- Pronounce most words accurately
- Use complete sentences
- Make eye contact

- Use appropriate gestures with speech
- Exhibit an awareness of audience and adjust content to fit the audience (adjust word choices and style to be appropriate for peers or adults)
- Ask relevant questions
- Respond appropriately when asked questions about information or an opinion, possibly also being able to provide reasons for opinions
- Speak in turn, not interrupt, and include others in conversations
- Provide a summary or report orally
- Participate in small and large group discussions and debates
- Read orally before an audience
- Conduct short interviews
- Provide directions and explanations orally, including explanations of class lessons

Viewing Skills Elementary/Intermediate School Children Should Have

Children of elementary school age should be developing or have attained the ability to understand the importance of **media** in people's lives. They should understand that television, radio, films, and the Internet have a role in everyday life. They should also be able to use media themselves (printing out material from the Internet or making an audio or video tape, for example). They should also be aware that the purpose of advertising is to sell. Children of intermediate school age should be developing or have attained the ability to **obtain and compare information** from newspapers, television, and the Internet. They should also be able to judge its **reliability and accuracy** to some extent. Children of this age should be able to tell the difference between fictional and non-fictional materials in media. They should also be able to use a variety of media, visuals, and sounds to make a presentation.

Listening Skills Children Should Develop Through Their Elementary/Intermediate School Years

Through the elementary/intermediate school years, children should develop the following listening skills:

- Follow oral instructions consistently
- Actively listen to peers and teachers
- Avoid creating distracting behavior or being distracted by the behavior of others most of the time
- Respond to listening activities and exhibit the ability to discuss, illustrate, or write about the activity and show knowledge of the content and quality of the listening activity
- Respond to listening activities and exhibit the ability to identify themes, similarities/differences, ideas, forms, and styles of activities
- Respond to a persuasive speaker and exhibit the ability to analyze and evaluate the credibility of the speaker and form an opinion describing whether they agree or disagree with the point made
- Demonstrate appropriate social behavior while part of an audience

Stages of Writing

The **three stages of writing** are drawing, dictating, and writing. During the **drawing stage**, young learners use scribbles or pictures to convey their message. When asked to "read" their drawing, children in the drawing stage will use their picture to tell a story, as if they were mimicking a book being read to them. In the **dictation stage**, learners will tell their thoughts to a literate person, who will in turn write the words for the child. During this stage, the student is aware that the written words on the page represent their thoughts and can sometimes recognize the beginning sounds of the words they are saying, including some sight words. In the third and final stage, the **writing stage**, students are able to write their own thoughts in a way that can be recognized by others. Both beginning and ending sounds are represented in the words, along with some vowels. Students in this stage also understand spacing between words and the idea of creating complete sentences.

Norm-Referenced and Criterion-Referenced Assessments

Norm-referenced assessments are used to gauge a student success by comparing his or her score to a theoretical "average" score achieved by students of the same age or grade level. With a norm-referenced assessment, a student's achievement is decided based on how much better or worse that student scored in comparison to his or her peers. In contrast, **criterion-referenced assessments** are scored based on each student's individual ability to show mastery of specific learning standards. Students are deemed successful if they are able to achieve mastery of concepts that are appropriate for their age or grade level, regardless of how their peers perform.

IRI

The **Informal Reading Inventory (IRI)**, also known as the **Qualitative Reading Inventory (QRI)** is a survey used to assess the instructional needs of individual readers. The IRI is used to determine a reader's grade-level reading, fluency, comprehension, vocabulary, oral reading accuracy, word recognition, word meaning, and reading strategies. The IRI is an ongoing assessment that should be administered several times a year starting from first grade through twelfth grade. Teachers should use the outcomes of these assessments to determine appropriate reading material for individual students and to identify and implement specific needs and strategies for individual learners or groups of learners.

Universal Screening Assessments, Diagnostic Assessments, and Progress Monitoring

Universal screening assessments are brief surveys given to all students at the beginning of each school year, which are used to determine the mastery of critical skills and concepts. These screenings should be repeated approximately three times a year to ensure that students are performing at age-appropriate levels. **Diagnostic assessments** are used to help educators make sense of universal screening assessment scores. Based on diagnostics, teachers can identify the specific educational gaps of individual students and use that information to modify and differentiate instruction. **Progress monitoring** is used to determine if the educational interventions and strategies put in place (based on the diagnostic testing) are actually working. Struggling students are often monitored more closely to ensure that educational gaps are being filled at an appropriate and sufficient rate.

Formal and Informal Assessments

Formal assessments, which include norm-based assessments, criterion-based assessments, intelligence tests, and diagnostic assessments are data driven. These types of assessments are used to determine a student's overall achievement and can be used to compare each student's abilities to his or her peers. Formal assessments are often shared with students and stakeholders to determine whether or not a student is performing at an appropriate level for his or her age or grade level. **Informal assessments**, which include running records, cloze tests, reading inventories, portfolios, and so on are not data driven. Instead, informal assessments use performance-driven tasks to guide instruction and provide informal ratings about each student's individual progress. During these assessments, each student's performance is used to monitor his or her progress and guide future instruction, often in preparation for a formal assessment.

Evaluating Appropriateness of Assessment Instrument or Practice

The two main factors that must be considered when evaluating the appropriateness of assessment instruction and practices are curriculum alignment and cultural bias. **Curriculum alignment** is the act of teaching students the concepts that they will eventually be tested on. To reach proficiency on the standards outlined by state or district mandates, teachers must continuously teach and assess the standards. Avoiding **cultural bias** ensures that all students are given access to all relevant lessons, instruction, and materials. Furthermore, avoiding cultural bias ensures that all students are given a fair opportunity to succeed on any given assessment. This includes accommodating students of certain subgroups with assessment modifications, such as additional testing time, taking the test in his or her native language, and creating types of assessments that are accessible and achievable for students of all backgrounds.

Example Evaluation of Scoring Method

A teacher is assessing a student's ability to identify the main idea of a text. The student correctly identifies the main idea but includes several spelling errors in her written response. The teacher lowers the student's grade, taking points off for misspellings. In this example, the teacher's scoring method is **inappropriate** for the concept being assessed. Although misspellings should be addressed and remedied, the question was designed to assess the student's ability to identify the main idea of the passage. It was not intended to assess the spelling abilities of the student. By lowering the student's score based on misspellings, the teacher is insinuating that the student is unable to correctly identify the main idea of a passage, which is not the case. When assessing a specific skill, it is important that teachers score students based on their ability to complete isolated skills for data to accurately drive future instruction.

Penmanship

Penmanship is a word used to describe a person's *handwriting*. The three main characteristics of penmanship are letter formation, size, and spacing. When teaching penmanship, teachers should start by helping students to correctly form each letter, using arrows to dictate the order and direction in which parts of each letter should be written. Once students have mastered each letter, teachers should focus on letter size or proportion. For example, smaller letters (like c, e, and n) should be half the size of larger letters (such as k, l, or t). Finally, proper spacing should be taught, both between letters and words. Once spacing between words has been mastered, students should begin to work on including punctuation and appropriate spacing between sentences.

Importance of Listening and Speaking Strategies

Both listening and speaking strategies are important skills for students in all areas of education. To achieve the highest success, students should be taught how to effectively **speak** and exchange dialogue in large- and small-group settings. In addition, students should be encouraged to question, retell, or reenact the words of others. Equally important, students must learn to actively **listen** and visualize the words of others so that they are able to understand the purpose of what someone else is saying. To check for listening, students should be encouraged to summarize what they have heard and complete graphic organizers outlining important concepts or facts. When given ample opportunity to both speak and listen, students are more likely to excel across all content areas.

Developing Listening and Speaking Skills with Dramatic Plays

Dramatic play is a type of play in which students are assigned specific roles and encouraged to act those roles out. In dramatic play, students are typically assigned a character but not a script. They are encouraged to take on the feelings and actions of the character they have been assigned and act as that character would act. Dramatic play is an excellent strategy for developing speaking skills as students must clearly identify and express the feelings of their characters. They must speak clearly and loud enough so that the other actors and audience can hear what they are saying. In addition, students must actively listen to what the other students in the play are saying to appropriately respond to the actions and words of the other characters in an effort to further develop the story line.

History and Social Science

World History

Important Contributions of Ancient Civilizations of Sumer, Egypt, and Indus Valley

These three ancient civilizations are distinguished by their unique contributions to the development of world civilization:

- **Sumer** used the first known writing system, which enabled the Sumerians to leave a sizeable written record of their myths and religion; advanced the development of the wheel and irrigation; and urbanized their culture with a cluster of cities.
- **Egypt** was united by the Nile River. Egyptians originally settled in villages on its banks; had a national religion that held their pharaohs as gods; had a central government that controlled civil and artistic affairs; and had writing and libraries.
- The **Indus Valley** was also called Harappan after the city of Harappa. This civilization started in the 3rd and 4th centuries BC and was widely dispersed over 400,000 square miles. It had a unified culture of luxury and refinement, no known national government, an advanced civic system, and prosperous trade routes.

Review Video: Early Mesopotamia: The Sumerians
Visit mometrix.com/academy and enter code: 939880

Review Video: Egyptians
Visit mometrix.com/academy and enter code: 398041

Common Traits and Cultural Identifiers of Early Empires of Mesopotamia, Egypt, Greece, and Rome

The common traits of these empires were: a strong military; a centralized government; control and standardization of commerce, money, and taxes; a weight system; and an official language. **Mesopotamia** had a series of short-term empires that failed because of their oppression of subject peoples. **Egypt** also had a series of governments after extending its territory beyond the Nile area. Compared to Mesopotamia, these were more stable and long-lived because they blended different peoples to create a single national identity. **Greece** started as a group of city-states that were united by Alexander the Great and joined to create an empire that stretched from the Indus River to Egypt and the Mediterranean coast. Greece blended Greek values with those of the local cultures, which collectively became known as Hellenistic society. **Rome** was an Italian city-state that grew into an empire extending from the British Isles across Europe to the Middle East. It lasted for 1,000 years and became the foundation of the Western world's culture, language, and laws.

Review Video: Ancient Greece
Visit mometrix.com/academy and enter code: 800829

Major Deities of Greek and Roman Mythology

The major gods of the **Greek/Roman mythological system** are:

- **Zeus/Jupiter** – Head of the Pantheon, god of the sky
- **Hera/Juno** – Wife of Zeus/Jupiter, goddess of marriage

- **Poseidon/Neptune** – God of the seas
- **Demeter/Ceres** – Goddess of grain
- **Apollo** – God of the sun, law, music, archery, healing, and truth
- **Artemis/Diana** – Goddess of the moon, wild creatures, and hunting
- **Athena/Minerva** – Goddess of civilized life, handicrafts, and agriculture
- **Hephaestus/Vulcan** – God of fire, blacksmith
- **Aphrodite/Venus** – Goddess of love and beauty
- **Ares/Mars** – God of war
- **Dionysus/Bacchus** – God of wine and vegetation
- **Hades/Pluto** – God of the underworld and the dead
- **Eros/Cupid** – Minor god of love
- **Hestia/Vesta** – Goddess of the hearth or home
- **Hermes/Mercury** – Minor god of gracefulness and swiftness

Characteristics of Chinese and Indian Empires

While the Chinese had the world's longest lasting and continuous empires, the Indians had more of a cohesive culture than an empire system. Their distinct characteristics are as follows:

- **China** – Since the end of the Warring States period in 221 BC, China has functioned as an empire. Although the dynasties changed several times, the basic governmental structure remained the same into the 20th century. The Chinese also have an extensive written record of their culture which heavily emphasizes history, philosophy, and a common religion.
- **India** – The subcontinent was seldom unified in terms of government until the British empire controlled the area in the 19th and 20th centuries. In terms of culture, India has had persistent institutions and religions that have loosely united the people, such as the caste system and guilds. These have regulated daily life more than any government.

Middle Ages in European History

The **Middle Ages**, or Medieval times, was a period that ran from approximately 500-1500 AD. During this time, the centers of European civilization moved from the Mediterranean countries to France, Germany, and England, where strong national governments were developing. Key events of this time include:

- **Roman Catholicism** was the cultural and religious center of medieval life, extending into politics and economics.
- **Knights**, with their systems of honor, combat, and chivalry, were loyal to their king. **Peasants**, or serfs, served a particular lord and his lands.
- Many **universities** were established that still function in modern times.
- The **Crusades**, the recurring wars between European Christians and Middle East Muslims, raged over the Holy Lands.
- One of the legendary leaders was Charles the Great, or **Charlemagne**, who created an empire across France and Germany around 800 AD.
- The **Black Death plague** swept across Europe from 1347-1350, leaving between one third and one half of the population dead.

Review Video: The Middle Ages
Visit mometrix.com/academy and enter code: 413133

Protestant Reformation

The dominance of the **Catholic Church** during the Middle Ages in Europe gave it immense power, which encouraged corrupt practices such as the selling of indulgences and clerical positions. The **Protestant Reformation** began as an attempt to reform the Catholic Church, but eventually led to the separation from it. In 1517, Martin Luther posted his *Ninety-Five Theses* on the door of a church in Saxony, which criticized unethical practices, various doctrines, and the authority of the pope. Other reformers such as John Calvin and John Wesley soon followed, but disagreed among themselves and divided along doctrinal lines. Consequently, the Lutheran, Reformed, Calvinist, and Presbyterian churches were founded, among others. In England, King Henry VIII was denied a divorce by the pope, so he broke away and established the **Anglican Church**. The Protestant reformation caused the Catholic Church to finally reform itself, but the Protestant movement continued, resulting in a proliferation of new denominations.

Renaissance

Renaissance is the French word for rebirth, and is used to describe the renewal of interest in ancient Greek and Latin art, literature, and philosophy that occurred in Europe, especially Italy, from the 14th through the 16th centuries. Historically, it was also a time of great scientific inquiry, the rise of individualism, extensive geographical exploration, and the rise of secular values.

Notable figures of the Renaissance include:

- **Petrarch** – An Italian scholar, writer, and key figure in northern Italy, which is where the Renaissance started and where chief patrons came from the merchant class
- **Leonardo da Vinci** – Artist and inventor
- Michelangelo and Raphael – Artists
- **Desiderius Erasmus** – Applied historical scholarship to the New Testament and laid the seeds for the Protestant Reformation
- **Sir Thomas More** – A lawyer and author who wrote *Utopia*
- **Niccolò Machiavelli** – Author of *Prince and Discourses*, which proposed a science of human nature and civil life
- **William Shakespeare** – A renowned playwright and poet

Review Video: Renaissance
Visit mometrix.com/academy and enter code: 123100

Industrial Revolution

The **Industrial Revolution** started in England with the construction of the first **cotton mill** in 1733. Other inventions and factories followed in rapid succession. The **steel industry** grew exponentially when it was realized that cheap, abundant English coal could be used instead of wood for melting metals. The **steam engine**, which revolutionized transportation and work power, came next. Around 1830, a factory-based, **technological era** was ushered into the rest of Europe. Society changed from agrarian to urban. A need for cheap, unskilled labor resulted in the extensive employment and abuse of women and children, who worked up to 14 hours a day, six days a week in deplorable conditions. Expanding populations brought crowded, unsanitary conditions to the cities, and the factories created air and water pollution. Societies had to deal with these new situations by enacting **child labor laws** and creating **labor unions** to protect the safety of workers.

Review Video: The Industrial Revolution
Visit mometrix.com/academy and enter code: 372796

Participants of World War I and World War II

World War I, which began in 1914, was fought by the **Allies** Britain, France, Russia, Greece, Italy, Romania, and Serbia. They fought against the **Central Powers** of Germany, Austria-Hungary, Bulgaria, and Turkey. In 1917, the United States joined the Allies, and Russia withdrew to pursue its own revolution. World War I ended in 1918.

World War II was truly a world war, with fighting occurring on nearly every continent. Germany occupied most of Europe and Northern Africa. It was opposed by the countries of the British Empire, free France and its colonies, Russia, and various national resistance forces. Japan, an **Axis** ally of Germany, had been forcefully expanding its territories in Korea, China, Indonesia, the Philippines, and the South Pacific for many years. When Japan attacked Pearl Harbor in 1941, the United States joined the **Allied** effort. Italy changed from the Axis to the Allied side mid-war after deposing its own dictator. The war ended in Europe in April 1945, and in Japan in August 1945.

Importance of Cross-Cultural Comparisons in World History Instruction

It is important to make **cross-cultural comparisons** when studying world history so that the subject is **holistic** and not oriented to just Western civilization. Not only are the contributions of civilizations around the world important, but they are also interesting and more representative of the mix of cultures present in the United States. It is also critical to the understanding of world relations to study the involvement of European countries and the United States in international commerce, colonization, and development. **Trade routes** from ancient times linked Africa, Asia, and Europe, resulting in exchanges and migrations of people, philosophies, and religions, as well as goods. While many civilizations in the Americas thrived and some became very sophisticated, many eventually became disastrously entangled in **European expansion**. The historic isolation of China and the modern industrialization of Japan have had huge impacts on relations with the rest of the world. The more students understand this history and its effects on the modern world, the better they will able to function in their own spheres.

U.S. History

Contributions of Early French Explorers

The **French** never succeeded in attracting settlers to their territories. Those who came were more interested in the fur and fish trades than in forming colonies. Eventually, the French ceded their southern possessions and New Orleans, founded in 1718, to Spain. However, the French made major contributions to the exploration of the new continent, including:

- **Giovanni da Verrazano** and **Jacques Cartier** explored the North American coast and the St. Lawrence Seaway for France.
- **Samuel de Champlain**, who founded Quebec and set up a fur empire on the St. Lawrence Seaway, also explored the coasts of Massachusetts and Rhode Island between 1604 and 1607.

- **Fr. Jacques Marquette**, a Jesuit missionary, and **Louis Joliet** were the first Europeans to travel down the Mississippi in 1673.
- **Rene-Robert de la Salle** explored the Great Lakes and the Illinois and Mississippi Rivers from 1679-1682, claiming all the land from the Great Lakes to the Gulf of Mexico and from the Appalachians to the Rockies for France.

Earliest Spanish Explorers

The **Spanish** claimed and explored huge portions of the United States after the voyages of Christopher Columbus. Among them were:

- **Juan Ponce de Leon** – In 1513, he became the first European in Florida; established the oldest European settlement in Puerto Rico; discovered the Gulf Stream; and searched for the fountain of youth.
- **Alonso Alvarez de Pineda** – He charted the Gulf Coast from Florida to Mexico in 1519. Probably the first European in Texas, he claimed it for Spain.
- **Panfilo de Narvaez** – He docked in Tampa Bay with Cabeza de Vaca in 1528, claimed Florida for Spain, and then sailed the Gulf Coast.
- **Alvar Nuñez Cabeza de Vaca** – He got lost on foot in Texas and New Mexico. Estevanico, or Esteban, a Moorish slave, was a companion who guided them to Mexico.
- **Francisco Vásquez de Coronado** – While searching for gold in 1540, he became the first European to explore Kansas, Oklahoma, Texas, New Mexico, and Arizona.
- **Hernando De Soto** – He was the first European to explore the southeastern United States from Tallahassee to Natchez.

Colonization of Virginia and the Virginia Company

In 1585, **Sir Walter Raleigh** landed on Roanoke Island and sent Arthur Barlow to the mainland, which they named **Virginia**. Two attempts to establish settlements failed. The first permanent English colony was founded by Captain John Smith in **Jamestown** in 1607. The **Virginia Company** and the **Chesapeake Bay Company** successfully colonized other Virginia sites. By 1619, Virginia had a House of Burgesses. The crown was indifferent to the colony, so local government grew strong and tobacco created wealth. The First Families of Virginia dominated politics there for two centuries, and four of the first five United States presidents came from these families. The Virginia Company sent 24 Puritan families, known as **Pilgrims**, to Virginia on the **Mayflower**. In 1620, it landed at Plymouth, Massachusetts instead. The **Plymouth Plantation** was established and survived with the help of natives. This is where the first Thanksgiving is believed to have occurred.

Colonization in Massachusetts, Maryland, Rhode Island, and Pennsylvania

In 1629, 400 Puritans arrived in **Salem**, which became an important port and was made famous by the witch trials in 1692. In 1628, the self-governed **Massachusetts Bay Company** was organized, and the Massachusetts Indians sold most of the land to the English. **Boston** was established in 1630 and **Harvard University** was established in 1636.

Maryland was established by Lord Baltimore in 1632 in the hopes of providing refuge for English Catholics. The Protestant majority, however, opposed this religious tolerance.

Roger Williams was banished from Massachusetts in 1636 because he called for separation of church and state. He established the **Rhode Island** colony in 1647 and had 800 settlers by 1650, including Anne Hutchinson and her "Antinomians," who attacked clerical authority.

In 1681, **William Penn** received a royal charter for the establishment of **Pennsylvania** as a colony for Quakers. However, religious tolerance allowed immigrants from a mixed group of denominations, who prospered from the beginning.

Reasons for American Revolution

The English colonies **rebelled** for the following reasons:

- England was remote yet **controlling**. By 1775, few Americans had ever been to England. They considered themselves Americans, not English.
- During the Seven Years' War (aka French and Indian War) from 1754-1763, Americans, including George Washington, served in the British army, but were treated as **inferiors**.
- It was feared that the Anglican Church might try to expand in the colonies and **inhibit religious freedom**.
- Heavy **taxation** such as the Sugar and Stamp Acts, which were created solely to create revenue for the crown, and business controls such as restricting trade of certain products to England only, were burdensome.
- The colonies had no official **representation** in the English Parliament and wanted to govern themselves.
- There were fears that Britain would block westward expansion and independent enterprise.
- **Local government**, established through elections by property holders, was already functioning.

Important Events and Groups Leading up to American Revolution

Over several years, various events and groups contributed to the rebellion that became a revolution:

- **Sons of Liberty** – This was the protest group headed by Samuel Adams that incited the Revolution.
- **Boston Massacre** – On March 5, 1770, soldiers fired on a crowd and killed five people.
- **Committees of Correspondence** – These were set up throughout the colonies to transmit revolutionary ideas and create a unified response.
- **The Boston Tea Party** – On December 6, 1773, the Sons of Liberty, dressed as Mohawks, dumped tea into the harbor from a British ship to protest the tea tax. The harsh British response further aggravated the situation.
- **First Continental Congress** – This was held in 1774 to list grievances and develop a response, including boycotts. It was attended by all the colonies with the exception of Georgia.
- **The Shot Heard Round the World** – In April, 1775, English soldiers on their way to confiscate arms in Concord passed through Lexington, Massachusetts and met the colonial militia called the Minutemen. A fight ensued. In Concord, a larger group of Minutemen forced the British to retreat.

Review Video: The First and Second Continental Congress
Visit mometrix.com/academy and enter code: 835211

Original 13 Colonies and Major Turning Points of the Revolution

The original **13 colonies** were: Connecticut, Delaware, Georgia, Maryland, Massachusetts, New Hampshire, New Jersey, New York, North Carolina, Pennsylvania, Rhode Island, South Carolina, and Virginia. Delaware was the first state to ratify the constitution.

The major turning points of the American Revolution were:

- The actions of the **Second Continental Congress** – This body established the Continental Army and chose George Washington as its commanding general. They allowed printing of money and created government offices.
- "**Common Sense**" – Published in 1776 by Thomas Paine, this pamphlet calling for independence was widely distributed.
- The **Declaration of Independence** – Written by Thomas Jefferson, it was ratified on July 4, 1776 by the Continental Congress assembled in Philadelphia.
- **Alliance with France** – Benjamin Franklin negotiated an agreement with France to fight with the Americans in 1778.
- **Treaty of Paris** – In 1782, it signaled the official end of the war, granted independence to the colonies, and gave them generous territorial rights.

Review Video: Declaration of Independence
Visit mometrix.com/academy and enter code: 256838

Review Video: Colonization of the Americas
Visit mometrix.com/academy and enter code: 438412

Articles of Confederation and the Constitution

The **Articles of Confederation**, designed to protect states' rights over those of the national government and sent to the colonies for ratification in 1777, had two major elements that proved unworkable. First, there was no centralized national government. Second, there was no centralized power to tax or regulate trade with other nations or between states. With no national tax, the Revolution was financed by printing more and more money, which caused inflation. In 1787, a convention was called to write a new **constitution**. This constitution created the three branches of government with checks and balances of power: **executive, legislative, and judicial**. It also created a **bicameral legislature** so that there would be equal representation for the states in the Senate and representation for the population in the House. Those who opposed the new constitution, the **Anti-Federalists**, wanted a bill of rights included. The **Federalist** platform was explained in the "Federalist Papers," written by James Madison, John Jay, and Alexander Hamilton. The Constitution went into effect in 1789, and the **Bill of Rights** was added in 1791.

Review Video: Articles of Confederation
Visit mometrix.com/academy and enter code: 927401

Louisiana Purchase

The **Louisiana Purchase** in 1803 for $15 million may be considered **Thomas Jefferson's** greatest achievement as president. The reasons for the purchase were to gain the vital port of New Orleans, remove the threat of French interference with trade along the Mississippi River, and double the territory of the United States. The purchase both answered and raised new questions about the use of federal power, including the constitutionality of the president making such a purchase, Jefferson asking Congress for permission, and Jefferson taking the biggest federalist action up to that time, even though he was an anti-federalist. Jefferson sent **Meriwether Lewis and William Clark** to map the new territory and find a means of passage all the way to the Pacific Ocean. Although there was no river that flowed all the way west, their expedition and the richness of the land and game started the great western migration of settlers.

War of 1812

A war between **France and Britain** caused blockades that hurt American trade and caused the British to attack American ships and impress sailors on them. An embargo against France and Britain was imposed by Jefferson, but rescinded by Madison with a renewed demand for respect for American sovereignty. However, Britain became more aggressive and war resulted. Native Americans under the leadership of **Tecumseh** sided with the British. The British captured Washington, D.C., and burned the White House, but Dolly Madison had enough forethought to save priceless American treasures, such as the Gilbert Stuart portrait of George Washington. Most battles, however, came to a draw. As a result, in 1815, when the British ended the war with France, they negotiated for peace with the United States as well under the **Treaty of Ghent**. A benefit of the war was that it motivated Americans to become more **self-sufficient** due to increased manufacturing and fewer imports.

Monroe Doctrine, Manifest Destiny, and Missouri Compromise

Three important political actions in the 19th century were:

- The **Monroe Doctrine** – Conceived by President James Monroe in 1823, this foreign policy warned European powers to cease colonization of Central and South America or face military intervention by the United States. In return, the United States would not meddle in the political affairs or standing colonies of Europe.
- The **Missouri Compromise** – In 1820, there were 11 free states and 11 slave states. The fear of a power imbalance between slave and free states when Missouri petitioned to become a slave state brought about this agreement. Maine was brought in as a free state; the southern border of Missouri was set as the northernmost line of any slave territory; and the western states could come in as free states, while Arkansas and Florida could be slave states.
- **Manifest Destiny** – This was a popular belief during the 1840s that it was the right and duty of the United States to expand westward to the Pacific. The idea became a slogan for the flood of settlers and expansionist power grabs.

Review Video: Monroe Doctrine
Visit mometrix.com/academy and enter code: 953021

Review Video: Missouri Compromise
Visit mometrix.com/academy and enter code: 848091

Review Video: Manifest Destiny
Visit mometrix.com/academy and enter code: 957409

Andrew Jackson Presidency

A number of important milestones occurred in American history during the presidency of **Andrew Jackson**. They included:

- Jackson's election is considered the beginning of the modern political party system and the start of the **Democratic Party**.
- Jeffersonian Democracy, a system governed by middle and upper class educated property holders, was replaced by **Jacksonian Democracy**, a system that allowed universal white male suffrage.
- The **Indian Removal Act of 1830** took natives out of territories that whites wanted to settle, most notably the Trail of Tears that removed Cherokees from Georgia and relocated them to Oklahoma.
- The issue of **nullification**, the right of states to nullify any federal laws they thought unconstitutional, came to a head over tariffs. However, a strong majority vote in Congress supporting the Tariff Acts cemented the policy that states must comply with federal laws.

Whig Party

The **Whig Party** existed from 1833 to 1856. It started in opposition to Jackson's **authoritarian policies** and was particularly concerned with defending the supremacy of Congress over the executive branch, states' rights, economic protectionism, and modernization. Notable members included: Daniel Webster, Henry Clay, Winfield Scott, and a young Abraham Lincoln. The Whigs had four presidents: William Henry Harrison, Zachary Taylor, John Tyler (expelled from the party), and Millard Fillmore. However, the Whigs won only two presidential elections. Harrison and Taylor were elected in 1840 and 1848, respectively. However, both died in office, so Tyler and Fillmore assumed the presidency. In 1852, the anti-slavery faction of the party kept Fillmore from getting the nomination. Instead, it went to Scott, who was soundly defeated. In 1856, the Whigs supported Fillmore and the National American Party, but lost badly. Thereafter, the **split over slavery** caused the party to dissolve.

Important 19th Century American Writers

In the 19th century, American literature became an entity of its own and provided a distinct voice for the American experience. **James Fenimore Cooper** was a great writer from this time period. He was the first to write about Native Americans, and was the author of the Leatherstocking series, which includes *The Last of the Mohicans* and *The Deerslayer*.

- **Ralph Waldo Emerson** – He was an essayist, philosopher, and poet, and also the leader of the Transcendentalist movement. His notable works include "Self-Reliance" and "The American Scholar."
- **Nathaniel Hawthorne** – This novelist and short story writer wrote *The Scarlet Letter*, *The House of Seven Gables*, "Young Goodman Brown," and "The Minister's Black Veil."
- **Herman Melville** – He was a novelist, essayist, short story writer, and poet who wrote *Moby Dick*, *Billy Budd*, and "Bartleby the Scrivener." **Edgar Allan Poe** – He was a poet, literary critic, and master of the short story, especially horror and detective stories. His notable works include "The Tell-Tale Heart," "The Pit and the Pendulum," "Annabel Lee," and "The Raven."
- **Harriet Beecher Stowe** – She was the author of *Uncle Tom's Cabin*.

- **Henry David Thoreau** – He was a poet, naturalist, and Transcendentalist who wrote *Walden* and *Civil Disobedience*.
- **Walt Whitman** – He was a poet, essayist, and journalist who wrote *Leaves of Grass* and "O Captain! My Captain!"

19th Century Social and Religious Leaders

Some of the important social and religious leaders from the 19th century were:

- **Susan B. Anthony** – A women's rights and abolition activist, she lectured across the nation for suffrage, property and wage rights, and labor organizations for women.
- **Dorothea Dix** – She created the first American asylums for the treatment of mental illness and served as the Superintendent of Army Nurses during the War Between the States.
- **Frederick Douglass** –An escaped slave who became an abolitionist leader, government official, and writer.
- **William Lloyd Garrison** –An abolitionist and the editor of the *Liberator*, the leading anti-slavery newspaper of the time.
- **Joseph Smith** – He founded the Latter-Day Saints (Mormonism) in 1829.
- **Horace Mann** – A leader of the common school movement that made public education a right of all Americans.
- **Elizabeth Cady Stanton** – With Lucretia Mott, she held the Seneca Falls Convention in 1848, demanding women's suffrage and other reforms.
- **Brigham Young** –The leader of the Mormons when they fled religious persecution, built Salt Lake City, and settled much of the West. He was the first governor of the Utah Territory.

Compromise of 1850, Fugitive Slave Law, Kansas-Nebraska Act, Bleeding Kansas, and Dred Scott Case

- The **Compromise of 1850**, calling upon the principle of popular sovereignty, allowed those who lived in the Mexican cession to decide for themselves whether to be a free or slave territory.
- The **Fugitive Slave Law of 1850** allowed slave owners to go into free states to retrieve their escaped slaves.
- The **Kansas-Nebraska Act of 1854** repealed the Missouri Compromise of 1820 to allow the lands from the Louisiana Purchase to settle the slavery issue by popular sovereignty. Outraged Northerners responded by defecting from the Whig Party and starting the Republican Party.
- **Bleeding Kansas** was the name applied to the state when a civil war broke out between pro- and anti-slavery advocates while Kansas was trying to formalize its statutes before being admitted as a state.
- The **Dred Scott vs. Sandford case** was decided by the Supreme Court in 1857. It was ruled that Congress had no authority to exclude slavery from the territories, which in effect meant that the Missouri Compromise had been unconstitutional.

States Forming the Confederacy and Leaders of the War Between the States

The states that **seceded** from the Union to form the Confederacy were: Georgia, Arkansas, South Carolina, North Carolina, Virginia, Florida, Mississippi, Alabama, Louisiana, Texas, and Tennessee.

The slave-holding states that were kept in the Union were Delaware, Maryland, Kentucky, and Missouri.

- **Jefferson Davis** of Mississippi, a former U. S. senator and cabinet member, was the president of the Confederacy.
- **Abraham Lincoln** of Illinois was the President of the United States. His election triggered the secession of the south. He was assassinated shortly after winning a second term.
- **Robert E. Lee** of Virginia was offered the position of commanding general of the Union Army, but declined because of loyalty to his home state. He led the Army of Northern Virginia and the central Confederate force, and is still considered a military mastermind.
- **Ulysses S. Grant** of Ohio wasn't appointed to command the Union Army until 1864, after a series of other commanders were unsuccessful. He received Lee's surrender at the Appomattox Court House in Virginia in April, 1865, and went on to become President from 1869 to 1877.

Reconstruction and 13th, 14th, and 15th Amendments

Reconstruction was the period from 1865 to 1877, during which the South was under strict control of the U.S. government. In March, 1867, all state governments of the former Confederacy were terminated, and **military occupation** began. Military commanders called for constitutional conventions to reconstruct the state governments, to which delegates were to be elected by universal male suffrage. After a state government was in operation and the state had **ratified the 14th Amendment**, its representatives were admitted to Congress. Three constitutional amendments from 1865 to 1870, which tried to rectify the problems caused by slavery, became part of the Reconstruction effort. The **13th Amendment** declared slavery illegal. The **14th Amendment** made all persons born or naturalized in the country U.S. citizens, and forbade any state to interfere with their fundamental civil rights. The **15th Amendment** made it illegal to deny individuals the right to vote on the grounds of race. In his 1876 election campaign, President **Rutherford B. Hayes** promised to withdraw the troops, and did so in 1877.

Major Changes in Industry in the Late 1800s

Important events during this time of enormous business growth and large-scale exploitation of natural resources were:

- **Industrialization** – Like the rest of the world, the United States' entry into the Industrial Age was marked by many new inventions and the mechanization of factories.
- **Railroad expansion** – The Transcontinental Railroad was built from 1865 to 1969. Railroad tracks stretched over 35,000 miles in 1865, but that distance reached 240,000 miles by 1910. The raw materials and manufactured goods needed for the railroads kept mines and factories very busy.
- **Gold and silver mining** – Mines brought many prospectors to the West from 1850 to about 1875, but mining corporations soon took over.
- **Cattle ranching** – This was a large-scale enterprise beginning in the late 1860s, but by the 1880s open ranges were being fenced and plowed for farming and pastures. Millions of farmers moved into the high plains, establishing the "Bread Basket," which was the major wheat growing area of the country.

Gilded Age and Infamous Robber Barons

The **Gilded Age**, from the 1870s to 1890, was so named because of the enormous wealth and grossly opulent lifestyle enjoyed by a handful of powerful families. This was the time when huge mansions were built as summer "cottages" in Newport, Rhode Island, and great lodges were built in mountain areas for the pleasure of families such as the Vanderbilts, Ascots, and Rockefellers. Control of the major industries was held largely by the following men, who were known as **Robber Barons** for their ruthless business practices and exploitation of workers: Jay Gould, railroads; Andrew Carnegie, steel; John D. Rockefeller, Sr., oil; Philip Danforth Armour, meatpacking; J. P. Morgan, banking; John Jacob Astor, fur pelts; and Cornelius Vanderbilt, steamboat shipping. Of course, all of these heads of industry diversified and became involved in multiple business ventures. To curb cutthroat competition, particularly among the railroads, and to prohibit restrained trade, Congress created the **Interstate Commerce Commission** and the **Sherman Anti-Trust Act**. Neither of these, however, was enforced.

Review Video: The Gilded Age: An Overview
Visit mometrix.com/academy and enter code: 684770

Review Video: The Gilded Age: Chinese Immigration
Visit mometrix.com/academy and enter code: 624166

Review Video: The Gilded Age: Labor Strikes
Visit mometrix.com/academy and enter code: 683116

Review Video: The Gilded Age: Labor Unions
Visit mometrix.com/academy and enter code: 749692

Immigration Trends in Late 1800s

The population of the United States doubled between 1860 and 1890, the period that saw 10 million **immigrants** arrive. Most lived in the north. Cities and their **slums** grew tremendously because of immigration and industrialization. While previous immigrants had come from Germany, Scandinavia, and Ireland, the 1880s saw a new wave of immigrants from Italy, Poland, Hungary, Bohemia, and Greece, as well as Jewish groups from central and eastern Europe, especially Russia. The Roman Catholic population grew from 1.6 million in 1850 to 12 million in 1900, a growth that ignited an anti-Catholic backlash from the anti-Catholic Know-Nothing Party of the 1880s and the Ku Klux Klan. Exploited immigrant workers started **labor protests** in the 1870s, and the **Knights of Labor** was formed in 1878, calling for sweeping social and economic reform. Its membership reached 700,000 by 1886. Eventually, this organization was replaced by the **American Federation of Labor**, headed by Samuel Gompers.

Effects of Progressive Movement on Foreign Affairs

The **Progressive Era**, which was the time period from the 1890s to the 1920s, got its name from progressive, reform-minded political leaders who wanted to export a just and rational social order to the rest of the world while increasing trade with foreign markets. Consequently, the United States interfered in a dispute between Venezuela and Britain. America invoked the **Monroe Doctrine** and sided with Cuba in its independence struggle against Spain. The latter resulted in the **Spanish-American Wars** in 1898 that ended with Cuba, Puerto Rico, the Philippines, and Guam becoming American protectorates at the same time the United States annexed Hawaii. In 1900, America declared an **Open Door policy** with China to support its independence and open markets.

In 1903, Theodore Roosevelt helped Panama become independent of Columbia, and then secured the right to build the **Panama Canal**. Roosevelt also negotiated the peace treaty to end the Russo-Japanese War, which earned him the Nobel Peace prize. He then sent the American fleet on a world cruise to display his country's power.

Review Video: The Progressive Era
Visit mometrix.com/academy and enter code: 722394

Domestic Accomplishments of Progressive Era

To the Progressives, promoting law and order meant cleaning up city governments to make them honest and efficient, bringing more democracy and humanity to state governments, and establishing a core of social workers to improve slum housing, health, and education. Also during the **Progressive Era**, the national government strengthened or created the following regulatory agencies, services, and acts to oversee business enterprise:

- Passed in 1906, the **Hepburn A**ct reinforced the Interstate Commerce Commission. In 1902, Roosevelt used the Justice Department and lawsuits to try to break monopolies and enforce the **Sherman Anti-Trust Act**. The **Clayton Anti-Trust Act** was added in 1914.
- From 1898 to 1910, the **Forest Service** guided lumber companies in the conservation and more efficient use of woodland resources under the direction of Gifford Pinchot.
- In 1906, the **Pure Food and Drug Act** was passed to protect consumers from fraudulent labeling and adulteration of products.
- In 1913, the **Federal Reserve System** was established to supervise banking and commerce. In 1914, the **Fair Trade Commission** was established to ensure fair competition.

US Involvement in World War I

When World War I broke out in 1914, America declared **neutrality**. The huge demand for war goods by the Allies broke a seven-year industrial stagnation and gave American factories full-time work. The country's sympathies lay mostly with the Allies, and before long American business and banking were heavily invested in an Allied victory. In 1916, **Woodrow Wilson** campaigned on the slogan "He kept us out of war." However, when the British ship the ***Lusitania*** was torpedoed in 1915 by a German submarine and many Americans were killed, Wilson had already warned the Germans that the United States would enter the war if Germany interfered with neutral ships at sea. Eventually, when it was proven that Germany was trying to incite Mexico and Japan into attacking the United States, Wilson declared war in 1917, even though America was unprepared. Nonetheless, America quickly armed and transferred sufficient troops to Europe, bringing the **Allies** to victory in 1918.

Review Video: WWI Overview
Visit mometrix.com/academy and enter code: 659767

Review Video: World War I: European Alliances
Visit mometrix.com/academy and enter code: 257458

Review Video: World War I: Outcomes
Visit mometrix.com/academy and enter code: 278666

Decade of Optimism

After World War I, **Warren Harding** ran for President on the slogan "return to normalcy" and concentrated on domestic affairs. The public felt optimistic because life improved due to affordable automobiles from Henry Ford's mass production system, better roads, electric lights, airplanes, new communication systems, and voting rights for women (19th Amendment, 1920). Radio and movies helped develop a national culture. For the first time, the majority of Americans lived in **cities.** Young people shortened dresses and haircuts, and smoked and drank in public despite Prohibition (18th Amendment, 1919). Meantime, the **Russian Revolution** caused a **Red Scare** that strengthened the already strong Ku Klux Klan that controlled some states' politics. In 1925, the **Scopes trial** in Tennessee convicted a high school teacher for presenting Darwinian theories. The **Teapot Dome scandal** rocked the Harding administration. After Harding died in 1923, **Calvin Coolidge** became president. He was followed by **Herbert Hoover**, a strong proponent of capitalism under whom unregulated business led to the 1929 stock crash.

Great Depression and Dust Bowl

In the 1920s, the rich got richer. After World War I, however, farmers were in a depression when foreign markets started growing their own crops again. Increased credit buying, bank war debts, a huge gap between rich and poor, and a belief that the stock market would always go up got the nation into financial trouble. The **Stock Market Crash** in October 1929 that destroyed fortunes dramatized the downward spiral of the whole economy. Banks failed, and customers lost all their money. By 1933, 14 million were unemployed, industrial production was down to one-third of its 1929 level, and national income had dropped by half. Adding to the misery of farmers, years of breaking sod on the prairies without adequate conservation techniques caused the topsoil to fly away in great **dust storms** that blackened skies for years, causing deaths from lung disease and failed crops.

US Role in World War II

World War II began in 1939. As with World War I, the United States tried to stay out of World War II, even though the **Lend-Lease program** transferred munitions to Great Britain. However, on December 7, 1941, Japan attacked **Pearl Harbor** in Hawaii. Since Japan was an ally of Germany, the United States declared war on all the Axis powers. Although there was fighting in both Europe and the Pacific, the decision was made to concentrate on defeating Hitler first. Since it did not have combat within its borders, the United States became the great manufacturer of goods and munitions for the war effort. Women went to work in the factories, while the men entered the military. All facets of American life were centered on the war effort, including rationing, metal collections, and buying war bonds. The benefit of this production was an **end to the economic depression**. The influx of American personnel and supplies eventually brought victory in Europe in April of 1945, and in Asia the following August.

Review Video: World War II
Visit mometrix.com/academy and enter code: 759402

Review Video: World War II: Germany
Visit mometrix.com/academy and enter code: 951452

Review Video: World War II: Japan
Visit mometrix.com/academy and enter code: 313104

Major Programs and Events Resulting from the Cold War

After World War II, the Soviet Union kept control of Eastern Europe, including half of Germany. **Communism** spread around the world. Resulting fears led to:

- The **Truman Doctrine** (1947) – This was a policy designed to protect free peoples everywhere against oppression.
- The **Marshall Plan** (1948) – This devoted $12 billion to rebuild Western Europe and strengthen its defenses.
- The **Organization of American States** (1948) – This was established to bolster democratic relations in the Americas.
- The **Berlin Blockade** (1948-49) – The Soviets tried to starve out West Berlin, so the United States provided massive supply drops by air.
- The **North Atlantic Treaty Organization** (1949) – This was formed to militarily link the United States and western Europe so that an attack on one was an attack on both.
- The **Korean War** (1950-53) – This divided the country into the communist North and the democratic South.
- The **McCarthy era** (1950-54) – Senator Joseph McCarthy of Wisconsin held hearings on supposed Communist conspiracies that ruined innocent reputations and led to the blacklisting of suspected sympathizers in the government, Hollywood, and the media.

Review Video: The Cold War: The United States and Russia
Visit mometrix.com/academy and enter code: 981433

Major Events of 1960s

The 1960s were a tumultuous time for the United States. Major events included:

- The **Cuban Missile Crisis** (1961) – This was a stand-off between the United States and the Soviet Union over a build-up of missiles in Cuba. Eventually, the Soviets stopped their shipments and a nuclear war was averted.
- The assassinations of President Kennedy (1963), Senator Robert Kennedy (1968), and Dr. Martin Luther King, Jr. (1968).
- The **Civil Rights Movement** – Protest marches held across the nation to draw attention to the plight of black citizens. From 1964 to 1968, race riots exploded in more than 100 cities.
- The **Vietnam War** (1964-73) – This resulted in a military draft. There was heavy involvement of American personnel and money. There were also protest demonstrations, particularly on college campuses. At Kent State, several students died after being shot by National Guardsmen.
- **Major legislation** – Legislation passed during this decade included the Civil Rights Act, the Clean Air Act, and the Water Quality Act. This decade also saw the creation of the Peace Corps, Medicare, and the War on Poverty, in which billions were appropriated for education, urban redevelopment, and public housing.

Presidents and Vice Presidents from 1972 to 1974

In a two-year time span, the United States had two presidents and two vice presidents. This situation resulted first from the resignation of Vice President **Spiro T. Agnew** in October of 1973 because of alleged kickbacks. President **Richard M. Nixon** then appointed House Minority Leader **Gerald R. Ford** to be vice president. This was accomplished through Senate ratification, a process that had been devised after Harry Truman succeeded to the presidency upon the death of Franklin

Roosevelt and went through nearly four years of his presidency without a vice president. Nixon resigned the presidency in August of 1974 because some Republican party members broke into Democratic headquarters at the **Watergate** building in Washington, DC, and the president participated in covering up the crime. Ford succeeded Nixon, and had to appoint another vice president. He chose **Nelson Rockefeller**, former governor of New York.

U.S. Government

Principles of the Constitution

The six basic principles of the Constitution are:

1. **Popular Sovereignty** – The people establish government and give power to it; the government can function only with the consent of the people.
2. **Limited Government** – The Constitution specifies limits on government authority, and no official or entity is above the law.
3. **Separation of Powers** – Power is divided among three government branches: the legislative (Congress), the executive (President), and the judicial (federal courts).
4. **Checks and Balances** – This is a system that enforces the separation of powers and ensures that each branch has the authority and ability to restrain the powers of the other two branches, thus preventing tyranny.
5. **Judicial Review** – Judges in the federal courts ensure that no act of government is in violation of the Constitution. If an act is unconstitutional, the judicial branch has the power to nullify it.
6. **Federalism** – This is the division of power between the central government and local governments, which limits the power of the federal government and allows states to deal with local problems.

Classic Forms of Government

Forms of government that have appeared throughout history include:

- **Feudalism** – This is based on the rule of local lords who are loyal to the king and control the lives and production of those who work on their land.
- **Classical republic** – This form is a representative democracy. Small groups of elected leaders represent the interests of the electorate.
- **Absolute monarchy** – A king or queen has complete control of the military and government.
- **Authoritarianism** – An individual or group has unlimited authority. There is no system in place to restrain the power of the government.
- **Dictatorship** – Those in power are not held responsible to the people.
- **Autocracy** – This is rule by one person (despot), not necessarily a monarch, who uses power tyrannically.
- **Oligarchy** – A small, usually self-appointed elite rules a region.
- **Liberal democracy** – This is a government based on the consent of the people that protects individual rights and freedoms from any intolerance by the majority.
- **Totalitarianism** – All facets of the citizens' lives are controlled by the government.

Influences of Philosophers on Political Study

Ancient Greek philosophers **Aristotle** and **Plato** believed political science would lead to order in political matters, and that this scientifically organized order would create stable, just societies.

Thomas Aquinas adapted the ideas of Aristotle to a Christian perspective. His ideas stated that individuals should have certain rights, but also certain duties, and that these rights and duties should determine the type and extent of government rule. In stating that laws should limit the role of government, he laid the groundwork for ideas that would eventually become modern constitutionalism. **Niccolò Machiavelli**, author of *The Prince*, was a proponent of politics based solely on power.

Parliamentary and Democratic Systems of Government

In a **parliamentary system**, government involves a legislature and a variety of political parties. The head of government, usually a Prime Minister, is typically the head of the dominant party. A head of state can be elected, or this position can be taken by a monarch, such as in Great Britain's constitutional monarchy system.

In a **democratic system** of government, the people elect their government representatives. The term democracy is a Greek term that means "for the rule of the people." There are two forms of democracy—direct and indirect. In a direct democracy, each issue or election is decided by a vote where each individual is counted separately. An indirect democracy employs a legislature that votes on issues that affect large number of people whom the legislative members represent. Democracy can exist as a Parliamentary system or a Presidential system. The US is a presidential, indirect democracy.

Bill of Rights

The **United States Bill of Rights** was based on principles established by the **Magna Carta** in 1215, the 1688 **English Bill of Rights**, and the 1776 **Virginia Bill of Rights**. In 1791, the federal government added 10 amendments to the United States Constitution that provided the following **protections**:

- Freedom of speech, religion, peaceful assembly, petition of the government, and petition of the press
- The right to keep and bear arms
- No quartering of soldiers on private property without the consent of the owner
- Regulations on government search and seizure
- Provisions concerning prosecution
- The right to a speedy, public trial and the calling of witnesses
- The right to trial by jury
- Freedom from excessive bail or cruel punishment
- These rights are not necessarily the only rights
- Powers not prohibited by the Constitution are reserved to the states.

Review Video: Bill of Rights
Visit mometrix.com/academy and enter code: 585149

Making a Formal Amendment to the Constitution

So far, there have been only **27 amendments** to the federal Constitution. There are four different ways to change the wording of the constitution: two methods for proposal and two methods for ratification:

1. An amendment is proposed by a two-thirds vote in each house of Congress and ratified by three-fourths of the state legislatures.
2. An amendment is proposed by a two-thirds vote in each house of Congress and ratified by three-fourths of the states in special conventions called for that purpose.
3. An amendment is proposed by a national convention that is called by Congress at the request of two-thirds of the state legislatures and ratified by three-fourths of the state legislatures.
4. An amendment is proposed by a national convention that is called by Congress at the request of two-thirds of the state legislatures and ratified by three-fourths of the states in special conventions called for that purpose.

Review Video: Amending the Constitution
Visit mometrix.com/academy and enter code: 147023

Division of Powers

The division of powers in the federal government system is as follows:

- **National** – This level can coin money, regulate interstate and foreign trade, raise and maintain armed forces, declare war, govern United States territories and admit new states, and conduct foreign relations.
- **Concurrent** – This level can levy and collect taxes, borrow money, establish courts, define crimes and set punishments, and claim private property for public use.
- **State** – This level can regulate trade and business within the state, establish public schools, pass license requirements for professionals, regulate alcoholic beverages, conduct elections, and establish local governments.

There are three types of delegated powers granted by the Constitution:

1. **Expressed or enumerated powers** – These are specifically spelled out in the Constitution.
2. **Implied** – These are not expressly stated, but are reasonably suggested by the expressed powers.
3. **Inherent** – These are powers not expressed by the Constitution but ones that national governments have historically possessed, such as granting diplomatic recognition.

Powers can also be classified or reserved or exclusive. **Reserved powers** are not granted to the national government, but not denied to the states. **Exclusive powers** are those reserved to the national government, including concurrent powers.

Stages of Extending Suffrage in US

Originally, the Constitution of 1789 provided the right to vote only to white male property owners. Through the years, suffrage was extended through the following five stages.

1. In the early1800s, states began to eliminate **property ownership** and **tax payment qualifications**.
2. By 1810, there were no more **religious tests** for voting. In the late 1800s, the 15th Amendment protected citizens from being denied the right to vote because of **race or color**.
3. In 1920, the 19th Amendment prohibited the denial of the right to vote because of **gender**, and women were given the right to vote.
4. Passed in 1961 and ratified in 1964, the 23rd Amendment added the voters of the **District of Columbia** to the presidential electorate and eliminated the poll tax as a condition for voting in federal elections. The **Voting Rights Act of 1965** prohibited disenfranchisement through literacy tests and various other means of discrimination.
5. In 1971, the 26th Amendment set the minimum voting age at **18 years of age**.

Major Supreme Court Cases

Out of the many Supreme Court rulings, several have had critical historical importance. These include:

- **Marbury v. Madison** (1803) – This ruling established judicial review as a power of the Supreme Court.
- **Dred Scott v. Sandford** (1857) – This decision upheld property rights over human rights in the case of a slave who had been transported to a free state by his master, but was still considered a slave.
- **Brown v. Board of Education** (1954) – The Court ruled that segregation was a violation of the Equal Protection Clause and that the "separate but equal" practice in education was unconstitutional. This decision overturned the 1896 Plessy v. Ferguson ruling that permitted segregation if facilities were equal.
- **Miranda v. Arizona** (1966) – This ruling made the reading of Miranda rights to those arrested for crimes the law. It ensured that confessions could not be illegally obtained and that citizen rights to fair trials and protection under the law would be upheld.

Review Video: Landmark Supreme Court Cases
Visit mometrix.com/academy and enter code: 753011

Famous Speeches in US History That Defined Government Policy, Foreign Relations, and American Spirit

Among the best-known speeches and famous lines known to modern Americans are the following:

- The **Gettysburg Address** – Made by Abraham Lincoln on November 19, 1863, it dedicated the battleground's cemetery.
- The **Fourteen Points** – Made by Woodrow Wilson on January 18, 1918, this outlined Wilson's plans for peace and the League of Nations.
- **Address to Congress** – Made by Franklin Roosevelt on December 8, 1941, it declared war on Japan and described the attack on Pearl Harbor as "a day which will live in infamy."

- **Inaugural Address** – Made by John F. Kennedy on January 20, 1961, it contained the famous line: "Ask not what your country can do for you, ask what you can do for your country."
- **Berlin Address** – Made by John F. Kennedy on June 26, 1963, it contained the famous line "Ich bin ein Berliner," which expressed empathy for West Berliners in their conflict with the Soviet Union.
- "**I Have a Dream**" and "**I See the Promised Land**" – Made by Martin Luther King, Jr. on August 28, 1963 and April 3, 1968, respectively, these speeches were hallmarks of the Civil Rights Movement.
- **Brandenburg Gate speech** – Made by Ronald Reagan on June 12, 1987, this speech was about the Berlin Wall and the end of the Cold War. It contained the famous line "Tear down this wall."

Closed and Open Primaries in a Direct Primary System

The **direct primary system** is a means for members of a political party to participate in the selection of a candidate from their party to compete against the other party's candidate in a general election. A **closed primary** is a party nominating election in which only declared party members can vote. Party membership is usually established by registration. Currently, 26 states and the District of Columbia use this system. An **open primary** is a party nominating election in which any qualified voter can take part. The voter makes a public choice at the polling place about which primary to participate in, and the choice does not depend on any registration or previous choices. A **blanket primary**, which allowed voters to vote in the primaries of both parties, was used at various times by three states. The Supreme Court ruled against this practice in 2000.

Important Documents in United States History and Government

The following are among the greatest **American documents** because of their impact on foreign and domestic policy:

- Declaration of Independence (1776)
- The Articles of Confederation (1777)
- The Constitution (1787) and the Bill of Rights (1791)
- The Northwest Ordinance (1787)
- The Federalist Papers (1787-88)
- George Washington's Inaugural Address (1789) and Farewell Address (1796)
- The Alien and Sedition Act (1798)
- The Louisiana Purchase Treaty (1803)
- The Monroe Doctrine (1823); The Missouri Compromise (1830)
- The Compromise of 1850
- The Kansas-Nebraska Act (1854)
- The Homestead Act (1862)
- The Emancipation Proclamation (1863)
- The agreement to purchase Alaska (1866)
- The Sherman Anti-Trust Act (1890)
- Theodore Roosevelt's Corollary to the Monroe Doctrine (1905)
- The Social Security Act (1935) and other acts of the New Deal in the 1930s; The Truman Doctrine (1947); The Marshall Plan (1948)
- The Civil Rights Act (1964)

Federal Taxes

The four types of **federal taxes** are:

- **Income taxes on individuals** – This is a complex system because of demands for various exemptions and rates. Further, the schedule of rates can be lowered or raised according to economic conditions in order to stimulate or restrain economic activity. For example, a tax cut can provide an economic stimulus, while a tax increase can slow down the rate of inflation. Personal income tax generates about five times as much as corporate taxes. Rates are based on an individual's income, and range from 10 to 35 percent.
- **Income taxes on corporations** – The same complexity of exemptions and rates exists for corporations as individuals. Taxes can be raised or lowered according to the need to stimulate or restrain the economy.
- **Excise taxes** – These are taxes on specific goods such as tobacco, liquor, automobiles, gasoline, air travel, and luxury items, or on activities such as highway usage by trucks.
- **Customs duties** – These are taxes imposed on imported goods. They serve to regulate trade between the United States and other countries.

United States Currency System

The Constitution of 1787 gave the United States Congress the central authority to **print or coin money** and to **regulate its value**. Before this time, states were permitted to maintain separate currencies. The currency system is based on a **modified gold standard**. There is an enormous store of gold to back up United States currency housed at Fort Knox, Kentucky. Paper money is actually **Federal Reserve notes** and coins. It is the job of the Bureau of Engraving and Printing in the Treasury Department to design plates, special types of paper, and other security measures for bills and bonds. This money is put into general circulation by the Treasury and Federal Reserve Banks, and is taken out of circulation when worn out. Coins are made at the Bureau of the Mint in Philadelphia, Denver, and San Francisco.

Employment Act of 1946

The **Employment Act of 1946** established the following entities to combat unemployment:

- The **Council of Economic Advisers** (CEA) – Composed of a chair and two other members appointed by the President and approved by the Senate, this council assists the President with the development and implementation of U.S. economic policy. The Council members and their staff, located in the Executive Office, are professionals in economics and statistics who forecast economic trends and provide analysis based on evidence-based research.
- The **Economic Report of the President** – This is presented every January by the President to Congress. Based on the work of the Council, the report recommends a program for maximizing employment, and may also recommend legislation.
- **Joint Economic Committee** (JEC) – This is a committee composed of 10 members of the House and 10 members of the Senate that makes a report early each year on its continuous study of the economy. Study is conducted through hearings and research, and the report is made in response to the president's recommendations.

Qualifications of a US Citizen

Anyone born in the US, born abroad to a US citizen, or who has gone through a process of **naturalization** to become a citizen, is considered a **citizen** of the United States. It is possible to lose

US citizenship as a result of conviction of certain crimes such as treason. Citizenship may also be lost if a citizen pledges an oath to another country or serves in the military of a country engaged in hostilities with the US. A US citizen can also choose to hold dual citizenship, work as an expatriate in another country without losing US citizenship, or even renounce citizenship if he or she so chooses.

Rights, Duties, and Responsibilities Granted to or Expected from US Citizens

Citizens are granted certain rights under the US government. The most important of these are defined in the **Bill of Rights**, and include freedom of speech, religion, assembly, and a variety of other rights the government is not allowed to remove.

Duties of a US citizen include:

- Paying taxes
- Loyalty to the government, though the US does not prosecute those who criticize or seek to change the government
- Support and defend the Constitution
- Serve in the Armed Forces as required by law
- Obeying laws as set forth by the various levels of government.

Responsibilities of a US citizen include:

- Voting in elections
- Respecting one another's rights and not infringing upon them
- Staying informed about various political and national issues
- Respecting one another's beliefs

Representative Democracy

In a system of government characterized as a representative democracy, voters elect **representatives** to act in their interests. Typically, a representative is elected by and responsible to a specific subset of the total population of eligible voters; this subset of the electorate is referred to as a representative's constituency. A **representative democracy** may foster a more powerful legislature than other forms of government systems; to compensate for a strong legislature, most constitutions stipulate that measures must be taken to balance the powers within government, such as the creation of a separate judicial branch. Representative democracy became popular in post-industrial nations where increasing numbers of people expressed an interest in politics, but where technology and census counts remained incompatible with systems of direct democracy. Today, the majority of the world's population resides in representative democracies, including constitutional monarchies that possess a strong representative branch.

Democracy

Democracy, or rule by the people, is a form of government in which power is vested in the people and in which policy decisions are made by the majority in a decision-making process such as an election that is open to all or most citizens. Definitions of democracy have become more generalized and include aspects of society and political culture in democratic societies that do not necessarily represent a form of government. What defines a democracy varies, but some of the characteristics of a democracy could include the presence of a middle class, the presence of a civil society, a free market, political pluralism, universal suffrage, and specific rights and freedoms. In practice however, democracies do have limits on specific freedoms, which are justified as being necessary to maintain democracy and ensure democratic freedoms. For example, freedom of association is limited in democracies for individuals and groups that pose a threat to government or to society.

Presidential/Congressional System

In a **presidential system**, also referred to as a **congressional system**, the legislative branch and the executive branches are elected separately from one another. The features of a presidential system include a *president* who serves as both the head of state and the head of the government, who has no formal relationship with the legislative branch, who is not a voting member, who cannot introduce bills, and who has a fixed term of office. *Elections* are held at scheduled times. The president's *cabinet* carries out the policies of the executive branch and the legislative branch.

Political Parties

A **political party** is an organization that advocates a particular ideology and seeks to gain power within government. The tendency of members of political parties to support their party's policies and interests relative to those of other parties is referred to as partisanship. Often, a political party is comprised of members whose positions, interests and perspectives on policies vary, despite having shared interests in the general ideology of the party. As such, many political parties will have divisions within them that have differing opinions on policy. Political parties are often placed on a political spectrum, with one end of the spectrum representing conservative, traditional values and policies and the other end of the spectrum representing radical, progressive value and policies.

Review Video: Political Parties
Visit mometrix.com/academy and enter code: 640197

Types of Party Systems

There is a variety of **party systems**, including single-party systems, dominant-party systems, and dual-party systems. In a **single-party system**, only one political party may hold power. In this type of system, minor parties may be permitted, but they must accept the leadership of the dominant party. **Dominant-party systems** allow for multiple parties in opposition of one another, however the dominant party is the only party considered to have power. A **two-party system**, such as in the United States, is one in which there are two dominant political parties. In such a system, it is very difficult for any other parties to win an election. In most two-party systems, there is typically one right wing party and one left wing party.

Democratic Party

The **Democratic Party** was founded in 1792. In the United States, it is one of the two dominant political parties, along with the Republican Party. The Democratic Party is to the left of the Republican Party. The Democratic Party began as a conservative party in the mid-1800s, shifting to the left during the 1900s. There are many factions within the Democratic Party in the United States. The **Democratic National Committee (DNC)** is the official organization of the Democratic Party, and it develops and promotes the party's platform and coordinates fundraising and election strategies. There are Democratic committees in every U.S. state and most U.S. counties. The official symbol of the Democratic Party is the donkey.

Republican Party

The **Republican Party** is often referred to as the **GOP**, which stands for *Grand Old Party*. The Republican Party is considered socially conservative and economically neoliberal relative to the

Democratic Party. Like the Democratic Party, there are factions within the Republic Party that agree with the party's overall ideology, but disagree with the party's positions on specific issues. The official symbol of the Republican Party is the elephant. The **Republican National Committee (RNC)** is the official organization of the Republican Party, and it develops and promotes the party's platform and coordinates fundraising and election strategies. There are Republican committees in every U.S. state and most U.S. counties.

Political Campaigns

A **political campaign** is an organized attempt to influence the decisions of a particular group of people . Examples of campaigns could include elections or efforts to influence policy changes. One of the first steps in a campaign is to develop a **campaign message**. The message must then be delivered to the individuals and groups that the campaign is trying to reach and influence through a campaign plan. There are various ways for a campaign to communicate its message to the intended audience, including public media; paid media such as television, radio and newspaper ads, billboards and the internet; public events such as protests and rallies; meetings with speakers; mailings; canvassing; fliers; and websites. Through these efforts, the campaign attempts to attract additional support and, ultimately, to reach the goal of the campaign.

Review Video: Political Campaigns
Visit mometrix.com/academy and enter code: 838608

Voting

Voting is a method of decision making that allows people to express their opinion or preference for a candidate or for a proposed resolution of an issue. In a democratic system, voting typically takes place as part of an **election**. An individual participates in the voting process by casting a vote, or a **ballot**; ballots are produced by states A *secret ballot* can be used at polls to protect voters' privacy. Individuals can also vote via *absentee ballot.* In some states voters can write-in a name to cast a vote for a candidate that is not on the ballot. Some states also use *straight ticket voting*, allowing the voter to vote for one party for all the elected positions on the ballot.

US Elections

In the United States, **officials** are elected at the federal, state and local levels. The first two articles of the Constitution, as well as various amendments, establish how **federal elections** are to be held. The **President** is elected indirectly, by electors of an electoral college. Members of the electoral college nearly always vote along the lines of the popular vote of their respective states. Members of **Congress** are directly elected. At the state level, state law establishes most aspects of how elections are held. There are many elected offices at the state level, including a governor and state legislature. There are also elected offices at the local level.

Voter Eligibility

The United States Constitution establishes that individual people are permitted to **vote** in elections if they are citizens of the United States and are at least eighteen years old. The **fifteenth** and **nineteenth amendments** of the United States Constitution stipulate that the right to vote cannot be denied to any United States citizen based on race or sex, respectively. States regulate voter eligibility beyond the minimum qualifications stipulated by the United States Constitution.

Depending on the regulations of individual states, individuals may be denied the right to vote if they are convicted criminals.

Review Video: Voter Behavior
Visit mometrix.com/academy and enter code: 976272

Advantages and Disadvantages to Two-Party System

Advocates of the **two-party system** argue that its advantages are that they are stable because they enable policies and government to change slowly rather than rapidly due to the relative lack of influence from small parties representing unconventional ideologies. In addition, they seem to drive voters toward a middle ground and are less susceptible to revolutions, coups, or civil wars. Among the critiques of the two-party system is the claim that stability in and of itself is not necessarily desirable, as it often comes at the expense of democracy. Critics also argue that the two-party system promotes negative political campaigns, in which candidates and their respective parties only take positions on issues that will differentiate themselves from their opponents, rather than focusing on policy issues that are of significance to citizens. Another concern is that if one of the two major parties becomes weak, a dominant-party system may develop.

Campaign Message

Political campaigns consist of three main elements, which are the campaign message, the money that is necessary to run the campaign and "machine," or the capital that is necessary run the campaign. A campaign message is a succinct statement expressing why voters should support the campaign and the individual or policy associated with that campaign. The message is one of the most significant aspects of a political campaign, and a considerable amount of time, money and effort is invested in devising a successful campaign message, as it will be repeated throughout the campaign and will be one of the most identifying factors of the campaign.

Modern Election Campaigns in US

Political campaigns in the U.S. have changed and continue to change as advances in technology permit varied campaign methods. Campaigns represent a civic practice, and today they are a high profit industry. The U.S. has an abundance of professional political consultants that employ highly sophisticated campaign management strategies and tools. The election process varies widely between the federal, state and local levels. Campaigns are typically controlled by individual candidates, rather than by the parties that they are associated with. Larger campaigns utilize a vast array of media to reach their targeted audiences, while smaller campaigns are typically limited to direct contact with voters, direct mailings and other forms of low-cost advertising to reach their audiences. In addition to fundraising and spending done by individual candidates, party committees and political action committees also raise money and spend it in ways that will advance the cause of the particular campaign they are associated with.

Voter Registration

Individuals have the responsibility of **registering to vote**. Every state except North Dakota requires citizens to register to vote. In an effort to increase voter turnout, Congress passed the **National Voter Registration Act** in 1993. The Act is also known as "Motor Voter," because it required states to make the voter registration process easier by providing registration services through drivers' license registration centers, as well as through disability centers, schools, libraries, and mail-in registration. Some states are exempt because they permit same-day voter registration, which enables voters to register to vote on the day of the election.

Presidential Elections

The President of the United States is elected **indirectly**, by members of an **electoral college**. Members of the electoral college nearly always vote along the lines of the popular vote of their respective states. The winner of a presidential election is the candidate with at least 270 electoral college votes. It is possible for a candidate to win the electoral vote, and lose the popular vote. Incumbent Presidents and challengers typically prefer a balanced ticket, where the President and Vice President are elected together and generally balance one another with regard to geography, ideology, or experience working in government. The nominated Vice Presidential candidate is referred to as the President's *running mate*.

Electoral College

Electoral college votes are cast by state by a group of electors; each elector casts one electoral college vote. State law regulates how states cast their electoral college votes. In all states except Maine and Nebraska, the candidate winning the most votes receives all the state's electoral college votes. In Maine and Nebraska two electoral votes are awarded based on the winner of the statewide election, and the rest go to the highest vote-winner in each of the state's congressional districts. Critics of the electoral college argue that it is undemocratic because the President is elected indirectly as opposed to directly, and that it creates inequality between voters in different states because candidates focus attention on voters in swing states who could influence election results. Critics argue that the electoral college provides more representation for voters in small states than large states, where more voters are represented by a single electoral than in small states and discriminates against candidates that do not have support concentrated in a given state.

Congressional Elections

Congressional elections are every two years. Members of the **House of Representatives** are elected for a two year term and elections occur every two years on the first Tuesday after November 1st in even years. A Representative is elected from each of 435 House districts in the U.S. House elections usually occur in the same year as Presidential elections. Members of the **Senate** are elected to six year terms; one-third of the Senate is elected every two years. Per the Seventeenth Amendment to the Constitution, which was passed in 1913, Senators are elected by the electorate of states. The country is divided into **Congressional districts**, and critics argue that this division eliminates voter choice, sometimes creating areas in which Congressional races are uncontested. Every ten years **redistricting** of Congressional districts occurs. However, redistricting is often partisan and therefore reduces the number of competitive districts. The division of voting districts resulting in an unfair advantage to one party in elections is known as gerrymandering. Gerrymandering has been criticized as being undemocratic.

State and Local Elections

State elections are regulated by state laws and constitutions. In keeping with the ideal of separation of powers, the legislature and the executive are elected separately at the state level, as they are at the federal level. In each state, a **Governor** and a **Lieutenant Governor** are elected. In some states, the Governor and Lieutenant Governor are elected on a joint ticket, while in other states they are elected separately from one another. In some states, executive positions such as Attorney General and Secretary of State are also elected offices. All members of state legislatures are elected, including state senators and state representatives. Depending on the state, members of the state supreme court and other members of the state judiciary may be chosen in elections. Local government can include the governments of counties and cities. At this level, nearly all government offices are filled through an election process. Elected local offices may include sheriffs, county school boards, and city mayors.

Campaign Finance and Independent Expenditures

An individual or group is legally permitted to make unlimited **independent expenditures** in association with federal elections. An independent expenditure is an expenditure that is made to pay for a form of communication that supports the election or defeat of a candidate; the expenditure must be made independently from the candidate's own campaign. To be considered independent, the communication may not be made with the cooperation or consultation with, or at the request or suggestion of, any candidate, any committees or political party associated with the candidate, or any agent that acts on behalf of the candidate. There are no restrictions on the amount that anyone may spend on an independent expenditure, however, any individual making an independent expenditure must report it and disclose the source of the funds they used.

Campaign Finance and Activities of Political Parties

Political parties participate in federal elections at the local, state and national levels. Most **party committees** must register with the **Federal Election Committee** and file reports disclosing federal campaign activities. While party committees may contribute funds directly to federal candidates, the amounts that they contribute are restricted by the campaign finance contribution limits. National and state party committees are permitted to make additional **coordinated expenditures**, within limits, to assist their nominees in general elections. However, national party committees are not permitted to make unlimited **independent expenditures** to support or oppose federal candidates using soft money. State and local party committees are also not permitted to use soft money for the purpose of supporting or opposing federal candidates, but they are allowed to spend soft money, up to a limit of $10,000 per source, on voter registration and on efforts aimed at increasing voter participation. All party committees are required to register themselves and file disclosure reports with the Federal Election Committee once their federal election activities exceed specified monetary limits.

Public Opinion

Public opinion represents the collective attitudes of individual members of the adult population in the United States of America. There are many varied forces that may influence public opinion. These forces include *public relations efforts* on the part of political campaigns and political parties. Another force affecting political opinion is the *political media* and the *mass media*. Public opinion is very important during elections, particularly Presidential elections, as it is an indicator of how candidates are perceived by the public and of how well candidates are doing during their election campaigns. Public opinion is often measured and evaluated using survey sampling.

Mass Media and Public Opinion

The **mass media** is critical in developing public opinion. In the short term people generally evaluate information they receive relative to their own beliefs; in the long term the media may have a considerable impact on people's beliefs. Due to the impact of the media on an individual's beliefs, some experts consider the effects of the media on an individual's independence and autonomy to be negative. Others view the impact of the media on individuals as a positive one, because the media provides information that expands worldviews and enriches life, and fosters the development of opinions that are informed by many sources of information. A critical aspect of the relationship between the media and public opinion is who is in control of the knowledge and information that is disseminated through the media. Whoever controls the media can propagate their own agenda. The extent to which an individual interprets and evaluates information received through the media can influence behaviors such as voting patterns or consumer behavior, as well as social attitudes.

Geography

Important Terms Related to Maps

The most important terms used when describing items on a map or globe are:

- **Latitude and longitude** – Latitude and longitude are the imaginary lines (horizontal and vertical, respectively) that divide the globe into a grid. Both are measured using the 360 degrees of a circle.
- **Coordinates** – These are the latitude and longitude measures for a place.
- **Absolute location** – This is the exact spot where coordinates meet. The grid system allows the location of every place on the planet to be identified.
- **Equator** – This is the line at 0° latitude that divides the earth into two equal halves called hemispheres.
- **Parallels** – This is another name for lines of latitude because they circle the earth in parallel lines that never meet.
- **Meridians** – This is another name for lines of longitude. The Prime Meridian is located at 0° longitude, and is the starting point for measuring distance (both east and west) around the globe. Meridians circle the earth and connect at the Poles.

Review Video: 5 Elements of any Map
Visit mometrix.com/academy and enter code: 437727

Four Hemispheres, North and South Poles, Tropics of Cancer and Capricorn, and Arctic and Antarctic Circles

The definitions for these terms are as follows:

- **Northern Hemisphere** – This is the area above, or north, of the equator.
- **Southern Hemisphere** – This is the area below, or south, of the equator.
- **Western Hemisphere** – This is the area between the North and South Poles. It extends west from the Prime Meridian to the International Date Line.
- **Eastern Hemisphere** – This is the area between the North and South Poles. It extends east from the Prime Meridian to the International Date Line.
- **North and South Poles** – Latitude is measured in terms of the number of degrees north and south from the equator. The North Pole is located at 90°N latitude, while the South Pole is located at 90°S latitude.
- **Tropic of Cancer** – This is the parallel, or latitude, 23½° north of the equator.
- **Tropic of Capricorn** – This is the parallel, or latitude, 23½° south of the equator. The region between these two parallels is the tropics. The subtropics is the area located between 23½° and 40° north and south of the equator.
- **Arctic Circle** – This is the parallel, or latitude, 66½° north of the equator.
- **Antarctic Circle** – This is the parallel, or latitude, 66½° south of the equator.

Review Video: Geographical Features
Visit mometrix.com/academy and enter code: 773539

GPS

Global Positioning System (GPS) is a system of satellites that orbit the Earth and communicate with mobile devices to pinpoint the mobile device's position. This is accomplished by determining the distance between the mobile device and at least three satellites. A mobile device might calculate a distance of 400 miles between it and the first satellite. The possible locations that are 400 miles from the first satellite and the mobile device will fall along a circle. The possible locations on Earth relative to the other two satellites will fall somewhere along different circles. The point on Earth at which these three circles intersect is the location of the mobile device. The process of determining position based on distance measurements from three satellites is called **trilateration**.

Review Video: Cartography and Technology
Visit mometrix.com/academy and enter code: 642071

Types of Maps

- A **physical map** is one that shows natural features such as mountains, rivers, lakes, deserts, and plains. Color is used to designate the different features.
- A **topographic map** is a type of physical map that shows the relief and configuration of a landscape, such as hills, valleys, fields, forest, roads, and settlements. It includes natural and human-made features.
- A **topological map** is one on which lines are stretched or straightened for the sake of clarity, but retain their essential geometric relationship. This type of map is used, for example, to show the routes of a subway system.
- A **political map** uses lines for state, county, and country boundaries; points or dots for cities and towns; and various other symbols for features such as airports and roads.

Physical and Cultural Features of Geographic Locations and Countries

Physical features:

- **Vegetation zones, or biomes** – Forests, grasslands, deserts, and tundra are the four main types of vegetation zones.
- **Climate zones** – Tropical, dry, temperate, continental, and polar are the five different types of climate zones. Climate is the long-term average weather conditions of a place.

Cultural features:

- **Population density** – This is the number of people living in each square mile or kilometer of a place. It is calculated by dividing population by area.
- **Religion** – This is the identification of the dominant religions of a place, whether Christianity, Hinduism, Judaism, Buddhism, Islam, Shinto, Taoism, or Confucianism. All of these originated in Asia.
- **Languages** – This is the identification of the dominant or official language of a place. There are 12 major language families. The Indo-European family (which includes English, Russian, German, French, and Spanish) is spoken over the widest geographic area, but Mandarin Chinese is spoken by the most people.

Review Video: Physical vs. Cultural Geography
Visit mometrix.com/academy and enter code: 912136

Coral Reefs

Coral reefs are formed from millions of tiny, tube-shaped **polyps**, an animal life form encased in tough limestone skeletons. Once anchored to a rocky surface, polyps eat plankton and miniscule shellfish caught with poisonous tentacles near the mouth. Polyps use calcium carbonate absorbed from chemicals given off by algae to harden their body armor and cement themselves together in fantastic shapes of many colors. Polyps reproduce through eggs and larvae, but the reef grows by branching out shoots of polyps. There are three types of coral reefs:

- **Fringing reefs** – These surround, or "fringe," an island.
- **Barrier reefs** – Over the centuries, a fringe reef grows so large that the island sinks down from the weight, and the reef becomes a barrier around the island. Water trapped between the island and the reef is called a lagoon.
- **Atolls** – Eventually, the sinking island goes under, leaving the coral reef around the lagoon.

Formation of Mountains

Mountains are formed by the movement of geologic plates, which are rigid slabs of rocks beneath the earth's crust that float on a layer of partially molten rock in the earth's upper mantle. As the plates collide, they push up the crust to form mountains. This process is called **orogeny**. There are three basic forms of orogeny:

- If the collision of continental plates causes the crust to buckle and fold, a chain of **folded mountains**, such as the Appalachians, the Alps, or the Himalayas, is formed.
- If the collision of the plates causes a denser oceanic plate to go under a continental plate, a process called **subduction**; strong horizontal forces lift and fold the margin of the continent. A mountain range like the Andes is the result.
- If an oceanic plate is driven under another oceanic plate, **volcanic mountains** such as those in Japan and the Philippines are formed.

Harmful or Potentially Harmful Interaction with Environment

Wherever humans have gone on the earth, they have made **changes** to their surroundings. Many are harmful or potentially harmful, depending on the extent of the alterations. Some of the changes and activities that can harm the **environment** include:

- Cutting into mountains by machine or blasting to build roads or construction sites
- Cutting down trees and clearing natural growth
- Building houses and cities
- Using grassland to graze herds
- Polluting water sources
- Polluting the ground with chemical and oil waste
- Wearing out fertile land and losing topsoil
- Placing communication lines cross country using poles and wires or underground cable
- Placing railway lines or paved roads cross country
- Building gas and oil pipelines cross country
- Draining wetlands

- Damming up or re-routing waterways
- Spraying fertilizers, pesticides, and defoliants
- Hunting animals to extinction or near extinction

Adaptation to Environmental Conditions

The environment influences the way people live. People **adapt** to **environmental conditions** in ways as simple as putting on warm clothing in a cold environment; finding means to cool their surroundings in an environment with high temperatures; building shelters from wind, rain, and temperature variations; and digging water wells if surface water is unavailable. More complex adaptations result from the physical diversity of the earth in terms of soil, climate, vegetation, and topography. Humans take advantage of opportunities and avoid or minimize limitations. Examples of environmental limitations are that rocky soils offer few opportunities for agriculture and rough terrain limits accessibility. Sometimes, **technology** allows humans to live in areas that were once uninhabitable or undesirable. For example, air conditioning allows people to live comfortably in hot climates; modern heating systems permit habitation in areas with extremely low temperatures, as is the case with research facilities in Antarctica; and airplanes have brought people to previously inaccessible places to establish settlements or industries.

Carrying Capacity and Natural Hazards

Carrying capacity is the maximum, sustained level of use of an environment can incur without sustaining significant environmental deterioration that would eventually lead to environmental destruction. Environments vary in terms of their carrying capacity, a concept humans need to learn to measure and respect before harm is done. Proper **assessment of environmental conditions** enables responsible decision making with respect to how much and in what ways the resources of a particular environment should be consumed. **Energy and water conservation** as well as recycling can extend an area's carrying capacity. In addition to carrying capacity limitations, the physical environment can also have occasional extremes that are costly to humans. **Natural hazards** such as hurricanes, tornadoes, earthquakes, volcanoes, floods, tsunamis, and some forest fires and insect infestations are processes or events that are not caused by humans, but may have serious consequences for humans and the environment. These events are not preventable, and their precise timing, location, and magnitude are not predictable. However, some precautions can be taken to reduce the damage.

Applying Geography to Interpretation of the Past

Space, environment, and chronology are three different points of view that can be used to study history. Events take place within **geographic contexts**. If the world is flat, then transportation choices are vastly different from those that would be made in a round world, for example. Invasions of Russia from the west have normally failed because of the harsh winter conditions, the vast distances that inhibit steady supply lines, and the number of rivers and marshes to be crossed, among other factors. Any invading or defending force anywhere must make choices based on consideration of space and environmental factors. For instance, lands may be too muddy or passages too narrow for certain equipment. Geography played a role in the building of the Panama Canal because the value of a shorter transportation route had to outweigh the costs of labor, disease, political negotiations, and equipment, not to mention a myriad of other effects from cutting a canal through an isthmus and changing a natural land structure as a result.

Applying Geography to Interpretation of the Present and Plans for the Future

The decisions that individual people as well as nations make that may **affect the environment** have to be made with an understanding of spatial patterns and concepts, cultural and transportation connections, physical processes and patterns, ecosystems, and the impact, or "footprint," of people on the physical environment. Sample issues that fit into these considerations are recycling programs, loss of agricultural land to further urban expansion, air and water pollution, deforestation, and ease of transportation and communication. In each of these areas, present and future uses have to be balanced against possible harmful effects. For example, wind is a clean and readily available resource for electric power, but the access roads to and noise of wind turbines can make some areas unsuitable for livestock pasture. Voting citizens need to have an understanding of **geographical and environmental connections** to make responsible decisions.

Spatial Organization

Spatial organization in geography refers to how things or people are grouped in a given space anywhere on earth. Spatial organization applies to the **placement of settlements**, whether hamlets, towns, or cities. These settlements are located to make the distribution of goods and services convenient. For example, in farm communities, people come to town to get groceries, to attend church and school, and to access medical services. It is more practical to provide these things to groups than to individuals. These settlements, historically, have been built close to water sources and agricultural areas. Lands that are topographically difficult, have few resources, or experience extreme temperatures do not have as many people as temperate zones and flat plains, where it is easier to live. Within settlements, a town or city will be organized into commercial and residential neighborhoods, with hospitals, fire stations, and shopping centers centrally located. All of these organizational considerations are spatial in nature.

Themes of Geography

The five themes of geography are:

- **Location** – This includes relative location (described in terms of surrounding geography such as a river, sea coast, or mountain) and absolute location (the specific point of latitude and longitude).
- **Place** – This includes physical characteristics (deserts, plains, mountains, and waterways) and human characteristics (features created by humans, such as architecture, roads, religion, industries, and food and folk practices).
- **Human-environmental interaction** – This includes human adaptation to the environment (using an umbrella when it rains), human modification of the environment (building terraces to prevent soil erosion), and human dependence on the environment for food, water, and natural resources.
- **Movement** –Interaction through trade, migration, communications, political boundaries, ideas, and fashions.
- **Regions** – This includes formal regions (a city, state, country, or other geographical organization as defined by political boundaries), functional regions (defined by a common function or connection, such as a school district), and vernacular regions (informal divisions determined by perceptions or one's mental image, such as the "Far East").

Review Video: Regional Geography
Visit mometrix.com/academy and enter code: 350378

Review Video: Human Geography
Visit mometrix.com/academy and enter code: 195767

Geomorphology

The study of landforms is call **geomorphology** or physiography, a science that considers the relationships between *geological structures* and *surface landscape features*. It is also concerned with the processes that change these features, such as erosion, deposition, and plate tectonics. Biological factors can also affect landforms. Examples are when corals build a coral reef or when plants contribute to the development of a salt marsh or a sand dune. Rivers, coastlines, rock types, slope formation, ice, erosion, and weathering are all part of geomorphology. A **landform** is a landscape feature or geomorphological unit. These include hills, plateaus, mountains, deserts, deltas, canyons, mesas, marshes, swamps, and valleys. These units are categorized according to elevation, slope, orientation, stratification, rock exposure, and soil type. Landform elements include pits, peaks, channels, ridges, passes, pools, and plains. The highest order landforms are continents and oceans. Elementary landforms such as segments, facets, and relief units are the smallest homogenous divisions of a land surface at a given scale or resolution.

Oceans, Seas, Lakes, Rivers, and Canals

- **Oceans** are the largest bodies of water on earth and cover nearly 71% of the earth's surface. There are five major oceans: Atlantic, Pacific (largest and deepest), Indian, Arctic, and Southern (surrounds Antarctica).
- **Seas** are smaller than oceans and are somewhat surrounded by land like a lake, but lakes are fresh water and seas are salt water. Seas include the Mediterranean, Baltic, Caspian, Caribbean, and Coral.
- **Lakes** are bodies of water in a depression on the earth's surface. Examples of lakes are the Great Lakes and Lake Victoria.
- **Rivers** are a channeled flow of water that start out as a spring or stream formed by runoff from rain or snow. Rivers flow from higher to lower ground, and usually empty into a sea or ocean. Great rivers of the world include the Amazon, Nile, Rhine, Mississippi, Ganges, Mekong, and Yangtze.
- **Canals** are artificial waterways constructed by humans to connect two larger water bodies. Examples of canals are the Panama and the Suez.

Mountains, Hills, Foothills, Valleys, Plateaus, and Mesas

The definitions for these geographical features are as follows:

- **Mountains** are elevated landforms that rise fairly steeply from the earth's surface to a summit of at least 1,000-2,000 feet (definitions vary) above sea level.
- **Hills** are elevated landforms that rise 500-2,000 feet above sea level.
- **Foothills** are a low series of hills found between a plain and a mountain range.
- **Valleys** are a long depression located between hills or mountains. They are usually products of river erosion. Valleys can vary in terms of width and depth, ranging from a few feet to thousands of feet.

- **Plateaus** are elevated landforms that are fairly flat on top. They may be as high as 10,000 feet above sea level and are usually next to mountains.
- **Mesas** are flat areas of upland. Their name is derived from the Spanish word for table. They are smaller than plateaus and often found in arid or semi-arid areas.

Plains, Deserts, Deltas, and Basins

- **Plains** are extensive areas of low-lying, flat, or gently undulating land, and are usually lower than the landforms around them. Plains near the seacoast are called lowlands.
- **Deserts** are large, dry areas that receive less than 10 inches of rain per year. They are almost barren, containing only a few patches of vegetation.
- **Deltas** are accumulations of silt deposited at river mouths into the seabed. They are eventually converted into very fertile, stable ground by vegetation, becoming important crop-growing areas. Examples include the deltas of the Nile, Ganges, and Mississippi River.
- **Basins** come in various types. They may be low areas that catch water from rivers; large hollows that dip to a central point and are surrounded by higher ground, as in the Donets and Kuznetsk basins in Russia; or areas of inland drainage in a desert when the water can't reach the sea and flows into lakes or evaporates in salt flats as a result. An example is the Great Salt Lake in Utah.

Marshes and Swamps and Tundra and Taiga

Marshes and swamps are both **wet lowlands**. The water can be fresh, brackish, or saline. Both host important ecological systems with unique wildlife. There are, however, some major differences. **Marshes** have no trees and are always wet because of frequent floods and poor drainage that leaves shallow water. Plants are mostly grasses, rushes, reeds, typhas, sedges, and herbs. **Swamps** have trees and dry periods. The water is very slow-moving, and is usually associated with adjacent rivers or lakes.

Both taiga and tundra regions have many plants and animals, but they have few humans or crops because of their harsh climates. **Taiga** has colder winters and hotter summers than tundra because of its distance from the Arctic Ocean. **Tundra** is a Russian word describing marshy plain in an area that has a very cold climate but receives little snow. The ground is usually frozen, but is quite spongy when it is not. Taiga is the world's largest forest region, located just south of the tundra line. It contains huge mineral resources and fur-bearing animals.

Humid Continental, Prairie, Subtropical, and Marine Climates

- A **humid continental climate** is one that has four seasons, including a cold winter and a hot summer, and sufficient rainfall for raising crops. Such climates can be found in the United States, Canada, and Russia. The best farmlands and mining areas are found in these countries.
- **Prairie climates**, or steppe regions, are found in the interiors of Asia and North America where there are dry flatlands (prairies that receive 10-20 inches of rain per year). These dry flatlands can be grasslands or deserts.
- **Subtropical climates** are very humid areas in the tropical areas of Japan, China, Australia, Africa, South America, and the United States. The moisture, carried by winds traveling over warm ocean currents, produces long summers and mild winters. It is possible to produce a continuous cycle of a variety of crops.

- A **marine climate** is one near or surrounded by water. Warm ocean winds bring moisture, mild temperatures year-round, and plentiful rain. These climates are found in Western Europe and parts of the United States, Canada, Chile, New Zealand, and Australia.

Physical and Cultural Geography and Physical and Political Locations

- **Physical geography** is the study of climate, water, and land and their relationships with each other and humans. Physical geography locates and identifies the earth's surface features and explores how humans thrive in various locations according to crop and goods production.
- **Cultural geography** is the study of the influence of the environment on human behaviors as well as the effect of human activities such as farming, building settlements, and grazing livestock on the environment. Cultural geography also identifies and compares the features of different cultures and how they influence interactions with other cultures and the earth.
- **Physical location** refers to the placement of the hemispheres and the continents.
- **Political location** refers to the divisions within continents that designate various countries. These divisions are made with borders, which are set according to boundary lines arrived at by legal agreements.

Both physical and political locations can be precisely determined by geographical surveys and by latitude and longitude.

Natural Resources, Renewable Resources, Nonrenewable Resources, and Commodities

Natural resources are things provided by nature that have commercial value to humans, such as minerals, energy, timber, fish, wildlife, and the landscape. **Renewable resources** are those that can be replenished, such as wind, solar radiation, tides, and water (with proper conservation and clean-up). Soil is renewable with proper conservation and management techniques, and timber can be replenished with replanting. Living resources such as fish and wildlife can replenish themselves if they are not over-harvested. **Nonrenewable resources** are those that cannot be replenished. These include fossil fuels such as oil and coal and metal ores. These cannot be replaced or reused once they have been burned, although some of their products can be recycled. **Commodities** are natural resources that have to be extracted and purified rather than created, such as mineral ores.

Geography

Geography involves learning about the world's primary **physical and cultural patterns** to help understand how the world functions as an interconnected and dynamic system. Combining information from different sources, geography teaches the basic patterns of climate, geology, vegetation, human settlement, migration, and commerce. Thus, geography is an **interdisciplinary** study of history, anthropology, and sociology. **History** incorporates geography in discussions of battle strategies, slavery (trade routes), ecological disasters (the Dust Bowl of the 1930s), and mass migrations. Geographic principles are useful when reading **literature** to help identify and visualize the setting, and also when studying **earth science**, **mathematics** (latitude, longitude, sun angle, and population statistics), and **fine arts** (song, art, and dance often reflect different cultures). Consequently, a good background in geography can help students succeed in other subjects as well.

Areas Covered by Geography

Geography is connected to many issues and provides answers to many everyday questions. Some of the areas covered by geography include:

- Geography investigates global climates, landforms, economies, political systems, human cultures, and migration patterns.
- Geography answers questions not only about where something is located, but also why it is there, how it got there, and how it is related to other things around it.
- Geography explains why people move to certain regions (climate, availability of natural resources, arable land, etc.).
- Geography explains world trade routes and modes of transportation.
- Geography identifies where various animals live and where various crops and forests grow.
- Geography identifies and locates populations that follow certain religions.
- Geography provides statistics on population numbers and growth, which aids in economic and infrastructure planning for cities and countries.

Globe and Map Projections

A **globe** is the only accurate representation of the earth's size, shape, distance, and direction since it, like the earth, is **spherical**. The flat surface of a map distorts these elements. To counter this problem, mapmakers use a variety of "**map projections**," a system for representing the earth's curvatures on a flat surface through the use of a grid that corresponds to lines of latitude and longitude. Some distortions are still inevitable, though, so mapmakers make choices based on the map scale, the size of the area to be mapped, and what they want the map to show. Some projections can represent a true shape or area, while others may be based on the equator and therefore become less accurate as they near the poles. In summary, all maps have some distortion in terms of the shape or size of features of the spherical earth.

<u>Types of Map Projections</u>

There are three main types of map projections:

- **Conical** – This type of projection superimposes a cone over the sphere of the earth, with two reference parallels secant to the globe and intersecting it. There is no distortion along the standard parallels, but distortion increases further from the chosen parallels. A Bonne projection is an example of a conical projection, in which the areas are accurately represented but the meridians are not on a true scale.
- **Cylindrical** – This is any projection in which meridians are mapped using equally spaced vertical lines and circles of latitude (parallels) are mapped using horizontal lines. A Mercator's projection is a modified cylindrical projection that is helpful to navigators because it allows them to maintain a constant compass direction between two points. However, it exaggerates areas in high latitudes.
- **Azimuthal** – This is a stereographic projection onto a plane so centered at any given point that a straight line radiating from the center to any other point represents the shortest distance. This distance can be measured to scale.

Physical Geographical Features to Know to Perform Well in National Geographic Bee

Organizing place names into categories of physical features helps students learn the type of information they need to know to compete in the **National Geographic Bee**. The physical features students need to be knowledgeable about are:

- The continents (Although everyone has been taught that there are seven continents, some geographers combine Europe and Asia into a single continent called Eurasia.)
- The five major oceans
- The highest and lowest points on each continent (Mt. Everest is the highest point in the world; the Dead Sea is the lowest point.)
- The 10 largest seas (The Coral Sea is the largest.)
- The 10 largest lakes (The Caspian Sea is actually the largest lake.)
- The 10 largest islands (Greenland is the largest island.)
- The longest rivers (The Nile is the longest river.)
- Major mountain ranges
- Earth's extremes such as the hottest (Ethiopia), the coldest (Antarctica), the wettest (India), and the driest (Atacama Desert) places; the highest waterfall (Angel Falls); the largest desert (Sahara); the largest canyon (Grand Canyon); the longest reef (Great Barrier Reef); and the highest tides.

Economics

Effects Economy Can Have on Purchasing Decisions of Consumers

The **economy** plays an important role in how careful consumers are when using their resources and what they perceive as needs as opposed to what they perceive as wants. When the economy is doing well, unemployment figures are low, which means that people can easily attain their basic necessities. As a result, consumers are typically more willing to spend their financial resources. Consumers will also be more willing to spend their resources on products and services that are not necessary to their survival, but are instead products and services that consumers enjoy having and believe increase their quality of life. On the other hand, when the economy is in a slump, consumers are much more likely to cut back on their spending because they perceive a significantly higher risk of being unable to acquire basic necessities due to a lack of financial resources.

Supply and Demand, Scarcity and Choice, and Money and Resources

Supply is the amount of a product or service available to consumers. **Demand** is how much consumers are willing to pay for the product or service. These two facets of the market determine the price of goods and services. The higher the demand, the higher the price the supplier will charge; the lower the demand, the lower the price.

Scarcity is a measure of supply in that demand is high when there is a scarcity, or low supply, of an item. **Choice** is related to scarcity and demand in that when an item in demand is scarce, consumers have to make difficult choices. They can pay more for an item, go without it, or go elsewhere for the item.

Money is the cash or currency available for payment. **Resources** are the items one can barter in exchange for goods. Money is also the cash reserves of a nation, while resources are the minerals, labor force, armaments, and other raw materials or assets a nation has available for trade.

Effects of Economic Downturn or Recession

When a **recession** happens, people at all levels of society feel the economic effects. For example:

- High **unemployment** results because businesses have to cut back to keep costs low, and may no longer have the work for the labor force they once did.
- **Mortgage rates** go up on variable-rate loans as banks try to increase their revenues, but the higher rates cause some people who cannot afford increased housing costs to sell or suffer foreclosure.
- **Credit** becomes less available as banks try to lessen their risk. This decreased lending affects business operations, home and auto loans, etc.
- **Stock market prices** drop, and the lower dividends paid to stockholders reduce their income. This is especially hard on retired people who rely on stock dividends.
- **Psychological depression and trauma** may occur in those who suffer bankruptcy, unemployment, or foreclosure during a depression.

Positive and Negative Economic Effects of Abundant Natural Resources

The **positive economic aspects** of abundant natural resources are an increase in **revenue and new jobs** where those resources have not been previously accessed. For example, the growing demand for oil, gas, and minerals has led companies to venture into new regions.

The **negative economic aspects** of abundant natural resources are:

- **Environmental degradation**, if sufficient regulations are not in place to counter strip mining, deforestation, and contamination.
- **Corruption**, if sufficient regulations are not in place to counter bribery, political favoritism, and exploitation of workers as greedy companies try to maximize their profits.
- **Social tension**, if the resources are privately owned such that the rich become richer and the poor do not reap the benefits of their national resources. Class divisions become wider, resulting in social unrest.
- **Dependence**, if the income from the natural resources is not used to develop other industries as well. In this situation, the economy becomes dependent on one source, and faces potential crises if natural disasters or depletion take away that income source.

Economics and Kinds of Economies

Economics is the study of the buying choices that people make, the production of goods and services, and how our market system works. The two kinds of economies are command and market. In a **command economy**, the government controls what and how much is produced, the methods used for production, and the distribution of goods and services. In a market economy, producers make decisions about methods and distribution on their own. These choices are based on what will sell and bring a profit in the marketplace. In a **market economy**, consumers ultimately affect these decisions by choosing whether or not to buy certain goods and services. The United States has a market economy.

Market Economy

The five characteristics of a **market economy** are:

- **Economic freedom** – There is freedom of choice with respect to jobs, salaries, production, and price.
- **Economic incentives** – A positive incentive is to make a profit. However, if the producer tries to make too high a profit, the consequences might be that no one will purchase the item at that price. A negative incentive would be a drop in profits, causing the producer to decrease or discontinue production. A boycott, which might cause the producer to change business practices or policies, is also a negative economic incentive.
- **Competition** – There is more than one producer for any given product. Consumers thereby have choices about what to buy, which are usually made based on quality and price. Competition is an incentive for a producer to make the best product at the best price. Otherwise, producers will lose business to the competition.
- **Private ownership** – Production and profits belong to an individual or to a private company, not to the government.
- **Limited government** – Government plays no role in the economic decisions of its individual citizens.

Factors of Production and Types of Markets That Create Economic Flow

The factors of **production** are:

- **Land** – This includes not only actual land, but also forests, minerals, water, etc.
- **Labor** – This is the work force required to produce goods and services, including factors such as talent, skills, and physical labor.
- **Capital** – This is the cash and material equipment needed to produce goods and services, including buildings, property, tools, office equipment, roads, etc.
- **Entrepreneurship** – Persons with initiative can capitalize on the free market system by producing goods and services.

The two types of markets are factor and product markets. The **factor market** consists of the people who exchange their services for wages. The people are sellers and companies are buyers. The **product market** is the selling of products to the people who want to buy them. The people are the buyers and the companies are the sellers. This exchange creates a circular economic flow in which money goes from the producers to workers as wages, and then flows back to producers in the form of payment for products.

Economic Impact of Technology

At the start of the 21st century, the role of **information and communications technologies** (ICT) grew rapidly as the economy shifted to a knowledge-based one. Output is increasing in areas where ICT is used intensively, which are service areas and knowledge-intensive industries such as finance; insurance; real estate; business services, health care, and environmental goods and services; and community, social, and personal services. Meanwhile, the economic share for manufacturers is declining in medium- and low-technology industries such as chemicals, food products, textiles, gas, water, electricity, construction, and transport and communication services. Industries that have traditionally been high-tech, such as aerospace, computers, electronics, and pharmaceuticals are remaining steady in terms of their economic share. Technology has become the strongest factor in determining **per capita income** for many countries. The ease of technology investments as compared to industries that involve factories and large labor forces has resulted in more foreign investments in countries that do not have natural resources to call upon.

Social Studies Skills

Essential Questions Used in Learning Process

Essential questions for learning include those that:

1. Ask for **evaluation, synthesis, and analysis** – the highest levels of Bloom's Taxonomy
2. Seek **information** that is important to know
3. Are worth the student's **awareness**
4. Will result in enduring **understanding**
5. Tend to focus on the questions "**why**?" or "**how** do we know this information?"
6. Are more open-ended and reflective in nature
7. Often address **interrelationships** or lend themselves to multi-disciplinary investigations
8. Spark **curiosity** and a sense of wonder, and invite investigation and activity
9. Can be asked **over and over** and in a variety of instances
10. Encourage related questions
11. Have answers that may be **extended** over time
12. Seek to identify key understandings
13. Engage students in **real-life**, applied problem solving
14. May not be answerable without a **lifetime of investigation**, and maybe not even then

Various Disciplines of Social Studies

- **Anthropology and sociology** provide an understanding of how the world's many cultures have developed and what these cultures and their values have to contribute to society.
- **Sociology, economics, and political science** provide an understanding of the institutions in society and each person's role within social groups. These topics teach the use of charts, graphs, and statistics.
- **Political science, civics, and government** teach how to see another person's point of view, accept responsibility, and deal with conflict. They also provide students with an understanding of democratic norms and values, such as justice and equality. Students learn how to apply these norms and values in their community, school, and family.
- **Economics** teaches concepts such as work, exchange (buying, selling, and other trade transactions), production of goods and services, the origins of materials and products, and consumption.
- **Geography** teaches students how to use maps, globes, and locational and directional terms. It also provides them with an understanding of spatial environments, landforms, climate, world trade and transportation, ecological systems, and world cultures.

Constructivist Learning Theory and Information Seeking Behavior Theory

The **Constructivist Learning Theory** supports a view of inquiry-based learning as an opportunity for students to experience learning through inquiry and problem solving. This process is characterized by exploration and risk taking, curiosity and motivation, engagement in critical and creative thinking, and connections with real-life situations and real audiences. The **Information Seeking Behavior Theory** purports that students progress through levels of question specificity, from vague notions of the information needed to clearly defined needs or questions. According to this theory, students are more successful in the search process if they have a realistic understanding of the information system and problem. They should understand that the inquiry process is not linear or confined to certain steps, but is a flexible, individual process that leads back to the original question.

Study of Cultures and Community Relations

An important part of social studies, whether anthropology, sociology, history, geography, or political science, is the study of **local and world cultures**, as well as individual community dynamics. Students should be able to:

- Identify **values** held by their own culture and community
- Identify **values** held by other cultures and communities
- Recognize the **influences** of other cultures on their own culture
- Identify major **social institutions** and their roles in the students' communities
- Understand how individuals and groups **interact** to obtain food, clothing, and shelter
- Understand the role of language, literature, the arts, and traditions in a culture
- Recognize the role of **media and technology** in cultures, particularly in the students' own cultures
- Recognize the influence of various types of **government, economics, the environment, and technology** on social systems and cultures
- Evaluate the effectiveness of **social institutions** in solving problems in a community or culture
- Examine changes in **population, climate, and production**, and evaluate their effects on the community or culture

Types of Maps and Scale

There are three basic types of maps:

- **Base maps** – Created from aerial and field surveys, base maps serve as the starting point for topographic and thematic maps.
- **Topographic maps** – These show the natural and human-made surface features of the earth, including mountain elevations, river courses, roads, names of lakes and towns, and county and state lines.
- **Thematic maps** – These use a base or topographic map as the foundation for showing data based on a theme, such as population density, wildlife distribution, hill-slope stability, economic trends, etc.

Scale is the size of a map expressed as a ratio of the actual size of the land (for example, 1 inch on a map represents 1 mile on land). In other words, it is the proportion between a distance on the map and its corresponding distance on earth. The scale determines the level of detail on a map. **Small-scale maps** depict larger areas, but include fewer details. **Large-scale maps** depict smaller areas, but include more details.

Time Zones

Time is linked to **longitude** in that a complete rotation of the Earth, or 360° of longitude, occurs every 24 hours. Each hour of time is therefore equivalent to 15° of longitude, or 4 minutes for each 1° turn. By the agreement of 27 nations at the 1884 International Meridian Conference, the time zone system consists of **24 time zones** corresponding to the 24 hours in a day. Although high noon technically occurs when the sun is directly above a meridian, calculating time that way would result in 360 different times for the 360 meridians. Using the 24-hour system, the time is the same for all locations in a 15° zone. The 1884 conference established the meridian passing through Greenwich, England, as the zero point, or **prime meridian**. The halfway point is found at the 180th meridian, a half day from Greenwich. It is called the **International Date Line**, and serves as the place where each day begins and ends on earth.

Cartography

Cartography is the art and science of **mapmaking**. Maps of local areas were drawn by the Egyptians as early as 1300 BC, and the Greeks began making maps of the known world in the 6th century BC. Cartography eventually grew into the field of geography. The first step in modern mapmaking is a **survey**. This involves designating a few key sites of known elevation as benchmarks to allow for measurement of other sites. **Aerial photography** is then used to chart the area by taking photos in sequence. Overlapping photos show the same area from different positions along the flight line. When paired and examined through a stereoscope, the cartographer gets a three-dimensional view that can be made into a **topographical map**. In addition, a field survey (on the ground) is made to determine municipal borders and place names. The second step is to compile the information and **computer-draft** a map based on the collected data. The map is then reproduced or printed.

Skills and Materials Needed to Be Successful in Social Studies Course

For classes in history, geography, civics/government, anthropology, sociology, and economics, the goal is for students to explore issues and learn key concepts. **Social studies** help improve communication skills in reading and writing, but students need sufficient **literacy skills** to be able to understand specialized vocabulary, identify key points in text, differentiate between fact and opinion, relate information across texts, connect prior knowledge and new information, and synthesize information into meaningful knowledge. These literacy skills will be enhanced in the process, and will extend into higher order thinking skills that enable students to compare and contrast, hypothesize, draw inferences, explain, analyze, predict, construct, and interpret. Social studies classes also depend on a number of different types of **materials beyond the textbook**, such as nonfiction books, biographies, journals, maps, newspapers (paper or online), photographs, and primary documents.

Benefits of Social Studies for Students

Social studies cover the political, economic, cultural, and environmental aspects of societies not only in the past, as in the study of history, but also in the present and future. Students gain an understanding of **current conditions** and learn how to prepare for the **future** and cope with **change** through studying geography, economics, anthropology, government, and sociology. Social studies classes teach assessment, problem solving, evaluation, and decision making skills in the context of good citizenship. Students learn about scope and sequence, designing investigations, and following up with research to collect, organize, and present information and data. In the process, students learn how to search for patterns and their meanings in society and in their own lives. Social studies build a **positive self-concept** within the context of understanding the similarities and differences of people. Students begin to understand that they are unique, but also share many feelings and concerns with others. As students learn that each individual can contribute to society, their self-awareness builds self-esteem.

Inquiry-Based Learning

Facilitated by the teacher who models, guides, and poses a starter question, **inquiry-based learning** is a process in which students are involved in their learning. This process involves formulating questions, investigating widely, and building new understanding and meaning. This combination of steps asks students to think independently, and enables them to answer their questions with new knowledge, develop solutions, or support a position or point of view. In inquiry-based learning activities, teachers engage students, ask for authentic assessments, require research using a variety of resources (books, interviews, Internet information, etc.), and involve students in cooperative interaction. All of these require the **application of processes and skills**. Consequently, new knowledge is usually shared with others, and may result in some type of action. Inquiry-based learning focuses on finding a solution to a question or a problem, whether it is a matter of curiosity, a puzzle, a challenge, or a disturbing confusion.

Credibility of Research Sources

Some sources are not reliable, so the student must have a means to evaluate the **credibility** of a source when doing research, particularly on the Internet. The value of a source depends on its intended use and whether it fits the subject. For example, students researching election campaigns in the 19th century would need to go to historical documents, but students researching current election practices could use candidate brochures, television advertisements, and web sites. A checklist for examining sources might include:

- Check the **authority and reputation** of the author, sponsoring group, or publication
- Examine the language and illustrations for **bias**
- Look for a clear, logical **arrangement** of information
- If online, check out the associated links, archives, contact ability, and the date of last update

Common Research Methods in Social Sciences

Social science research relies heavily on **empirical research**, which is original data gathering and analysis through direct observation or experiment. It also involves using the library and Internet to obtain raw data, locate information, or review expert opinion. Because social science projects are often interdisciplinary, students may need assistance from the librarian to find related search terms. While arguments still exist about the superiority of quantitative versus qualitative research, most social scientists understand that research is an eclectic mix of the two methods. **Quantitative research** involves using techniques to gather data, which is information dealing with numbers and measurable values. Statistics, tables, and graphs are often the products. **Qualitative research** involves non-measurable factors, and looks for meaning in the numbers produced by quantitative research. Qualitative research takes data from observations and analyzes it to find underlying meanings and patterns of relationships.

PBA

The acronym **PBA** stands for **performance-based assessment**. A PBA is an alternative assessment, defined as a multistep task or project aligned to meet the specific state standards of any given subject. In social sciences, PBAs are used to assess a student's ability to use the concepts learned in a unit and apply those concepts to complete tasks that require higher-order thinking skills. The goal of most PBAs is to create a product or complete a process in which students connect what they have learned to their own experience or environment. These assessments are typically graded using a rubric, which focuses on both the final product and the process followed throughout the project.

Assessment of Social Sciences

Assessment **social sciences** should be assessed before, during, and after instruction. The data from these assessments should be used to guide, monitor, and revise instruction at both the whole-class and individual levels. Before instruction, assessments should be used to plan for an upcoming unit, whereas assessments that occur during instruction should be used to identify students who may need modified instruction or provide for an expansion of the current curriculum for accelerated learners. Assessments occurring after instruction should be used to gauge whether or not students have mastered the intended standards, at which point reteaching may need to occur.

Mathematics

Numbers and Operations

Classifications of Numbers

- **Numbers** are the basic building blocks of mathematics. Specific features of numbers are identified by the following terms:
- **Integer** – any positive or negative whole number, including zero. Integers do not include fractions $\left(\frac{1}{3}\right)$, decimals (0.56), or mixed numbers $\left(7\frac{3}{4}\right)$.
- **Prime number** – any whole number greater than 1 that has only two factors, itself and 1; that is, a number that can be divided evenly only by 1 and itself.
- **Composite number** – any whole number greater than 1 that has more than two different factors; in other words, any whole number that is not a prime number. For example: The composite number 8 has the factors of 1, 2, 4, and 8.
- **Even number** – any integer that can be divided by 2 without leaving a remainder. For example: 2, 4, 6, 8, and so on.
- **Odd number** – any integer that cannot be divided evenly by 2. For example: 3, 5, 7, 9, and so on.
- **Decimal number** – any number that uses a decimal point to show the part of the number that is less than one. Example: 1.234.
- **Decimal point** – a symbol used to separate the ones place from the tenths place in decimals or dollars from cents in currency.
- **Decimal place** – the position of a number to the right of the decimal point. In the decimal 0.123, the 1 is in the first place to the right of the decimal point, indicating tenths; the 2 is in the second place, indicating hundredths; and the 3 is in the third place, indicating thousandths.
- The **decimal**, or base 10, system is a number system that uses ten different digits (0, 1, 2, 3, 4, 5, 6, 7, 8, 9). An example of a number system that uses something other than ten digits is the **binary**, or base 2, number system, used by computers, which uses only the numbers 0 and 1. It is thought that the decimal system originated because people had only their 10 fingers for counting.
- **Rational numbers** include all integers, decimals, and fractions. Any terminating or repeating decimal number is a rational number.
- **Irrational numbers** cannot be written as fractions or decimals because the number of decimal places is infinite and there is no recurring pattern of digits within the number. For example, pi (π) begins with 3.141592 and continues without terminating or repeating, so pi is an irrational number.
- **Real numbers** are the set of all rational and irrational numbers.

Review Video: Numbers and Their Classifications
Visit mometrix.com/academy and enter code: 461071

Place Value

Write the place value of each digit in the following number: 14,059.826

1: ten-thousands
4: thousands

0: hundreds
5: tens
9: ones
8: tenths
2: hundredths
6: thousandths

Review Video: Number Place Value
Visit mometrix.com/academy and enter code: 205433

Writing Numbers in Word Form

Example 1

Write each number in words.
29: twenty-nine

478: four hundred seventy-eight

9,435: nine thousand four hundred thirty-five

98,542: ninety-eight thousand five hundred forty-two

302, 876: three hundred two thousand eight hundred seventy-six

Example 2

Write each decimal in words.
0.06: six hundredths

0.6: six tenths

6.0: six

0.009: nine thousandths

0.113: one hundred thirteen thousandths

0.901: nine hundred one-thousandths

Rounding and Estimation

Rounding is reducing the digits in a number while still trying to keep the value similar. The result will be less accurate, but will be in a simpler form, and will be easier to use. Whole numbers can be rounded to the nearest ten, hundred or thousand.

Example 1

Round each number:
a. Round each number to the nearest ten: 11, 47, 118

b. Round each number to the nearest hundred: 78, 980, 248

c. Round each number to the nearest thousand: 302, 1274, 3756

<u>Answer</u>

a. Remember, when rounding to the nearest ten, anything ending in 5 or greater rounds up. So, 11 rounds to 10, 47 rounds to 50, and 118 rounds to 120

b. Remember, when rounding to the nearest hundred, anything ending in 50 or greater rounds up. So, 78 rounds to 100, 980 rounds to 1000, and 248 rounds to 200.

c. Remember, when rounding to the nearest thousand, anything ending in 500 or greater rounds up. So, 302 rounds to 0, 1274 rounds to 1000, and 3756 rounds to 4000.

When you are asked for the solution a problem, you may need to provide only an approximate figure or **estimation** for your answer. In this situation, you can round the numbers that will be calculated to a non-zero number. This means that the first digit in the number is not zero, and the following numbers are zeros.

<u>Example 2</u>

Estimate the solution to $345{,}932 + 96{,}369$.

Start by rounding each number to have only one digit as a non-zero number: 345,932 becomes 300,000 and 96,369 becomes 100,000.

Then, add the rounded numbers: $300{,}000 + 100{,}000 = 400{,}000$. So, the answer is approximately 400,000.

The exact answer would be $345{,}932 + 96{,}369 = 442{,}301$. So, the estimate of 400,000 is a similar value to the exact answer.

<u>Example 3</u>

A runner's heart beats 422 times over the course of six minutes. About how many times did the runner's heart beat during each minute?

"About how many" indicates that you need to estimate the solution. In this case, look at the numbers you are given. 422 can be rounded down to 420, which is easily divisible by 6. A good estimate is $420 \div 6 = 70$ beats per minute. More accurately, the patient's heart rate was just over 70 beats per minute since his heart actually beat a little more than 420 times in six minutes.

Review Video: <u>Rounding and Estimation</u>
Visit mometrix.com/academy and enter code: 126243

Measurement Conversion

When going from a larger unit to a smaller unit, multiply the number of the known amount by the **equivalent amount**. When going from a smaller unit to a larger unit, divide the number of the known amount by the equivalent amount.

Also, you can set up conversion fractions. In these fractions, one fraction is the **conversion factor**. The other fraction has the unknown amount in the numerator. So, the known value is placed in the denominator. Sometimes the second fraction has the known value from the problem in the numerator, and the unknown in the denominator. Multiply the two fractions to get the converted measurement.

Conversion Units

Metric Conversions

1000 mcg (microgram)	1 mg
1000 mg (milligram)	1 g
1000 g (gram)	1 kg
1000 kg (kilogram)	1 metric ton
1000 mL (milliliter)	1 L
1000 um (micrometer)	1 mm
1000 mm (millimeter)	1 m
100 cm (centimeter)	1 m
1000 m (meter)	1 km

U.S. and Metric Equivalents

Unit	U.S. equivalent	Metric equivalent
Inch	1 inch	2.54 centimeters
Foot	12 inches	0.305 meters
Yard	3 feet	0.914 meters
Mile	5280 feet	1.609 kilometers

Capacity Measurements

Unit	U.S. equivalent	Metric equivalent
Ounce	8 drams	29.573 milliliters
Cup	8 ounces	0.237 liter
Pint	16 ounces	0.473 liter
Quart	2 pints	0.946 liter
Gallon	4 quarts	3.785 liters

Weight Measurements

Unit	U.S. equivalent	Metric equivalent
Ounce	16 drams	28.35 grams
Pound	16 ounces	453.6 grams
Ton	2,000 pounds	907.2 kilograms

Fluid Measurements

Unit	English equivalent	Metric equivalent
1 tsp	1 fluid dram	5 milliliters
3 tsp	4 fluid drams	15 or 16 milliliters
2 tbsp	1 fluid ounce	30 milliliters
1 glass	8 fluid ounces	240 milliliters

Measurement Conversion Practice Problems

Example 1

a. Convert 1.4 meters to centimeters.

b. Convert 218 centimeters to meters.

Example 2

a. Convert 42 inches to feet.

b. Convert 15 feet to yards.

Example 3

a. How many pounds are in 15 kilograms?

b. How many pounds are in 80 ounces?

Example 4

a. How many kilometers are in 2 miles?

b. How many centimeters are in 5 feet?

Example 5

a. How many gallons are in 15.14 liters?

b. How many liters are in 8 quarts?

Example 6

a. How many grams are in 13.2 pounds?

b. How many pints are in 9 gallons?

Measurement Conversion Practice Solutions

Example 1

Write ratios with the conversion factor $\frac{100\text{ cm}}{1\text{ m}}$. Use proportions to convert the given units.

a. $\frac{100\text{ cm}}{1\text{ m}} = \frac{x\text{ cm}}{1.4\text{ m}}$. Cross multiply to get $x = 140$. So, 1.4 m is the same as 140 cm.

b. $\frac{100\text{ cm}}{1\text{ m}} = \frac{218\text{ cm}}{x\text{ m}}$. Cross multiply to get $100x = 218$, or $x = 2.18$. So, 218 cm is the same as 2.18 m.

Example 2

Write ratios with the conversion factors $\frac{12\text{ in}}{1\text{ ft}}$ and $\frac{3\text{ ft}}{1\text{ yd}}$. Use proportions to convert the given units.

a. $\frac{12\text{ in}}{1\text{ ft}} = \frac{42\text{ in}}{x\text{ ft}}$. Cross multiply to get $12x = 42$, or $x = 3.5$. So, 42 inches is the same as 3.5 feet.

b. $\frac{3\text{ ft}}{1\text{ yd}} = \frac{15\text{ ft}}{x\text{ yd}}$. Cross multiply to get $3x = 15$, or $x = 5$. So, 15 feet is the same as 5 yards.

Example 3

a. 15 kilograms $\times \frac{2.2\text{ pounds}}{1\text{ kilogram}} = 33$ pounds

b. 80 ounces $\times \frac{1\text{ pound}}{16\text{ ounces}} = 5$ pounds

Example 4

a. 2 miles $\times \frac{1.609 \text{ kilometers}}{1 \text{ mile}} = 3.218$ kilometers

b. 5 feet $\times \frac{12 \text{ inches}}{1 \text{ foot}} \times \frac{2.54 \text{ centimeters}}{1 \text{ inch}} = 152.4$ centimeters

Example 5

a. 15.14 liters $\times \frac{1 \text{ gallon}}{3.785 \text{ liters}} = 4$ gallons

b. 8 quarts $\times \frac{1 \text{ gallon}}{4 \text{ quarts}} \times \frac{3.785 \text{ liters}}{1 \text{ gallon}} = 7.57$ liters

Example 6

a. 13.2 pounds $\times \frac{1 \text{ kilogram}}{2.2 \text{ pounds}} \times \frac{1000 \text{ grams}}{1 \text{ kilogram}} = 6000$ grams

b. 9 gallons $\times \frac{4 \text{ quarts}}{1 \text{ gallon}} \times \frac{2 \text{ pints}}{1 \text{ quarts}} = 72$ pints

Operations

There are four basic mathematical operations:

Addition and Subtraction

Addition increases the value of one quantity by the value of another quantity. Example: $2 + 4 = 6$; $8 + 9 = 17$. The result is called the **sum**. With addition, the order does not matter. $4 + 2 = 2 + 4$.

Subtraction is the opposite operation to addition; it decreases the value of one quantity by the value of another quantity. Example: $6 - 4 = 2$; $17 - 8 = 9$. The result is called the **difference**. Note that with subtraction, the order does matter. $6 - 4 \neq 4 - 6$.

Review Video: Addition and Subtraction
Visit mometrix.com/academy and enter code: 521157

Multiplication and Division

Multiplication can be thought of as repeated addition. One number tells how many times to add the other number to itself. Example: 3×2 (three times two) $= 2 + 2 + 2 = 6$. With multiplication, the order does not matter. $2 \times 3 = 3 \times 2$ or $3 + 3 = 2 + 2 + 2$.

Division is the opposite operation to multiplication; one number tells us how many parts to divide the other number into. Example: $20 \div 4 = 5$; if 20 is split into 4 equal parts, each part is 5. With division, the order of the numbers does matter. $20 \div 4 \neq 4 \div 20$.

Review Video: Multiplication and Division
Visit mometrix.com/academy and enter code: 643326

Order of Operations

Order of operations is a set of rules that dictates the order in which we must perform each operation in an expression so that we will evaluate it accurately. If we have an expression that includes multiple different operations, order of operations tells us which operations to do first. The most common mnemonic for order of operations is **PEMDAS**, or "Please Excuse My Dear Aunt

Sally." PEMDAS stands for parentheses, exponents, multiplication, division, addition, and subtraction. It is important to understand that multiplication and division have equal precedence, as do addition and subtraction, so those pairs of operations are simply worked from left to right in order.

Example
Evaluate the expression $5 + 20 \div 4 \times (2 + 3) - 6$ using the correct order of operations.

P: Perform the operations inside the parentheses: $(2 + 3) = 5$

E: Simplify the exponents.

The equation now looks like this: $5 + 20 \div 4 \times 5 - 6$

MD: Perform multiplication and division from left to right: $20 \div 4 = 5$; then $5 \times 5 = 25$

The equation now looks like this: $5 + 25 - 6$

AS: Perform addition and subtraction from left to right: $5 + 25 = 30$; then $30 - 6 = 24$

Review Video: Order of Operations
Visit mometrix.com/academy and enter code: 259675

Subtraction with Regrouping

Example 1
Demonstrate how to subtract 189 from 525 using regrouping.

First, set up the subtraction problem:

$$\begin{array}{r} 525 \\ -\ 189 \\ \hline \end{array}$$

Notice that the numbers in the ones and tens columns of 525 are smaller than the numbers in the ones and tens columns of 189. This means you will need to use regrouping to perform subtraction.

	5	2	5
–	1	8	9

To subtract 9 from 5 in the ones column you will need to borrow from the 2 in the tens columns:

	5	1	15
–	1	8	9
			6

Next, to subtract 8 from 1 in the tens column you will need to borrow from the 5 in the hundreds column:

	4	11	15
–	1	8	9
		3	6

Last, subtract the 1 from the 4 in the hundreds column:

	4	11	15
–	1	8	9
	3	3	6

Example 2

Demonstrate how to subtract 477 from 620 using regrouping.

First, set up the subtraction problem:

	620
–	477

Notice that the numbers in the ones and tens columns of 620 are smaller than the numbers in the ones and tens columns of 477. This means you will need to use regrouping to perform subtraction.

	6	2	0
–	4	7	7

To subtract 7 from 0 in the ones column you will need to borrow from the 2 in the tens column.

	6	1	10
–	4	7	7
			3

Next, to subtract 7 from the 1 that's still in the tens column you will need to borrow from the 6 in the hundreds column.

	5	11	10
–	4	7	7
		4	3

Lastly, subtract 4 from the 5 remaining in the hundreds column to get:

	5	11	10
–	4	7	7
	1	4	3

Real World One or Multi-Step Problems with Rational Numbers

Example 1
A woman's age is thirteen more than half of 60. How old is the woman?

"More than" indicates addition, and "of" indicates multiplication. The expression can be written as $\frac{1}{2}(60) + 13$. So, the woman's age is equal to $\frac{1}{2}(60) + 13 = 30 + 13 = 43$. The woman is 43 years old.

Example 2
A patient was given pain medicine at a dosage of 0.22 grams. The patient's dosage was then increased to 0.80 grams. By how much was the patient's dosage increased?

The first step is to determine what operation (addition, subtraction, multiplication, or division) the problem requires. Notice the keywords and phrases "by how much" and "increased." "Increased" means that you go from a smaller amount to a larger amount. This change can be found by subtracting the smaller amount from the larger amount: $0.80 \text{ grams} - 0.22 \text{ grams} = 0.58 \text{ grams}$.

Remember to line up the decimal when subtracting.

$$\begin{array}{rr} & 0.80 \\ - & 0.22 \\ & 0.58 \end{array}$$

Example 3

At a hotel, $\frac{3}{4}$ of the 100 rooms are occupied today. Yesterday, $\frac{4}{5}$ of the 100 rooms were occupied. On which day were more of the rooms occupied and by how much more?

First, find the number of rooms occupied each day. To do so, multiply the fraction of rooms occupied by the number of rooms available:

$$\text{Number occupied} = \text{Fraction occupied} \times \text{Total number}$$

Today:

$$\text{Number of rooms occupied} = \frac{3}{4} \times 100 = 75$$

Today, 75 rooms are occupied.

Yesterday:

$$\text{Number of rooms occupied} = \frac{4}{5} \times 100 = 80$$

Yesterday, 80 rooms were occupied.

The difference in the number of rooms occupied is

$$80 - 75 = 5 \text{ rooms}$$

Therefore, five more rooms were occupied yesterday than today.

Review Video: Rational Numbers
Visit mometrix.com/academy and enter code: 280645

Example 4

At a school, 40% of the teachers teach English. If 20 teachers teach English, how many teachers work at the school?

To answer this problem, first think about the number of teachers that work at the school. Will it be more or less than the number of teachers who work in a specific department such as English? More teachers work at the school, so the number you find to answer this question will be greater than 20.

40% of the teachers are English teachers. "Of" indicates multiplication, and words like "is" and "are" indicate equivalence. Translating the problem into a mathematical sentence gives $40\% \times t = 20$, where t represents the total number of teachers. Solving for t gives $t = \frac{20}{40\%} = \frac{20}{0.40} = 50$. Fifty teachers work at the school.

Example 5

A patient was given blood pressure medicine at a dosage of 2 grams. The patient's dosage was then decreased to 0.45 grams. By how much was the patient's dosage decreased?

The decrease is represented by the difference between the two amounts:

$$2 \text{ grams} - 0.45 \text{ grams} = 1.55 \text{ grams}.$$

Remember to line up the decimal point before subtracting.

$$\begin{array}{r} 2.00 \\ -\quad 0.45 \\ \hline 1.55 \end{array}$$

Example 6

Two weeks ago, $\frac{2}{3}$ of the 60 customers at a skate shop were male. Last week, $\frac{3}{6}$ of the 80 customers were male. During which week were there more male customers?

First, you need to find the number of male customers that were in the skate shop each week. You are given this amount in terms of fractions. To find the actual number of male customers, multiply the fraction of male customers by the number of customers in the store.

Actual number of male customers = fraction of male customers × total number of customers.

Two weeks ago: Actual number of male customers $= \frac{2}{3} \times 60$.

$$\frac{2}{3} \times \frac{60}{1} = \frac{2 \times 60}{3 \times 1} = \frac{120}{3} = 40$$

Two weeks ago, 40 of the customers were male.

Last week: Actual number of male customers $= \frac{3}{6} \times 80$.

$$\frac{3}{6} \times \frac{80}{1} = \frac{3 \times 80}{6 \times 1} = \frac{240}{6} = 40$$

Last week, 40 of the customers were male.

The number of male customers was the same both weeks.

Example 7

Jane ate lunch at a local restaurant. She ordered a \$4.99 appetizer, a \$12.50 entrée, and a \$1.25 soda. If she wants to tip her server 20%, how much money will she spend in all?

To find total amount, first find the sum of the items she ordered from the menu and then add 20% of this sum to the total.

In other words:

$$\$4.99 + \$12.50 + \$1.25 = \$18.74$$

Then 20% of \$18.74 is $(20\%)(\$18.74) = (0.20)(\$18.74) = \$3.75$.

So, the total she spends is cost of the meal plus the tip or $\$18.74 + \$3.75 = \$22.49$.

Another way to find this sum is to multiply 120% by the cost of the meal.

$$\$18.74(120\%) = \$18.74(1.20) = \$22.49.$$

Parentheses

Parentheses are used to designate which operations should be done first when there are multiple operations. Example: $4 - (2 + 1) = 1$; the parentheses tell us that we must add 2 and 1, and then subtract the sum from 4, rather than subtracting 2 from 4 and then adding 1 (this would give us an answer of 3).

Review Video: Mathematical Parentheses
Visit mometrix.com/academy and enter code: 978600

Exponents

An **exponent** is a superscript number placed next to another number at the top right. It indicates how many times the base number is to be multiplied by itself. Exponents provide a shorthand way to write what would be a longer mathematical expression. Example: $a^2 = a \times a$; $2^4 = 2 \times 2 \times 2 \times 2$. A number with an exponent of 2 is said to be "squared," while a number with an exponent of 3 is said to be "cubed." The value of a number raised to an exponent is called its power. So, 8^4 is read as "8 to the 4th power," or "8 raised to the power of 4." A negative exponent is the same as the **reciprocal** of a positive exponent. Example: $a^{-2} = \frac{1}{a^2}$.

Review Video: Exponents
Visit mometrix.com/academy and enter code: 600998

Roots

A **root**, such as a square root, is another way of writing a fractional exponent. Instead of using a superscript, roots use the radical symbol ($\sqrt{\ }$) to indicate the operation. A radical will have a number underneath the bar, and may sometimes have a number in the upper left: $\sqrt[n]{a}$, read as "the nth root of a." The relationship between radical notation and exponent notation can be described by this equation: $\sqrt[n]{a} = a^{\frac{1}{n}}$. The two special cases of $n = 2$ and $n = 3$ are called square roots and cube roots. If there is no number to the upper left, it is understood to be a square root ($n = 2$). Nearly all of the roots you encounter will be square roots. A square root is the same as a number raised to the one-half power. When we say that a is the square root of b ($a = \sqrt{b}$), we mean that a multiplied by itself equals b: ($a \times a = b$).

Review Video: Roots
Visit mometrix.com/academy and enter code: 795655

Review Video: Square Root and Perfect Square
Visit mometrix.com/academy and enter code: 648063

A **perfect square** is a number that has an integer for its square root. There are 10 perfect squares from 1 to 100: 1, 4, 9, 16, 25, 36, 49, 64, 81, 100 (the squares of integers 1 through 10).

Parentheses are used to designate which operations should be done first when there are multiple operations. Example: $4-(2+1)=1$; the parentheses tell us that we must add 2 and 1, and then subtract the sum from 4, rather than subtracting 2 from 4 and then adding 1 (this would give us an answer of 3).

Absolute Value

A precursor to working with negative numbers is understanding what **absolute values** are. A number's absolute value is simply the distance away from zero a number is on the number line. The absolute value of a number is always positive and is written $|x|$.

Example
Show that $|3| = |-3|$.

The absolute value of 3, written as $|3|$, is 3 because the distance between 0 and 3 on a number line is three units. Likewise, the absolute value of –3, written as $|-3|$, is 3 because the distance between 0 and –3 on a number line is three units. So, $|3| = |-3|$.

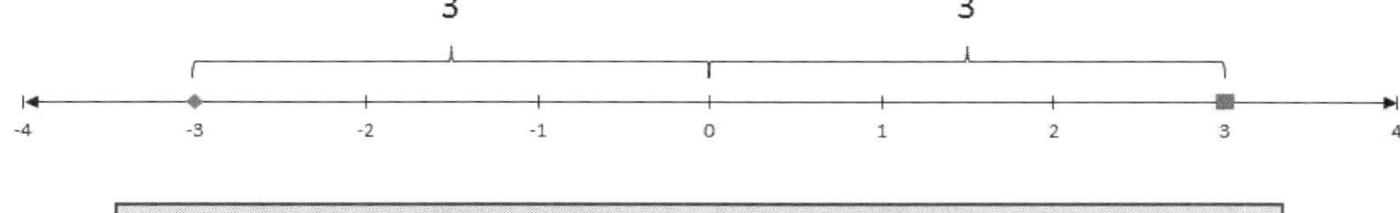

Review Video: Absolute Value
Visit mometrix.com/academy and enter code: 314669

Operations with Positive and Negative Numbers

Addition
When adding signed numbers, if the signs are the same simply add the absolute values of the addends and apply the original sign to the sum. For example, $(+4) + (+8) = +12$ and $(-4) + (-8) = -12$. When the original signs are different, take the absolute values of the addends and subtract the smaller value from the larger value, then apply the original sign of the larger value to the difference. For instance, $(+4) + (-8) = -4$ and $(-4) + (+8) = +4$.

Subtraction
For subtracting signed numbers, change the sign of the number after the minus symbol and then follow the same rules used for addition. For example, $(+4) - (+8) = (+4) + (-8) = -4$.

Multiplication

If the signs are the same the product is positive when multiplying signed numbers. For example, $(+4) \times (+8) = +32$ and $(-4) \times (-8) = +32$. If the signs are opposite, the product is negative. For example, $(+4) \times (-8) = -32$ and $(-4) \times (+8) = -32$. When more than two factors are multiplied together, the sign of the product is determined by how many negative factors are present. If there are an odd number of negative factors then the product is negative, whereas an even number of negative factors indicates a positive product. For instance, $(+4) \times (-8) \times (-2) = +64$ and $(-4) \times (-8) \times (-2) = -64$.

Division

The rules for dividing signed numbers are similar to multiplying signed numbers. If the dividend and divisor have the same sign, the quotient is positive. If the dividend and divisor have opposite signs, the quotient is negative. For example, $(-4) \div (+8) = -0.5$.

The Number Line

A number line is a graph to see the distance between numbers. Basically, this graph shows the relationship between numbers. So, a number line may have a point for zero and may show negative numbers on the left side of the line. Also, any positive numbers are placed on the right side of the line.

Example

Name each point on the number line below:

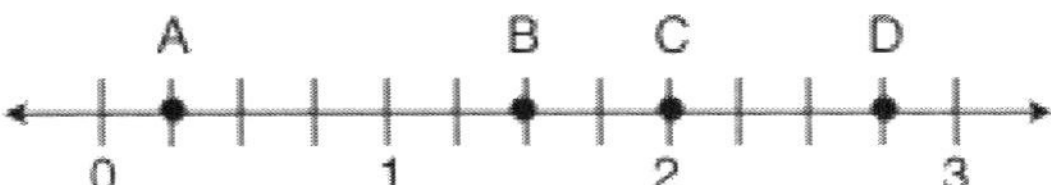

Use the dashed lines on the number line to identify each point. Each dashed line between two whole numbers is $\frac{1}{4}$. The line halfway between two numbers is $\frac{1}{2}$.

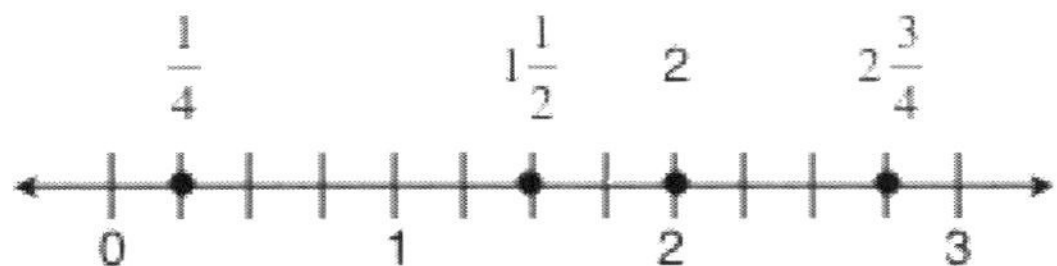

Review Video: Negative and Positive Number Line
Visit mometrix.com/academy and enter code: 816439

Fractions, Decimals, and Percentages

Fractions

A **fraction** is a number that is expressed as one integer written above another integer, with a dividing line between them $\left(\frac{x}{y}\right)$. It represents the **quotient** of the two numbers "x divided by y." It can also be thought of as x out of y equal parts.

The top number of a fraction is called the **numerator**, and it represents the number of parts under consideration. The 1 in $\frac{1}{4}$ means that 1 part out of the whole is being considered in the calculation. The bottom number of a fraction is called the **denominator**, and it represents the total number of equal parts. The 4 in $\frac{1}{4}$ means that the whole consists of 4 equal parts. A fraction cannot have a denominator of zero; this is referred to as "*undefined*."

Fractions can be manipulated, without changing the value of the fraction, by multiplying or dividing (but not adding or subtracting) both the numerator and denominator by the same number. If you divide both numbers by a common factor, you are **reducing** or simplifying the fraction. Two fractions that have the same value but are expressed differently are known as **equivalent fractions**. For example, $\frac{2}{10}, \frac{3}{15}, \frac{4}{20}$, and $\frac{5}{25}$ are all equivalent fractions. They can also all be reduced or simplified to $\frac{1}{5}$.

When two fractions are manipulated so that they have the same denominator, this is known as finding a **common denominator**. The number chosen to be that common denominator should be the least common multiple of the two original denominators. Example: $\frac{3}{4}$ and $\frac{5}{6}$; the least common multiple of 4 and 6 is 12. Manipulating to achieve the common denominator: $\frac{3}{4} = \frac{9}{12}; \frac{5}{6} = \frac{10}{12}$.

Proper Fractions and Mixed Numbers

A fraction whose denominator is greater than its numerator is known as a **proper fraction**, while a fraction whose numerator is greater than its denominator is known as an **improper fraction**. Proper fractions have values *less than one* and improper fractions have values *greater than one.*

A **mixed number** is a number that contains both an integer and a fraction. Any improper fraction can be rewritten as a mixed number. Example: $\frac{8}{3} = \frac{6}{3} + \frac{2}{3} = 2 + \frac{2}{3} = 2\frac{2}{3}$. Similarly, any mixed number can be rewritten as an improper fraction. Example: $1\frac{3}{5} = 1 + \frac{3}{5} = \frac{5}{5} + \frac{3}{5} = \frac{8}{5}$.

Review Video: Proper and Improper Fractions and Mixed Numbers
Visit mometrix.com/academy and enter code: 211077

Review Video: Fractions
Visit mometrix.com/academy and enter code: 262335

Decimals

Decimal Illustration

Use a model to represent the decimal: 0.24. Write 0.24 as a fraction.

The decimal 0.24 is twenty-four hundredths. One possible model to represent this fraction is to draw 100 pennies, since each penny is worth one-hundredth of a dollar. Draw one hundred circles to represent one hundred pennies. Shade 24 of the pennies to represent the decimal twenty-four hundredths.

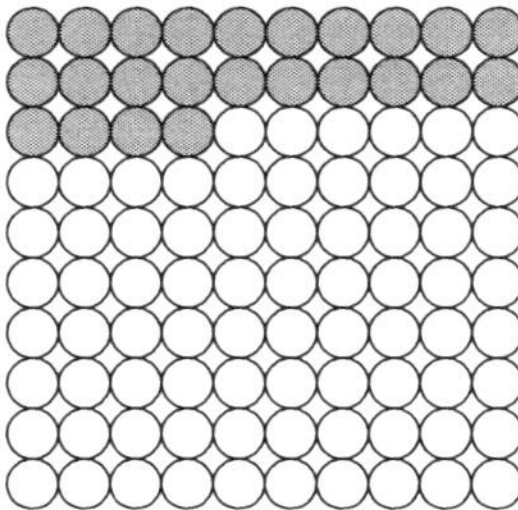

To write the decimal as a fraction, write a fraction: $\frac{\text{\# shaded spaces}}{\text{\# total spaces}}$. The number of shaded spaces is 24, and the total number of spaces is 100, so as a fraction 0.24 equals $\frac{24}{100}$. This fraction can then be reduced to $\frac{6}{25}$.

Review Video: Decimals
Visit mometrix.com/academy and enter code: 837268

Percentages

Percentages can be thought of as fractions that are based on a whole of 100; that is, one whole is equal to 100%. The word percent means "per hundred." Fractions can be expressed as a percentage by finding equivalent fractions with a denomination of 100. Example: $\frac{7}{10} = \frac{70}{100} = 70\%$; $\frac{1}{4} = \frac{25}{100} = 25\%$.

To express a *percentage as a fraction*, divide the percentage number by 100 and reduce the fraction to its simplest possible terms. Example: $60\% = \frac{60}{100} = \frac{3}{5}$; $96\% = \frac{96}{100} = \frac{24}{25}$.

Review Video: Percentages
Visit mometrix.com/academy and enter code: 141911

Real World Problems with Percentages

A percentage problem can be presented three main ways: (1) Find what percentage of some number another number is. Example: What percentage of 40 is 8? (2) Find what number is some percentage of a given number. Example: What number is 20% of 40? (3) Find what number another number is a given percentage of. Example: What number is 8 20% of?

The three components in all of these cases are the same: a **whole** (W), a **part** (P), and a **percentage** (%). These are related by the equation: $\boldsymbol{P = W \times \%}$. This is the form of the equation you would use to solve problems of type (2). To solve types (1) and (3), you would use these two forms:

$$\% = \frac{P}{W} \text{ and } W = \frac{P}{\%}$$

The thing that frequently makes percentage problems difficult is that they are most often also word problems, so a large part of solving them is figuring out which quantities are what. Example: In a school cafeteria, 7 students choose pizza, 9 choose hamburgers, and 4 choose tacos. Find the percentage that chooses tacos. To find the whole, you must first add all of the parts: $7 + 9 + 4 = 20$. The percentage can then be found by dividing the part by the whole ($\% = \frac{P}{W}$): $\frac{4}{20} = \frac{20}{100} = 20\%$.

Example 1

What is 30% of 120?

The word "of" indicates multiplication, so 30% of 120 is found by multiplying 30% by 120. First, change 30% to a fraction or decimal. Recall that "percent" means per hundred, so $30\% = \frac{30}{100} = 0.30$. 120 times 0.3 is 36.

Review Video: Finding Percentage of Number Given Whole
Visit mometrix.com/academy and enter code: 932623

Example 2

What is 150% of 20?

150% of 20 is found by multiplying 150% by 20. First, change 150% to a fraction or decimal. Recall that "percent" means per hundred, so $150\% = \frac{150}{100} = 1.50$. So, $(1.50)(20) = 30$. Notice that 30 is greater than the original number of 20. This makes sense because you are finding a number that is more than 100% of the original number.

Example 3

What is 14.5% of 96?

Change 14.5% to a decimal before multiplying. $0.145 \times 96 = 13.92$. Notice that 13.92 is much smaller than the original number of 96. This makes sense because you are finding a small percentage of the original number.

Example 4

According to a survey, about 82% of engineers were highly satisfied with their job. If 145 engineers were surveyed, how many reported that they were highly satisfied?

82% of $145 = 0.82 \times 145 = 118.9$. Because you can't have 0.9 of a person, we must round up to say that 119 engineers reported that they were highly satisfied with their jobs.

Example 5

On Monday, Lucy spent 5 hours observing sales, 3 hours working on advertising, and 4 hours doing paperwork. On Tuesday, she spent 4 hours observing sales, 6 hours working on advertising, and 2 hours doing paperwork. What was the percent change for time spent on each task between the two days?

The three tasks are observing sales, working on advertising, and doing paperwork. To find the amount of change, compare the first amount with the second amount for each task. Then, write this difference as a percentage compared to the initial amount.

Amount of change for observing sales:

$$5 \text{ hours} - 4 \text{ hours} = 1 \text{ hour}$$

The percent of change is

$$\frac{\text{amount of change}}{\text{original amount}} \times 100\%. \frac{1 \text{ hour}}{5 \text{ hours}} \times 100\% = 20\%.$$

Lucy spent 20% less time observing sales on Tuesday than she did on Monday.

Amount of change for working on advertising:

$$6 \text{ hours} - 3 \text{ hours} = 3 \text{ hours}$$

The percent of change is

$$\frac{\text{amount of change}}{\text{original amount}} \times 100\%. \frac{3 \text{ hours}}{3 \text{ hours}} \times 100\% = 100\%.$$

Lucy spent 100% more time (or twice as much time) working on advertising on Tuesday than she did on Monday.

Amount of change for doing paperwork:

$$4 \text{ hours} - 2 \text{ hours} = 2 \text{ hours}$$

The percent of change is

$$\frac{\text{amount of change}}{\text{original amount}} \times 100\%. \frac{2 \text{ hours}}{4 \text{ hours}} \times 100\% = 50\%.$$

Lucy spent 50% less time (or half as much time) working on paperwork on Tuesday than she did on Monday.

<u>Example 6</u>
A patient was given 40 mg of a certain medicine. Later, the patient's dosage was increased to 45 mg. What was the percent increase in his medication?

To find the percent increase, first compare the original and increased amounts. The original amount was 40 mg, and the increased amount is 45 mg, so the dosage of medication was increased by 5 mg ($45 - 40 = 5$). Note, however, that the question asks not by how much the dosage increased but by what percentage it increased. Percent increase $= \frac{\text{new amount} - \text{original amount}}{\text{original amount}} \times 100\%$.

So, $\frac{45 \text{ mg} - 40 \text{ mg}}{40 \text{ mg}} \times 100\% = \frac{5}{40} \times 100\% = 0.125 \times 100\% = 12.5\%$

The percent increase is 12.5%.

<u>Example 7</u>
A patient was given 100 mg of a certain medicine. The patient's dosage was later decreased to 88 mg. What was the percent decrease?

The medication was decreased by 12 mg:

$$(100 \text{ mg} - 88 \text{ mg} = 12 \text{ mg})$$

To find by what percent the medication was decreased, this change must be written as a percentage when compared to the original amount.

In other words, $\frac{\text{new amount} - \text{original amount}}{\text{original amount}} \times 100\% = \text{percent change}$

So $\frac{12 \text{ mg}}{100 \text{ mg}} \times 100\% = 0.12 \times 100\% = 12\%$.

The percent decrease is 12%.

Example 8

A barista used 125 units of coffee grounds to make a liter of coffee. The barista later reduced the amount of coffee to 100 units. By what percentage was the amount of coffee grounds reduced?

In this problem you must determine which information is necessary to answer the question. The question asks by what percentage the coffee grounds were reduced. Find the two amounts and perform subtraction to find their difference. The first pot of coffee used 125 units. The second time, the barista used 100 units. Therefore, the difference is 125 units − 100 units = 25 units. The percentage reduction can then be calculated as:

$$\frac{\text{change}}{\text{original}} = \frac{25}{125} = \frac{1}{5} = 20\%$$

Example 9

In a performance review, an employee received a score of 70 for efficiency and 90 for meeting project deadlines. Six months later, the employee received a score of 65 for efficiency and 96 for meeting project deadlines. What was the percent change for each score on the performance review?

To find the percent change, compare the first amount with the second amount for each score; then, write this difference as a percentage of the initial amount.

Percent change for efficiency score:

$$70 - 65 = 5; \ \frac{5}{70} \approx 7.1\%$$

The employee's efficiency decreased by about 7.1%.

Percent change for meeting project deadlines score:

$$96 - 90 = 6; \ \frac{6}{90} \approx 6.7\%$$

The employee increased his ability to meet project deadlines by about 6.7%.

Simplify

Example 1

How to simplify:

$$\frac{\frac{2}{5}}{\frac{4}{7}}$$

Dividing a fraction by a fraction may appear tricky, but it's not if you write out your steps carefully. Follow these steps to divide a fraction by a fraction.

Step 1: Rewrite the problem as a multiplication problem. Dividing by a fraction is the same as multiplying by its **reciprocal**, also known as its **multiplicative inverse**. The product of a number and its reciprocal is 1. Because $\frac{4}{7}$ times $\frac{7}{4}$ is 1, these numbers are reciprocals. Note that reciprocals can be found by simply interchanging the numerators and denominators. So, rewriting the problem as a multiplication problem gives $\frac{2}{5} \times \frac{7}{4}$.

Step 2: Perform multiplication of the fractions by multiplying the numerators by each other and the denominators by each other. In other words, multiply across the top and then multiply across the bottom.

$$\frac{2}{5} \times \frac{7}{4} = \frac{2 \times 7}{5 \times 4} = \frac{14}{20}$$

Step 3: Make sure the fraction is reduced to lowest terms. Both 14 and 20 can be divided by 2.

$$\frac{14}{20} = \frac{14 \div 2}{20 \div 2} = \frac{7}{10}$$

The answer is $\frac{7}{10}$.

<u>Example 2</u>

How to simplify:

$$\frac{1}{4} + \frac{3}{6}$$

Fractions with common denominators can be easily added or subtracted. Recall that the denominator is the bottom number in the fraction and that the numerator is the top number in the fraction.

The denominators of $\frac{1}{4}$ and $\frac{3}{6}$ are 4 and 6, respectively. The lowest common denominator of 4 and 6 is 12 because 12 is the least common multiple of 4 (multiples 4, 8, 12, 16, ...) and 6 (multiples 6, 12, 18, 24, ...). Convert each fraction to its equivalent with the newly found common denominator of 12.

$$\frac{1 \times 3}{4 \times 3} = \frac{3}{12}; \quad \frac{3 \times 2}{6 \times 2} = \frac{6}{12}$$

Now that the fractions have the same denominator, you can add them.

$$\frac{3}{12} + \frac{6}{12} = \frac{9}{12}$$

Be sure to write your answer in lowest terms. Both 9 and 12 can be divided by 3, so the answer is $\frac{3}{4}$.

Example 3

How to simplify:

$$\frac{7}{8} - \frac{8}{16}$$

Fractions with common denominators can be easily added or subtracted. Recall that the denominator is the bottom number in the fraction and that the numerator is the top number in the fraction.

The denominators of $\frac{7}{8}$ and $\frac{8}{16}$ are 8 and 16, respectively. The lowest common denominator of 8 and 16 is 16 because 16 is the least common multiple of 8 (multiples 8, 16, 24 ...) and 16 (multiples 16, 32, 48, ...). Convert each fraction to its equivalent with the newly found common denominator of 16.

$$\frac{7 \times 2}{8 \times 2} = \frac{14}{16}; \ \frac{8 \times 1}{16 \times 1} = \frac{8}{16}$$

Now that the fractions have the same denominator, you can subtract them.

$$\frac{14}{16} - \frac{8}{16} = \frac{6}{16}$$

Be sure to write your answer in lowest terms. Both 6 and 16 can be divided by 2, so the answer is $\frac{3}{8}$.

Example 4

How to simplify:

$$\frac{1}{2} + \left(3\left(\frac{3}{4}\right) - 2\right) + 4$$

When simplifying expressions, first perform operations within groups. Within the set of parentheses are multiplication and subtraction operations. Perform the multiplication first to get $\frac{1}{2} + \left(\frac{9}{4} - 2\right) + 4$. Then, subtract two to obtain $\frac{1}{2} + \frac{1}{4} + 4$. Finally, perform addition from left to right:

$$\frac{1}{2} + \frac{1}{4} + 4 = \frac{2}{4} + \frac{1}{4} + \frac{16}{4} = \frac{19}{4}$$

Example 5

How to simplify: $0.22 + 0.5 - (5.5 + 3.3 \div 3)$

First, evaluate the terms in the parentheses $(5.5 + 3.3 \div 3)$ using order of operations. $3.3 \div 3 = 1.1$, and $5.5 + 1.1 = 6.6$.

Next, rewrite the problem: $0.22 + 0.5 - 6.6$.

Finally, add and subtract from left to right: $0.22 + 0.5 = 0.72$; $0.72 - 6.6 = -5.88$. The answer is -5.88.

Example 6

How to simplify:

$$\frac{3}{2} + (4(0.5) - 0.75) + 2$$

First, simplify within the parentheses:

$$\frac{3}{2} + (2 - 0.75) + 2 =$$

$$\frac{3}{2} + 1.25 + 2$$

Finally, change the fraction to a decimal and perform addition from left to right:

$$1.5 + 1.25 + 2 = 4.75$$

Example 7

How to simplify: $1.45 + 1.5 + (6 - 9 \div 2) + 45$

First, evaluate the terms in the parentheses using proper order of operations.

$$1.45 + 1.5 + (6 - 4.5) + 45$$

$$1.45 + 1.5 + 1.5 + 45$$

Finally, add from left to right.

$$1.45 + 1.5 + 1.5 + 45 = 49.45$$

Converting Percentages, Fractions, and Decimals

Converting decimals to percentages and percentages to decimals is as simple as moving the decimal point. To *convert from a decimal to a percentage*, move the decimal point **two places to the right**. To *convert from a percentage to a decimal*, move it **two places to the left**. Example: $0.23 = 23\%$; $5.34 = 534\%$; $0.007 = 0.7\%$; 700% 7.00; $86\% = 0.86$; $0.15\% = 0.0015$.

It may be helpful to remember that the percentage number will always be larger than the equivalent decimal number.

Review Video: Converting Decimals to Fractions and Percentages
Visit mometrix.com/academy and enter code: 986765

Example 1

Convert 15% to both a fraction and a decimal.

First, write the percentage over 100 because percent means "per one hundred." So, 15% can be written as $\frac{15}{100}$. Fractions should be written in the simplest form, which means that the numbers in the numerator and denominator should be reduced if possible. Both 15 and 100 can be divided by 5:

$$\frac{15 \div 5}{100 \div 5} = \frac{3}{20}$$

As before, write the percentage over 100 because percent means "per one hundred." So, 15% can be written as $\frac{15}{100}$. Dividing a number by a power of ten (10, 100, 1000, etc.) is the same as moving the decimal point to the left by the same number of spaces that there are zeros in the divisor. Since 100 has 2 zeros, move the decimal point two places to the left:

$$15\% = 0.15$$

In other words, when converting from a percentage to a decimal, drop the percent sign and move the decimal point two places to the left.

Example 2

Write 24.36% as a fraction and then as a decimal. Explain how you made these conversions.

24.36% written as a fraction is $\frac{24.36}{100}$, or $\frac{2436}{10{,}000}$, which reduces to $\frac{609}{2500}$. 24.36% written as a decimal is 0.2436. Recall that dividing by 100 moves the decimal two places to the left.

Review Video: Converting Percentages to Decimals and Fractions
Visit mometrix.com/academy and enter code: 287297

Example 3

Convert $\frac{4}{5}$ to a decimal and to a percentage.

To convert a fraction to a decimal, simply divide the numerator by the denominator in the fraction. The numerator is the top number in the fraction and the denominator is the bottom number in a fraction. So $\frac{4}{5} = 4 \div 5 = 0.80 = 0.8$.

Percent means "per hundred." $\frac{4 \times 20}{5 \times 20} = \frac{80}{100} = 80\%$.

Example 4

Convert $3\frac{2}{5}$ to a decimal and to a percentage.

The mixed number $3\frac{2}{5}$ has a whole number and a fractional part. The fractional part $\frac{2}{5}$ can be written as a decimal by dividing 5 into 2, which gives 0.4. Adding the whole to the part gives 3.4. Alternatively, note that $3\frac{2}{5} = 3\frac{4}{10} = 3.4$

To change a decimal to a percentage, multiply it by 100.

$3.4(100) = 340\%$. Notice that this percentage is greater than 100%. This makes sense because the original mixed number $3\frac{2}{5}$ is greater than 1.

Review Video: Converting Fractions to Percentages and Decimals
Visit mometrix.com/academy and enter code: 306233

Scientific Notation

Scientific notation is a way of writing large numbers in a shorter form. The form $a \times 10^n$ is used in scientific notation, where a is greater than or equal to 1, but less than 10, and n is the number of places the decimal must move to get from the original number to a. Example: The number 230,400,000 is cumbersome to write. To write the value in scientific notation, place a decimal point between the first and second numbers, and include all digits through the last non-zero digit ($a = 2.304$). To find the appropriate power of 10, count the number of places the decimal point had to move ($n = 8$). The number is positive if the decimal moved to the left, and negative if it moved to the right. We can then write 230,400,000 as 2.304×10^8. If we look instead at the number 0.00002304, we have the same value for a, but this time the decimal moved 5 places to the right ($n = -5$). Thus, 0.00002304 can be written as 2.304×10^{-5}. Using this notation makes it simple to compare very large or very small numbers. By comparing exponents, it is easy to see that 3.28×10^4 is smaller than 1.51×10^5, because 4 is less than 5.

Review Video: Scientific Notation
Visit mometrix.com/academy and enter code: 976454

Operations with Decimals

Adding and Subtracting Decimals

When adding and subtracting decimals, the decimal points must always be aligned. Adding decimals is just like adding regular whole numbers. Example: $4.5 + 2 = 6.5$.

If the problem-solver does not properly align the decimal points, an incorrect answer of 4.7 may result. An easy way to add decimals is to align all of the decimal points in a vertical column visually. This will allow one to see exactly where the decimal should be placed in the final answer. Begin adding from right to left. Add each column in turn, making sure to carry the number to the left if a column adds up to more than 9. The same rules apply to the subtraction of decimals.

Review Video: Adding and Subtracting Decimals
Visit mometrix.com/academy and enter code: 381101

Multiplying Decimals

A simple multiplication problem has two components: a **multiplicand** and a **multiplier**. When multiplying decimals, work as though the numbers were whole rather than decimals. Once the final product is calculated, count the number of places to the right of the decimal in both the multiplicand and the multiplier. Then, count that number of places from the right of the product and place the decimal in that position.

For example, 12.3×2.56 has three places to the right of the respective decimals. Multiply 123×256 to get 31488. Now, beginning on the right, count three places to the left and insert the decimal. The final product will be 31.488.

Review Video: Multiplying Decimals
Visit mometrix.com/academy and enter code: 731574

Dividing Decimals

Every division problem has a **divisor** and a **dividend**. The dividend is the number that is being divided. In the problem $14 \div 7$, 14 is the dividend and 7 is the divisor. In a division problem with decimals, the divisor must be converted into a whole number. Begin by moving the decimal in the divisor to the right until a whole number is created. Next, move the decimal in the dividend the same number of spaces to the right. For example, 4.9 into 24.5 would become 49 into 245. The decimal was moved one space to the right to create a whole number in the divisor, and then the same was done for the dividend. Once the whole numbers are created, the problem is carried out normally: $245 \div 49 = 5$.

Review Video: Dividing Decimals
Visit mometrix.com/academy and enter code: 560690

Operations with Fractions

Adding and Subtracting Fractions

If two fractions have a common denominator, they can be added or subtracted simply by adding or subtracting the two numerators and retaining the same denominator. Example: $\frac{1}{2} + \frac{1}{4} = \frac{2}{4} + \frac{1}{4} = \frac{3}{4}$. If the two fractions do not already have the same denominator, one or both of them must be manipulated to achieve a common denominator before they can be added or subtracted.

Review Video: Adding and Subtracting Fractions
Visit mometrix.com/academy and enter code: 378080

Multiplying Fractions

Two fractions can be multiplied by multiplying the two numerators to find the new numerator and the two denominators to find the new denominator. Example: $\frac{1}{3} \times \frac{2}{3} = \frac{1\times2}{3\times3} = \frac{2}{9}$.

Review Video: Multiplying Fractions
Visit mometrix.com/academy and enter code: 638849

Dividing Fractions

Two fractions can be divided by flipping the numerator and denominator of the second fraction and then proceeding as though it were a multiplication. Example: $\frac{2}{3} \div \frac{3}{4} = \frac{2}{3} \times \frac{4}{3} = \frac{8}{9}$.

Review Video: Dividing Fractions
Visit mometrix.com/academy and enter code: 300874

Rational Numbers from Least to Greatest

Example

Order the following rational numbers from least to greatest: 0.55, 17%, $\sqrt{25}$, $\frac{64}{4}$, $\frac{25}{50}$, 3.

Recall that the term **rational** simply means that the number can be expressed as a ratio or fraction. The set of rational numbers includes integers and decimals. Notice that each of the numbers in the problem can be written as a decimal or integer:

$$17\% = 0.1717$$
$$\sqrt{25} = 5$$
$$\frac{64}{4} = 16$$

$$\frac{25}{50} = \frac{1}{2} = 0.5$$

So, the answer is 17%, $\frac{25}{50}$, 0.55, 3, $\sqrt{25}$, $\frac{64}{4}$.

Rational Numbers from Greatest to Least

Example

Order the following rational numbers from greatest to least: 0.3, 27%, $\sqrt{100}$, $\frac{72}{9}$, $\frac{1}{9}$, 4.5

Recall that the term **rational** simply means that the number can be expressed as a ratio or fraction. The set of rational numbers includes integers and decimals. Notice that each of the numbers in the problem can be written as a decimal or integer:

$$27\% = 0.27$$
$$\sqrt{100} = 10$$
$$\frac{72}{9} = 8$$
$$\frac{1}{9} \approx 0.11$$

So, the answer is $\sqrt{100}$, $\frac{72}{9}$, 4.5, 0.3, 27%, $\frac{1}{9}$.

Review Video: Ordering Rational Numbers
Visit mometrix.com/academy and enter code: 419578

Common Denominators with Fractions

When two fractions are manipulated so that they have the same denominator, this is known as finding a **common denominator**. The number chosen to be that common denominator should be the **least common multiple** of the two original denominators. Example: $\frac{3}{4}$ and $\frac{5}{6}$; the least common multiple of 4 and 6 is 12. Manipulating to achieve the common denominator: $\frac{3}{4} = \frac{9}{12}$; $\frac{5}{6} = \frac{10}{12}$.

Factors and Greatest Common Factor

Factors are numbers that are multiplied together to obtain a **product**. For example, in the equation $2 \times 3 = 6$, the numbers 2 and 3 are factors. A **prime number** has only two factors (1 and itself), but other numbers can have many factors.

A **common factor** is a number that divides exactly into two or more other numbers. For example, the factors of 12 are 1, 2, 3, 4, 6, and 12, while the factors of 15 are 1, 3, 5, and 15. The common factors of 12 and 15 are 1 and 3.

A **prime factor** is also a prime number. Therefore, the prime factors of 12 are 2 and 3. For 15, the prime factors are 3 and 5.

Review Video: Factors
Visit mometrix.com/academy and enter code: 920086

The **greatest common factor** (**GCF**) is the largest number that is a factor of two or more numbers. For example, the factors of 15 are 1, 3, 5, and 15; the factors of 35 are 1, 5, 7, and 35. Therefore, the greatest common factor of 15 and 35 is 5.

Review Video: Greatest Common Factor (GCF)
Visit mometrix.com/academy and enter code: 838699

Multiples and Least Common Multiple

The least common multiple (**LCM**) is the smallest number that is a multiple of two or more numbers. For example, the multiples of 3 include 3, 6, 9, 12, 15, etc.; the multiples of 5 include 5, 10, 15, 20, etc. Therefore, the least common multiple of 3 and 5 is 15.

Review Video: Multiples
Visit mometrix.com/academy and enter code: 626738

Review Video: Multiples and Least Common Multiple (LCM)
Visit mometrix.com/academy and enter code: 520269

Pre-Algebra

Proportions and Ratios

Proportions

A proportion is a relationship between two quantities that dictates how one changes when the other changes. A **direct proportion** describes a relationship in which a quantity increases by a set amount for every increase in the other quantity, or decreases by that same amount for every decrease in the other quantity. Example: Assuming a constant driving speed, the time required for a car trip increases as the distance of the trip increases. The distance to be traveled and the time required to travel are directly proportional.

Inverse proportion is a relationship in which an increase in one quantity is accompanied by a decrease in the other, or vice versa. Example: the time required for a car trip decreases as the speed increases, and increases as the speed decreases, so the time required is inversely proportional to the speed of the car.

Review Video: Proportions
Visit mometrix.com/academy and enter code: 505355

Ratios

A **ratio** is a comparison of two quantities in a particular order. Example: If there are 14 computers in a lab, and the class has 20 students, there is a student to computer ratio of 20 to 14, commonly written as 20:14. Ratios are normally reduced to their smallest whole number representation, so 20:14 would be reduced to 10:7 by dividing both sides by 2.

Review Video: Ratios
Visit mometrix.com/academy and enter code: 996914

Real World Problems with Proportions and Ratios

Example 1

A child was given 100 mg of chocolate every two hours. How much chocolate will the child receive in five hours?

Using proportional reasoning, since five hours is two and a half times as long as two hours, the child will receive two and a half times as much chocolate, $2.5 \times 100 \text{ mg} = 250 \text{ mg}$, in five hours.

To compute the answer methodically, first write the amount of chocolate per 2 hours as a ratio.

$$\frac{100 \text{ mg}}{2 \text{ hours}}$$

Next create a proportion to relate the different time increments of 2 hours and 5 hours.

$\frac{100 \text{ mg}}{2 \text{ hours}} = \frac{x \text{ mg}}{5 \text{ hours}}$, where x is the amount of chocolate the child receives in five hours. Make sure to keep the same units in either the numerator or denominator. In this case the numerator units must be mg for both ratios and the denominator units must be hours for both ratios.

Use cross multiplication and division to solve for x:

$$\begin{aligned} \frac{100 \text{ mg}}{2 \text{ hours}} &= \frac{x \text{ mg}}{5 \text{ hours}} \\ 100(5) &= 2(x) \\ 500 &= 2x \\ 500 \div 2 &= 2x \div 2 \\ 250 &= x \end{aligned}$$

Therefore, the child receives 250 mg every five hours.

Review Video: Proportions in the Real World
Visit mometrix.com/academy and enter code: 221143

Example 2

At a school, for every 20 female students there are 15 male students. This same student ratio happens to exist at another school. If there are 100 female students at the second school, how many male students are there?

One way to find the number of male students is to set up and solve a proportion.

$$\frac{\text{number of female students}}{\text{number of male students}} = \frac{20}{15} = \frac{100}{\text{number of male students}}$$

Represent the unknown number of male students as the variable x.

$$\frac{20}{15} = \frac{100}{x}$$

Follow these steps to solve for x:

1. Cross multiply. $20 \times x = 15 \times 100$.

$$20x = 1500$$

2. Divide each side of the equation by 20.

$$x = 75$$

Or, notice that: $\frac{20 \times 5}{15 \times 5} = \frac{100}{75}$, so $x = 75$.

Example 3

In a hospital emergency room, there are 4 nurses for every 12 patients. What is the ratio of nurses to patients? If the nurse-to-patient ratio remains constant, how many nurses must be present to care for 24 patients?

The ratio of nurses to patients can be written as 4 to 12, 4:12, or $\frac{4}{12}$. Because four and twelve have a common factor of four, the ratio should be reduced to 1:3, which means that there is one nurse present for every three patients. If this ratio remains constant, there must be eight nurses present to care for 24 patients.

Example 4

In a bank, the banker-to-customer ratio is 1:2. If seven bankers are on duty, how many customers are currently in the bank?

Use proportional reasoning or set up a proportion to solve. Because there are twice as many customers as bankers, there must be fourteen customers when seven bankers are on duty. Setting up and solving a proportion gives the same result:

$$\frac{\text{number of bankers}}{\text{number of customers}} = \frac{1}{2} = \frac{7}{\text{number of customers}}$$

Represent the unknown number of patients as the variable *x*.

$$\frac{1}{2} = \frac{7}{x}$$

To solve for *x*, cross multiply:

$1 \times x = 7 \times 2$, so $x = 14$.

Constant of Proportionality

When two quantities have a proportional relationship, there exists a **constant of proportionality** between the quantities; the product of this constant and one of the quantities is equal to the other quantity. For example, if one lemon costs $0.25, two lemons cost $0.50, and three lemons cost $0.75, there is a proportional relationship between the total cost of lemons and the number of lemons purchased. The constant of proportionality is the **unit price**, namely $0.25/lemon. Notice that the total price of lemons, *t*, can be found by multiplying the unit price of lemons, *p*, and the number of lemons, *n*: $t = pn$.

Slope

On a graph with two points, (x_1, y_1) and (x_2, y_2), the **slope** is found with the formula $m = \frac{y_2 - y_1}{x_2 - x_1}$; where $x_1 \neq x_2$ and m stands for slope. If the value of the slope is **positive**, the line has an *upward* *direction* from left to right. If the value of the slope is **negative**, the line has a *downward direction* from left to right.

Unit Rate as the Slope

A new book goes on sale in bookstores and online stores. In the first month, 5,000 copies of the book are sold. Over time, the book continues to grow in popularity. The data for the number of copies sold is in the table below.

# of Months on Sale	1	2	3	4	5
# of Copies Sold (In Thousands)	5	10	15	20	25

So, the number of copies that are sold and the time that the book is on sale is a proportional relationship. In this example, an equation can be used to show the data: $y = 5x$, where x is the number of months that the book is on sale. Also, y is the number of copies sold. So, the slope is $\frac{\text{rise}}{\text{run}} = \frac{5}{1}$. This can be reduced to 5.

Review Video: Finding the Slope of a Line
Visit mometrix.com/academy and enter code: 766664

Work/Unit Rate

Unit rate expresses a quantity of one thing in terms of one unit of another. For example, if you travel 30 miles every two hours, a unit rate expresses this comparison in terms of one hour: in one hour you travel 15 miles, so your unit rate is 15 miles per hour. Other examples are how much one ounce of food costs (price per ounce) or figuring out how much one egg costs out of the dozen (price per 1 egg, instead of price per 12 eggs). The denominator of a unit rate is always 1. Unit rates are used to compare different situations to solve problems. For example, to make sure you get the best deal when deciding which kind of soda to buy, you can find the unit rate of each. If Soda #1 costs $1.50 for a 1-liter bottle, and soda #2 costs $2.75 for a 2-liter bottle, it would be a better deal to buy Soda #2, because its unit rate is only $1.375 per 1-liter, which is cheaper than Soda #1. Unit rates can also help determine the length of time a given event will take. For example, if you can paint 2 rooms in 4.5 hours, you can determine how long it will take you to paint 5 rooms by solving for the unit rate per room and then multiplying that by 5.

Review Video: Rates and Unit Rates
Visit mometrix.com/academy and enter code: 185363

Example 1

Janice made $40 during the first 5 hours she spent babysitting. She will continue to earn money at this rate until she finishes babysitting in 3 more hours. Find how much money Janice earned babysitting and how much she earns per hour.

Janice will earn $64 babysitting in her 8 total hours (adding the first 5 hours to the remaining 3 gives the 8 hour total). This can be found by setting up a proportion comparing money earned to babysitting hours. Since she earns $40 for 5 hours and since the rate is constant, she will earn a proportional amount in 8 hours: $\frac{40}{5} = \frac{x}{8}$. Cross multiplying will yield $5x = 320$, and division by 5 shows that $x = 64$.

Janice earns \$8 per hour. This can be found by taking her total amount earned, \$64, and dividing it by the total number of hours worked, 8. Since $\frac{64}{8} = 8$, Janice makes \$8 in one hour. This can also be found by finding the unit rate, money earned per hour: $\frac{64}{8} = \frac{x}{1}$. Since cross multiplying yields $8x = 64$, and division by 8 shows that $x = 8$, Janice earns \$8 per hour.

Example 2

The McDonalds are taking a family road trip, driving 300 miles to their cabin. It took them 2 hours to drive the first 120 miles. They will drive at the same speed all the way to their cabin. Find the speed at which the McDonalds are driving and how much longer it will take them to get to their cabin.

The McDonalds are driving 60 miles per hour. This can be found by setting up a proportion to find the unit rate, the number of miles they drive per one hour: $\frac{120}{2} = \frac{x}{1}$. Cross multiplying yields $2x = 120$ and division by 2 shows that $x = 60$.

Since the McDonalds will drive this same speed, it will take them another 3 hours to get to their cabin. This can be found by first finding how many miles the McDonalds have left to drive, which is $300 - 120 = 180$. The McDonalds are driving at 60 miles per hour, so a proportion can be set up to determine how many hours it will take them to drive 180 miles: $\frac{180}{x} = \frac{60}{1}$. Cross multiplying yields $60x = 180$, and division by 60 shows that $x = 3$. This can also be found by using the formula $D = r \times t$ (or Distance = rate × time), where $180 = 60 \times t$, and division by 60 shows that $t = 3$.

Example 3

It takes Andy 10 minutes to read 6 pages of his book. He has already read 150 pages in his book that is 210 pages long. Find how long it takes Andy to read 1 page and also find how long it will take him to finish his book if he continues to read at the same speed.

It takes Andy 1 minute and 40 seconds to read one page in his book. This can be found by finding the unit rate per one page, by dividing the total time it takes him to read 6 pages by 6. Since it takes him 10 minutes to read 6 pages, $\frac{10}{6} = 1\frac{2}{3}$ minutes, which is 1 minute and 40 seconds.

It will take Andy another 100 minutes, or 1 hour and 40 minutes to finish his book. This can be found by first figuring out how many pages Andy has left to read, which is $210 - 150 = 60$. Since it is now known that it takes him $1\frac{2}{3}$ minutes to read each page, then that rate must be multiplied by however many pages he has left to read (60) to find the time he'll need: $60 \times 1\frac{2}{3} = 100$, so it will take him 100 minutes, or 1 hour and 40 minutes, to read the rest of his book.

Algebra

Function and Relation

When expressing functional relationships, the **variables** x and y are typically used. These values are often written as the **coordinates** (x, y). The x-value is the independent variable and the y-value is the dependent variable. A **relation** is a set of data in which there is not a unique y-value for each x-value in the dataset. This means that there can be two of the same x-values assigned to different y-

values. A relation is simply a relationship between the x and y-values in each coordinate but does not apply to the relationship between the values of x and y in the data set. A **function** is a relation where one quantity depends on the other. For example, the amount of money that you make depends on the number of hours that you work. In a function, each x-value in the data set has one unique y-value because the y-value depends on the x-value.

Review Video: Definition of a Function
Visit mometrix.com/academy and enter code: 784611

Determining a Function

You can determine whether an equation is a **function** by substituting different values into the equation for x. These values are called input values. All possible input values are referred to as the **domain**. The result of substituting these values into the equation is called the output, or **range**. You can display and organize these numbers in a data table. A **data table** contains the values for x and y, which you can also list as coordinates. In order for a function to exist, the table cannot contain any repeating x-values that correspond with different y-values. If each x-coordinate has a unique y-coordinate, the table contains a function. However, there can be repeating y-values that correspond with different x-values. An example of this is when the function contains an exponent. For example, if $x^2 = y$, $2^2 = 4$, and $(-2)^2 = 4$.

Review Video: Basics of Functions
Visit mometrix.com/academy and enter code: 822500

Equation Using Independent and Dependent Variables

To write an equation, you must first assign **variables** to the unknown values in the problem and then translate the words and phrases into expressions containing numbers and symbols. For example, if Ray earns $10 an hour, this can be represented by the expression $10x$, where x is equal to the number of hours that Ray works. The value of x represents the number of hours because it is the **independent variable**, or the amount that you can choose and can manipulate. To find out how much money he earns in y hours, you would write the equation $10x = y$. The variable y is the **dependent variable** because it depends on x and cannot be manipulated. Once you have the equation for the function, you can choose any number of hours to find the corresponding amount that he earns. For example, if you want to know how much he would earn working 36 hours, you would substitute 36 in for x and multiply to find that he would earn $360.

Review Video: Dependent and Independent Variables and Inverting Functions
Visit mometrix.com/academy and enter code: 704764

Writing a Function Rule Using a Table

If given a set of data, place the corresponding x and y-values into a table and analyze the relationship between them. Consider what you can do to each x-value to obtain the corresponding y-value. Try adding or subtracting different numbers to and from x and then try multiplying or dividing different numbers to and from x. If none of these **operations** give you the y-value, try combining the operations. Once you find a rule that works for one pair, make sure to try it with each additional set of ordered pairs in the table. If the same operation or combination of operations satisfies each set of coordinates, then the table contains a function. The rule is then used to write the equation of the function in "y =" form.

Equations and Graphing

When algebraic functions and equations are shown graphically, they are usually shown on a *Cartesian coordinate plane*. The Cartesian coordinate plane consists of two number lines placed perpendicular to each other, and intersecting at the zero point, also known as the origin. The horizontal number line is known as the x-axis, with positive values to the right of the origin, and negative values to the left of the origin. The vertical number line is known as the y-axis, with positive values above the origin, and negative values below the origin. Any point on the plane can be identified by an ordered pair in the form (x,y), called coordinates. The x-value of the coordinate is called the abscissa, and the y-value of the coordinate is called the ordinate. The two number lines divide the plane into *four quadrants*: I, II, III, and IV.

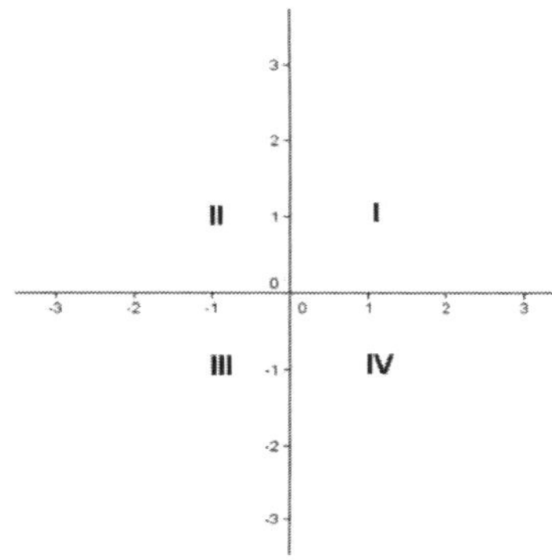

Before learning the different forms in which equations can be written, it is important to understand some terminology. A ratio of the change in the vertical distance to the change in horizontal distance is called the *slope*. On a graph with two points, (x_1, y_1) and (x_2, y_2), the slope is represented by the formula $s = \frac{y_2 - y_1}{x_2 - x_1}$; $x_1 \neq x_2$. If the value of the slope is positive, the line slopes upward from left to right. If the value of the slope is negative, the line slopes downward from left to right. If the y-coordinates are the same for both points, the slope is 0 and the line is a *horizontal line*. If the x-coordinates are the same for both points, there is no slope and the line is a *vertical line*. Two or more lines that have equal slopes are *parallel lines*. *perpendicular lines* have slopes that are negative reciprocals of each other, such as $\frac{a}{b}$ and $\frac{-b}{a}$.

Review Video: Graphs of Functions
Visit mometrix.com/academy and enter code: 492785

Equations are made up of monomials and polynomials. A *monomial* is a single variable or product of constants and variables, such as x, $2x$, or $\frac{2}{x}$. There will never be addition or subtraction symbols in a monomial. Like monomials have like variables, but they may have different coefficients. *Polynomials* are algebraic expressions which use addition and subtraction to combine two or more monomials. Two terms make a binomial; three terms make a trinomial; etc.. The *degree of a monomial* is the sum of the exponents of the variables. The *degree of a polynomial* is the highest degree of any individual term.

As mentioned previously, equations can be written many ways. Below is a list of the many forms equations can take.

- Standard Form: $Ax + By = C$; the slope is $\frac{-A}{B}$ and the y-intercept is $\frac{C}{B}$
- *Slope Intercept Form*: $y = mx + b$, where m is the slope and b is the y-intercept
- Point-Slope Form: $y - y_1 = m(x - x_1)$, where m is the slope and (x_1, y_1) is a point on the line
- Two-Point Form: $\frac{y-y_1}{x-x_1} = \frac{y_2-y_1}{x_2-x_1}$, where (x_1, y_1) and (x_2, y_2) are two points on the given line
- *Intercept Form*: $\frac{x}{x_1} + \frac{y}{y_1} = 1$, where $(x_1, 0)$ is the point at which a line intersects the x-axis, and $(0, y_1)$ is the point at which the same line intersects the y-axis

Review Video: Slope-Intercept and Point-Slope Forms
Visit mometrix.com/academy and enter code: 113216

Equations can also be written as $ax + b = 0$, where $a \neq 0$. These are referred to as **one variable linear equations**. A solution to such an equation is called a **root**. In the case where we have the equation $5x + 10 = 0$, if we solve for x we get a solution of $x = -2$. In other words, the root of the equation is -2. This is found by first subtracting 10 from both sides, which gives $5x = -10$. Next, simply divide both sides by the coefficient of the variable, in this case 5, to get $x = -2$. This can be checked by plugging -2 back into the original equation $(5)(-2) + 10 = -10 + 10 = 0$.

The **solution set** is the set of all solutions of an equation. In our example, the solution set would simply be -2. If there were more solutions (there usually are in multivariable equations) then they would also be included in the solution set. When an equation has no true solutions, this is referred to as an **empty set**. Equations with identical solution sets are ***equivalent equations***. An **identity** is a term whose value or determinant is equal to 1.

Manipulation of Functions

Horizontal and vertical shift occur when values are added to or subtracted from the x or y values, respectively.

If a constant is added to the y portion of each point, the graph shifts up. If a constant is subtracted from the y portion of each point, the graph shifts down. This is represented by the expression $f(x) \pm k$, where k is a constant.

If a constant is added to the x portion of each point, the graph shifts left. If a constant is subtracted from the x portion of each point, the graph shifts right. This is represented by the expression $f(x \pm k)$, where k is a constant.

Stretch, compression, and reflection occur when different parts of a function are multiplied by different groups of constants. If the function as a whole is multiplied by a real number constant greater than 1, $(k \times f(x))$, the graph is stretched vertically. If k in the previous equation is greater than zero but less than 1, the graph is compressed vertically. If k is less than zero, the graph is reflected about the x-axis, in addition to being either stretched or compressed vertically if k is less than or greater than -1, respectively. If instead, just the x-term is multiplied by a constant greater than 1 $(f(k \times x))$, the graph is compressed horizontally. If k in the previous equation is greater than zero but less than 1, the graph is stretched horizontally. If k is less than zero, the graph is reflected about the y-axis, in addition to being either stretched or compressed horizontally if k is greater than or less than -1, respectively.

Classification of Functions

There are many different ways to classify functions based on their structure or behavior. Listed here are a few common classifications.

Constant functions are given by the equation y=b or $f(x) = b$, where b is a real number. There is no independent variable present in the equation, so the function has a constant value for all x. The graph of a constant function is a horizontal line of slope 0 that is positioned b units from the x-axis. If b is positive, the line is above the x-axis; if b is negative, the line is below the x-axis.

Identity functions are identified by the equation y=x or $f(x) = x$, where every value of y is equal to its corresponding value of x. The only zero is the point (0, 0). The graph is a diagonal line with slope 1.

In **linear functions**, the value of the function changes in direct proportion to x. The rate of change,represented by the slope on its graph, is constant throughout. The standard form of a linear equation is $ax + by = c$, where a, b, and c are real numbers. As a function, this equation is commonly written as $y = mx + b$ or $f(x) = mx + b$. This is known as the slope-intercept form, because the coefficients give the slope of the graphed function (m) and its y-intercept (b). Solve the equation $mx + b = 0$ for x to get $x = -\frac{b}{m}$, which is the only zero of the function. The domain and range are both the set of all real numbers.

A **polynomial function** is a function with multiple terms and multiple powers of x, such as:

$$f(x) = a_n x^n + a_{n-1} x^{n-1} + a_{n-2} x^{n-2} + \cdots + a_1 x + a_0$$

where n is a non-negative integer that is the highest exponent in the polynomial, and $a_n \neq 0$. The domain of a polynomial function is the set of all real numbers. If the greatest exponent in the polynomial is even, the polynomial is said to be of even degree and the range is the set of real numbers that satisfy the function. If the greatest exponent in the polynomial is odd, the polynomial is said to be odd and the range, like the domain, is the set of all real numbers.

Review Video: Simplifying Rational Polynomial Functions
Visit mometrix.com/academy and enter code: 351038

A **quadratic function** is a polynomial function that follows the equation pattern $y = ax^2 + bx + c$, or $f(x) = ax^2 + bx + c$, where a, b, and c are real numbers and $a \neq 0$. The domain of a quadratic function is the set of all real numbers. The range is also real numbers, but only those in the subset of the domain that satisfy the equation. The root(s) of any quadratic function can be found by plugging the values of a, b, and c into the **quadratic formula**:

$$x = \frac{-b \pm \sqrt{b^2 - 4ac}}{2a}$$

If the expression $b^2 - 4ac$ is negative, you will instead find complex roots.

A quadratic function has a parabola for its graph. In the equation $f(x) = ax^2 + bx + c$, if a is positive, the parabola will open upward. If a is negative, the parabola will open downward. The axis of symmetry is a vertical line that passes through the vertex. To determine whether or not the parabola will intersect the x-axis, check the number of real roots. An equation with two real roots will cross the x-axis twice. An equation with one real root will have its vertex on the x-axis. An equation with no real roots will not contact the x-axis.

> **Review Video: Deriving the Quadratic Formula**
> Visit mometrix.com/academy and enter code: 317436
>
> **Review Video: Using the Quadratic Formula**
> Visit mometrix.com/academy and enter code: 163102
>
> **Review Video: Changing Constants in Graphs of Functions: Quadratic Equations**
> Visit mometrix.com/academy and enter code: 476276

A **rational function** is a function that can be constructed as a ratio of two polynomial expressions: $f(x) = \frac{p(x)}{q(x)}$, where $p(x)$ and $q(x)$ are both polynomial expressions and $q(x) \neq 0$. The domain is the set of all real numbers, except any values for which $q(x) = 0$. The range is the set of real numbers that satisfies the function when the domain is applied. When you graph a rational function, you will have vertical asymptotes wherever $q(x) = 0$. If the polynomial in the numerator is of lesser degree than the polynomial in the denominator, the x-axis will also be a horizontal asymptote. If the numerator and denominator have equal degrees, there will be a horizontal asymptote not on the x-axis. If the degree of the numerator is exactly one greater than the degree of the denominator, the graph will have an oblique, or diagonal, asymptote. The asymptote will be along the line $y = \frac{p_n}{q_{n-1}}x + \frac{p_{n-1}}{q_{n-1}}$, where p_n and q_{n-1} are the coefficients of the highest degree terms in their respective polynomials.

A **square root function** is a function that contains a radical and is in the format $f(x) = \sqrt{ax + b}$. The domain is the set of all real numbers that yields a positive radicand or a radicand equal to zero. Because square root values are assumed to be positive unless otherwise identified, the range is all real numbers from zero to infinity. To find the zero of a square root function, set the radicand equal to zero and solve for x. The graph of a square root function is always to the right of the zero and always above the x-axis.

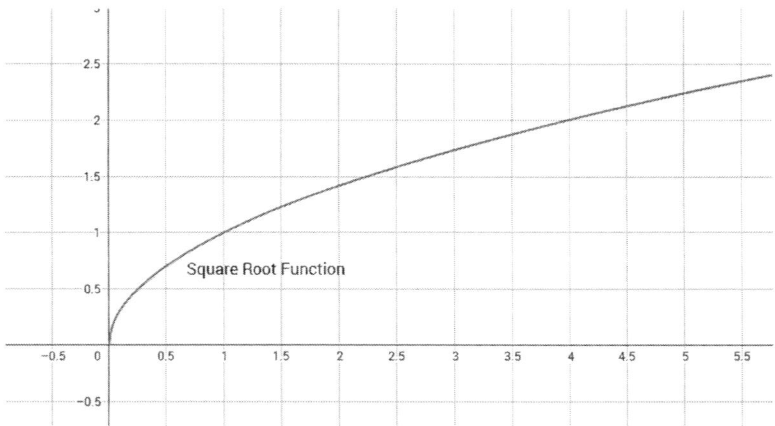

An **absolute value function** is in the format $f(x) = |ax + b|$. Like other functions, the domain is the set of all real numbers. However, because absolute value indicates positive numbers, the range is limited to positive real numbers. To find the zero of an absolute value function, set the portion inside the absolute value sign equal to zero and solve for x.

An absolute value function is also known as a piecewise function because it must be solved in pieces – one for if the value inside the absolute value sign is positive, and one for if the value is negative. The function can be expressed as

$$f(x) = \begin{cases} ax + b \text{ if } ax + b \geq 0 \\ -(ax + b) \text{ if } ax + b < 0 \end{cases}$$

This will allow for an accurate statement of the range.

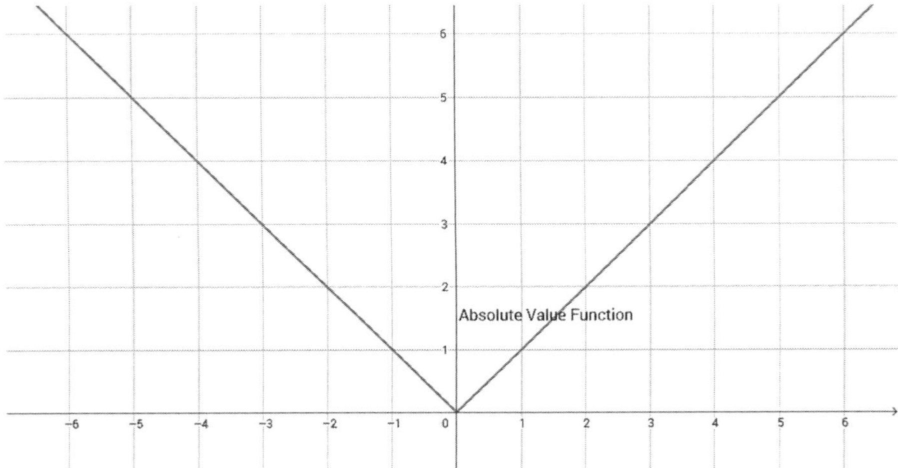

Exponential functions are equations that have the format $y = b^x$, where base $b > 0$ and $b \neq 1$. The exponential function can also be written $f(x) = b^x$.

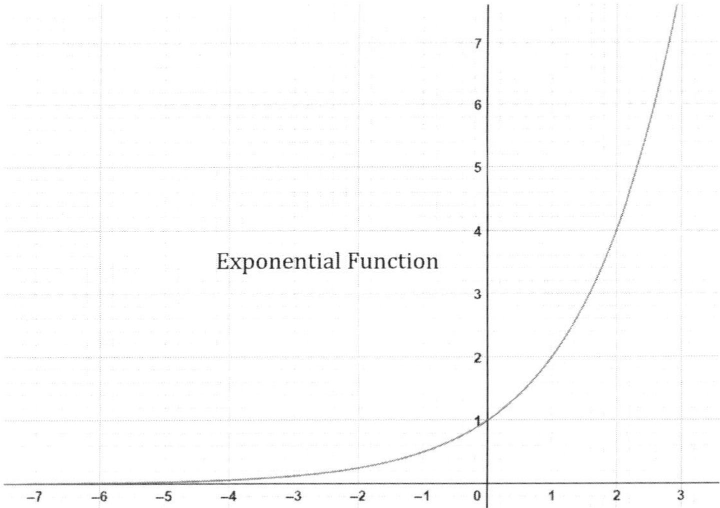

Logarithmic functions are equations that have the format $y = \log_b x$ or $f(x) = \log_b x$. The base b may be any number except one; however, the most common bases for logarithms are base 10 and base *e*. The log base *e* is known the natural logarithm, or *ln*, expressed by the function $f(x) = \ln x$.

Any logarithm that does not have an assigned value of b is assumed to be base 10: $\log x = \log_{10} x$. Exponential functions and logarithmic functions are related in that one is the inverse of the other. If $f(x) = b^x$, then $f^{-1}(x) = \log_b x$. This can perhaps be expressed more clearly by the two equations: $y = b^x$ and $x = \log_b y$.

The following properties apply to logarithmic expressions:

$$\log_b 1 = 0$$
$$\log_b b = 1$$
$$\log_b b^p = p$$
$$\log_b MN = \log_b M + \log_b N$$
$$\log_b \frac{M}{N} = \log_b M - \log_b N$$
$$\log_b M^p = p \log_b M$$

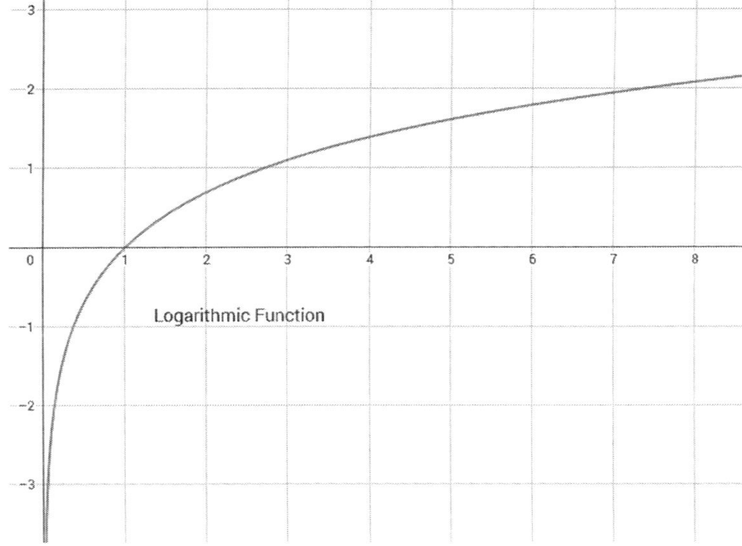

In a **one-to-one function**, each value of x has exactly one value for y (this is the definition of a function) *and* each value of y has exactly one value for x. While the vertical line test will determine if a graph is that of a function, the horizontal line test will determine if a function is a one-to-one function. If a horizontal line drawn at any value of y intersects the graph in more than one place, the graph is not that of a one-to-one function. Do not make the mistake of using the horizontal line test exclusively in determining if a graph is that of a one-to-one function. A one-to-one function must pass both the vertical line test and the horizontal line test. One-to-one functions are also **invertible functions**.

A **monotone function** is a function whose graph either constantly increases or constantly decreases. Examples include the functions $f(x) = x$, $f(x) = -x$, or $f(x) = x^3$.

An **even function** has a graph that is symmetric with respect to the y-axis and satisfies the equation $f(x) = f(-x)$. Examples include the functions $f(x) = x^2$ and $f(x) = ax^n$, where a is any real number and n is a positive even integer.

An **odd function** has a graph that is symmetric with respect to the origin and satisfies the equation $f(x) = -f(-x)$. Examples include the functions $f(x) = x^3$ and $f(x) = ax^n$, where a is any real number and n is a positive odd integer.

Algebraic functions are those that exclusively use polynomials and roots. These would include polynomial functions, rational functions, square root functions, and all combinations of these functions, such as polynomials as the radicand. These combinations may be joined by addition, subtraction, multiplication, or division, but may not include variables as exponents.

Transcendental functions are all functions that are non-algebraic. Any function that includes logarithms, trigonometric functions, variables as exponents, or any combination that includes any of these is not algebraic in nature, even if the function includes polynomials or roots.

Related Concepts

According to the **fundamental theorem of algebra**, every non-constant, single variable polynomial has exactly as many roots as the polynomial's highest exponent. For example, if x^4 is the largest exponent of a term, the polynomial will have exactly 4 roots. However, some of these roots may have multiplicity or be non-real numbers. For instance, in the polynomial function $f(x) = x^4 - 4x + 3$, the only real roots are 1 and -1. The root 1 has multiplicity of 2 and there is one non-real root $(-1 - \sqrt{2}i)$.

The **remainder theorem** is useful for determining the remainder when a polynomial is divided by a binomial. The Remainder Theorem states that if a polynomial function $f(x)$ is divided by a binomial $x - a$, where a is a real number, the remainder of the division will be the value of $f(a)$. If $f(a) = 0$, then a is a root of the polynomial.

The **factor theorem** is related to the Remainder Theorem and states that if $f(a) = 0$ then $(x- a)$ is a factor of the function.

According to the **rational root theorem,** any rational root of a polynomial function $f(x) = a_n x^n + a_{n-1}x^{n-1} + \cdots + a_1 x + a_0$ with integer coefficients will, when reduced to its lowest terms, be a positive or negative fraction such that the numerator is a factor of a_0 and the denominator is a factor of a_n. For instance, if the polynomial function $f(x) = x^3 + 3x^2 - 4$ has any rational roots, the numerators of those roots can only be factors of 4 (1, 2, 4), and the denominators can only be factors of 1 (1). The function in this example has roots of 1 $\left(\text{or } \frac{1}{1}\right)$ and -2 $\left(\text{or } -\frac{2}{1}\right)$.

Variables that vary directly are those that either both increase at the same rate or both decrease at the same rate. For example, in the functions $f(x) = kx$ or $f(x) = kx^n$, where k and n are positive, the value of $f(x)$ increases as the value of x increases and decreases as the value of x decreases.

Variables that vary inversely are those where one increases while the other decreases. For example, in the functions $f(x) = \frac{k}{x}$ or $f(x) = \frac{k}{x^n}$ where k is a positive constant, the value of y increases as the value of x decreases, and the value of y decreases as the value of x increases.

In both cases, k is the constant of variation.

Applying the Basic Operations to Functions

For each of the basic operations, we will use these functions as examples: $f(x) = x^2$ and $g(x) = x$.

To find the sum of two functions f and g, assuming the domains are compatible, simply add the two functions together: $(f + g)(x) = f(x) + g(x) = x^2 + x$

To find the difference of two functions f and g, assuming the domains are compatible, simply subtract the second function from the first: $(f - g)(x) = f(x) - g(x) = x^2 - x$.

To find the product of two functions f and g, assuming the domains are compatible, multiply the two functions together: $(f \cdot g)(x) = f(x) \cdot g(x) = x^2 \cdot x = x^3$.

To find the quotient of two functions f and g, assuming the domains are compatible, divide the first function by the second: $\frac{f}{g}(x) = \frac{f(x)}{g(x)} = \frac{x^2}{x} = x\,; x \neq 0$.

The example given in each case is fairly simple, but on a given problem, if you are looking only for the value of the sum, difference, product or quotient of two functions at a particular x-value, it may be simpler to solve the functions individually and then perform the given operation using those values.

The composite of two functions f and g, written as $(f \circ g)(x)$ simply means that the output of the second function is used as the input of the first. This can also be written as $f\big(g(x)\big)$. In general, this can be solved by substituting $g(x)$ for all instances of x in $f(x)$ and simplifying. Using the example functions $f(x) = x^2 - x + 2$ and $g(x) = x + 1$, we can find that $(f \circ g)(x)$ or $f\big(g(x)\big)$ is equal to $f(x+1) = (x+1)^2 - (x+1) + 2$, which simplifies to $x^2 + x + 2$.

It is important to note that $(f \circ g)(x)$ is not necessarily the same as $(g \circ f)(x)$. The process is not commutative like addition or multiplication expressions. If $(f \circ g)(x)$ does equal $(g \circ f)(x)$, the two functions are inverses of each other.

Solve Equations in One Variable

Manipulating Equations

Sometimes you will have variables missing in equations. So, you need to find the missing variable. To do this, you need to remember one important thing: *whatever you do to one side of an equation, you need to do to the other side.* If you subtract 100 from one side of an equation, you need to subtract 100 from the other side of the equation. This will allow you to change the form of the equation to find missing values.

Example

Ray earns \$10 an hour at his job. Write an equation for his earnings as a function of time spent working. Determine how long Ray has to work in order to earn \$360.

The number of dollars that Ray earns is dependent on the number of hours he works, so earnings will be represented by the dependent variable y and hours worked will be represented by the independent variable x. He earns 10 dollars per hour worked, so his earning can be calculated as

$$y = 10x$$

To calculate the number of hours Ray must work in order to earn \$360, plug in 360 for y and solve for x:

$$360 = 10x$$

$$x = \frac{360}{10} = 36$$

So, Ray must work 36 hours in order to earn \$360.

Solving One Variable Linear Equations

Another way to write an equation is $ax + b = 0$ where $a \neq 0$. This is known as a **one-variable linear equation**. A solution to an equation is called a **root**. Consider the following equation:

$$5x + 10 = 0$$

If we solve for x, the solution is $x = -2$. In other words, the root of the equation is –2.

The first step is to subtract 10 from both sides. This gives $5x = -10$.

Next, divide both sides by the **coefficient** of the variable. For this example, that is 5. So, you should have $x = -2$. You can make sure that you have the correct answer by substituting –2 back into the original equation. So, the equation now looks like this: $(5)(-2) + 10 = -10 + 10 = 0$.

Example 1

$\frac{45\%}{12\%} = \frac{15\%}{x}$. Solve for x.

First, cross multiply; then, solve for x: $\frac{45\%}{12\%} = \frac{15\%}{x}$

$$\frac{0.45}{0.12} = \frac{0.15}{x}$$
$$0.45(x) = 0.12(0.15)$$
$$0.45x = 0.0180$$
$$0.45x \div 0.45 = 0.0180 \div 0.45$$
$$x = 0.04 = 4\%$$

Alternatively, notice that $\frac{45\% \div 3}{12\% \div 3} = \frac{15\%}{4\%}$. So, $x = 4\%$.

Example 2

How do you solve for x in the proportion $\frac{0.50}{2} = \frac{1.50}{x}$?

First, cross multiply; then, solve for x.

$$\frac{0.50}{2} = \frac{1.50}{x}$$
$$0.50(x) = 2(1.50)$$
$$0.50x = 3$$
$$0.50x \div 0.50 = 3 \div 0.50$$
$$x = 6$$

Or, notice that $\frac{0.50 \times 3}{2 \times 3} = \frac{1.50}{6}$, so $x = 6$.

Example 3

$\frac{40}{8} = \frac{x}{24}$. Find x.

One way to solve for x is to first cross multiply.

$$\frac{40}{8} = \frac{x}{24}$$

$$40(24) = 8(x)$$
$$960 = 8x$$
$$960 \div 8 = 8x \div 8$$
$$x = 120$$

Or, notice that:

$$\frac{40 \times 3}{8 \times 3} = \frac{120}{24}, \text{so } x = 120$$

Other Important Concepts

Commonly in algebra and other upper-level fields of math you find yourself working with mathematical expressions that do not equal each other. The statement comparing such expressions with symbols such as < (less than) or > (greater than) is called an *inequality*. An example of an inequality is $7x > 5$. To solve for x, simply divide both sides by 7 and the solution is shown to be $x > \frac{5}{7}$. Graphs of the solution set of inequalities are represented on a number line. Open circles are used to show that an expression approaches a number but is never quite equal to that number.

Review Video: Inequalities
Visit mometrix.com/academy and enter code: 347842

Conditional inequalities are those with certain values for the variable that will make the condition true and other values for the variable where the condition will be false. **Absolute inequalities** can have any real number as the value for the variable to make the condition true, while there is no real number value for the variable that will make the condition false. Solving inequalities is done by following the same rules as for solving equations with the exception that when multiplying or dividing by a negative number the direction of the inequality sign must be flipped or reversed. **double inequalities** are situations where two inequality statements apply to the same variable expression. An example of this is $-c < ax + b < c$.

A **weighted mean**, or weighted average, is a mean that uses "weighted" values. The formula is weighted mean $= \frac{w_1x_1+w_2x_2+w_3x_3...+w_nx_n}{w_1+w_2+w_3+\cdots+w_n}$. Weighted values, such as $w_1, w_2, w_3, \ldots w_n$ are assigned to each member of the set $x_1, x_2, x_3, \ldots x_n$. If calculating weighted mean, make sure a weight value for each member of the set is used.

Graphing Inequalities

Graph the inequality $10 > -2x + 4$.

In order to **graph the inequality** $10 > -2x + 4$, you must first solve for x. The opposite of addition is subtraction, so subtract 4 from both sides. This results in $6 > -2x$. Next, the opposite of multiplication is division, so divide both sides by -2. Don't forget to flip the inequality symbol since you are dividing by a negative number. This results in $-3 < x$. You can rewrite this as $x > -3$. To graph an inequality, you create a number line and put a circle around the value that is being compared to x. If you are graphing a greater than or less than inequality, as the one shown, the circle remains open. This represents all of the values excluding -3. If the inequality happens to be a greater than or equal to or less than or equal to, you draw a closed circle around the value. This would represent all of the values including the number. Finally, take a look at the values that the solution represents and shade the number line in the appropriate direction. You are graphing all of the values greater than -3 and since this is all of the numbers to the right of -3, shade this region on the number line.

Determining Solutions to Inequalities

Determine whether $(-2, 4)$ is a solution of the inequality $y \geq -2x + 3$.

To determine whether a coordinate is a **solution of an inequality**, you can either use the inequality or its graph. Using $(-2, 4)$ as (x, y), substitute the values into the inequality to see if it makes a true statement. This results in $4 \geq -2(-2) + 3$. Using the integer rules, simplify the right side of the inequality by multiplying and then adding. The result is $4 \geq 7$, which is a false statement. Therefore, the coordinate is not a solution of the inequality. You can also use the **graph** of an inequality to see if a coordinate is a part of the solution. The graph of an inequality is shaded over the section of the coordinate grid that is included in the solution. The graph of $y \geq -2x + 3$ includes the solid line $y = -2x + 3$ and is shaded to the right of the line, representing all of the points greater than and including the points on the line. This excludes the point $(-2, 4)$, so it is not a solution of the inequality.

Calculations Using Points

Sometimes you need to perform calculations using only points on a graph as input data. Using points, you can determine what the **midpoint** and **distance** are. If you know the equation for a line you can calculate the distance between the line and the point.

To find the **midpoint** of two points (x_1, y_1) and (x_2, y_2), average the x-coordinates to get the x-coordinate of the midpoint, and average the y-coordinates to get the y-coordinate of the midpoint. The formula is Midpoint $= \left(\frac{x_1+x_2}{2}, \frac{y_1+y_2}{2}\right)$.

The **distance** between two points is the same as the length of the hypotenuse of a right triangle with the two given points as endpoints, and the two sides of the right triangle parallel to the x-axis and y-axis, respectively. The length of the segment parallel to the x-axis is the difference between the x-coordinates of the two points. The length of the segment parallel to the y-axis is the difference between the y-coordinates of the two points. Use the Pythagorean theorem $a^2 + b^2 = c^2$ or $c = \sqrt{a^2 + b^2}$ to find the distance. The formula is distance $= \sqrt{(x_2 - x_1)^2 + (y_2 - y_1)^2}$.

When a line is in the format $Ax + By + C = 0$, where A, B, and C are coefficients, you can use a point (x_1, y_1) not on the line and apply the formula $d = \frac{|Ax_1+By_1+C|}{\sqrt{A^2+B^2}}$ to find the distance between the line and the point (x_1, y_1).

Example

Find the distance and midpoint between points (2, 4) and (8,6).

Midpoint

$$\text{Midpoint} = \left(\frac{x_1 + x_2}{2}, \frac{y_1 + y_2}{2}\right)$$
$$\text{Midpoint} = \left(\frac{2 + 8}{2}, \frac{4 + 6}{2}\right)$$
$$\text{Midpoint} = \left(\frac{10}{2}, \frac{10}{2}\right)$$
$$\text{Midpoint} = (5,5)$$

Distance

$$\text{Distance} = \sqrt{(x_2 - x_1)^2 + (y_2 - y_1)^2}$$
$$\text{Distance} = \sqrt{(8-2)^2 + (6-4)^2}$$
$$\text{Distance} = \sqrt{(6)^2 + (2)^2}$$
$$\text{Distance} = \sqrt{36+4}$$
$$\text{Distance} = \sqrt{40} \text{ or } 2\sqrt{10}$$

Systems of Equations

Systems of equations are a set of simultaneous equations that all use the same variables. A solution to a system of equations must be true for each equation in the system. *Consistent systems* are those with at least one solution. *Inconsistent systems* are systems of equations that have no solution.

Review Video: Systems of Equations
Visit mometrix.com/academy and enter code: 658153

Substitution

To solve a system of linear equations by *substitution*, start with the easier equation and solve for one of the variables. Express this variable in terms of the other variable. Substitute this expression in the other equation and solve for the other variable. The solution should be expressed in the form (x, y). Substitute the values into both of the original equations to check your answer. Consider the following problem.

Solve the system using substitution:

$$x + 6y = 15$$
$$3x - 12y = 18$$

Solve the first equation for x:

$$x = 15 - 6y$$

Substitute this value in place of x in the second equation, and solve for y:

$$3(15 - 6y) - 12y = 18$$
$$45 - 18y - 12y = 18$$
$$30y = 27$$
$$y = \frac{27}{30} = \frac{9}{10} = 0.9$$

Plug this value for y back into the first equation to solve for x:

$$x = 15 - 6(0.9) = 15 - 5.4 = 9.6$$

Check both equations if you have time:

$$9.6 + 6(0.9) = 9.6 + 5.4 = 15$$

$$3(9.6) - 12(0.9) = 28.8 - 10.8 = 18$$

Therefore, the solution is (9.6, 0.9).

Elimination

To solve a system of equations using *elimination*, begin by rewriting both equations in standard form $Ax + By = C$. Check to see if the coefficients of one pair of like variables add to zero. If not, multiply one or both of the equations by a non-zero number to make one set of like variables add to zero. Add the two equations to solve for one of the variables. Substitute this value into one of the original equations to solve for the other variable. Check your work by substituting into the other equation. Next, we will solve the same problem as above, but using the addition method.

Solve the system using elimination:

$$x + 6y = 15$$

$$3x - 12y = 18$$

If we multiply the first equation by 2, we can eliminate the y terms:

$$2x + 12y = 30$$

$$3x - 12y = 18$$

Add the equations together and solve for x:

$$5x = 48$$

$$x = \frac{48}{5} = 9.6$$

Plug the value for x back into either of the original equations and solve for y:

$$9.6 + 6y = 15$$

$$y = \frac{15 - 9.6}{6} = 0.9$$

Check both equations if you have time:

$$9.6 + 6(0.9) = 9.6 + 5.4 = 15$$

$$3(9.6) - 12(0.9) = 28.8 - 10.8 = 18$$

Therefore, the solution is (9.6, 0.9).

Graphically

To solve a system of linear equations **graphically**, plot both equations on the same graph. The solution of the equations is the point where both lines cross. If the lines do not cross (are parallel), then there is **no solution**.

For example, consider the following system of equations:

$$y = 2x + 7$$
$$y = -x + 1$$

Since these equations are given in slope-intercept form, they are easy to graph; the y intercepts of the lines are $(0, 7)$ and $(0, 1)$. The respective slopes are 2 and –1, thus the graphs look like this:

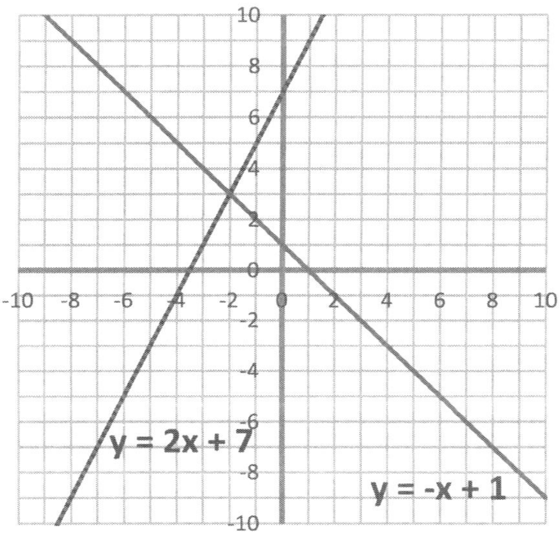

The two lines intersect at the point $(-2, 3)$, thus this is the solution to the system of equations.

Solving a system graphically is generally only practical if both coordinates of the solution are integers; otherwise the intersection will lie between gridlines on the graph and the coordinates will be difficult or impossible to determine exactly. It also helps if, as in this example, the equations are in slope-intercept form or some other form that makes them easy to graph. Otherwise, another method of solution (by substitution or elimination) is likely to be more useful.

Solving A System of Equations Consisting of a Linear Equation and a Quadratic Equation

<u>Algebraically</u>

Generally, the simplest way to solve a system of equations consisting of a linear equation and a quadratic equation algebraically is through the method of **substitution**. One possible strategy is to solve the linear equation for y and then substitute that expression into the quadratic equation. After expansion and combining like terms, this will result in a new quadratic equation for x which, like all quadratic equations, may have zero, one, or two solutions. Plugging each solution for x back into one of the original equations will then produce the corresponding value of y.

For example, consider the following system of equations:

$$x + y = 1$$
$$y = (x + 3)^2 - 2$$

We can solve the linear equation for y to yield $y = -x + 1$.

Substituting this expression into the quadratic equation produces $-x + 1 = (x + 3)^2 - 2$

We can simplify this equation:

$$-x + 1 = (x + 3)^2 - 2$$

$$-x + 1 = x^2 + 6x + 9 - 2$$

$$-x + 1 = x^2 + 6x + 7$$

$$x^2 + 7x + 6 = 0$$

This quadratic equation can be factored as $(x + 1)(x + 6) = 0$. It therefore has two solutions: $x_1 = -1$ and $x_2 = -6$. Plugging each of these back into the original linear equation yields $y_1 = -x_1 + 1 = -(-1) + 1 = 2$ and $y_2 = -x_2 + 1 = -(-6) + 1 = 7$. Thus this system of equations has two solutions, $(-1, 2)$ and $(-6, 7)$.

It may help to check your work by putting each *x* and *y* value back into the original equations and verifying that they do provide a solution.

<u>Graphically</u>

To solve a system of equations consisting of a linear equation and a quadratic equation **graphically**, plot both equations on the same graph. The linear equation will of course produce a straight line, while the quadratic equation will produce a parabola. These two graphs will intersect at zero, one, or two points; each point of intersection is a solution of the system.

For example, consider the following system of equations:

$$y = -2x + 2$$
$$y = -2x^2 + 4x + 2$$

The linear equation describes a line with a y-intercept of $(0, 2)$ and a slope of -2.

To graph the quadratic equation, we can first find the vertex of the parabola: the x-coordinate of the vertex is $h = -\frac{b}{2a} = -\frac{4}{2(-2)} = 1$, and the y coordinate is $k = -2(1)^2 + 4(1) + 2 = 4$. Thus, the vertex lies at $(1, 4)$. To get a feel for the rest of the parabola, we can plug in a few more values of x to find more points; by putting in $x = 2$ and $x = 3$ in the quadratic equation, we find that the points $(2, 2)$ and $(3, -4)$ lie on the parabola; by symmetry thus do $(0, 2)$ and $(-1, -4)$. We can now plot both equations:

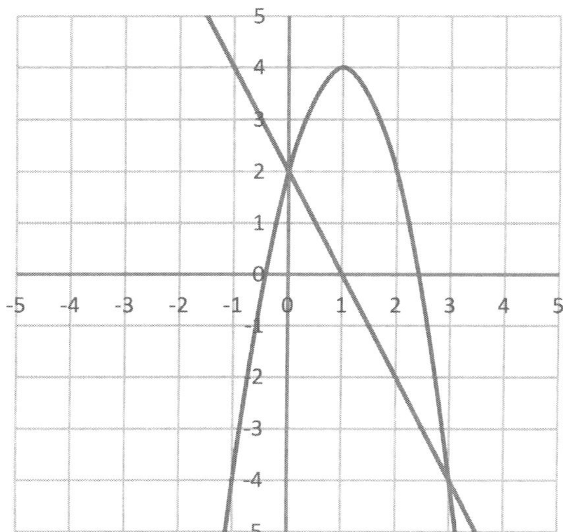

These two curves intersect at the points $(0, 2)$ and $(3, -4)$, thus these are the solutions of the equation.

Polynomial Algebra

To multiply two binomials, follow the **FOIL** method. FOIL stands for:

- First: Multiply the first term of each binomial
- Outer: Multiply the outer terms of each binomial
- Inner: Multiply the inner terms of each binomial
- Last: Multiply the last term of each binomial

Using FOIL $(Ax + By)(Cx + Dy) = ACx^2 + ADxy + BCxy + BDy^2$.

Example

Use the FOIL method on binomials $(x + 2)$ and $(x - 3)$.

$$\text{First: } (x + 2)(x - 3) = (x)(x) = x^2$$

$$\text{Outer: } (x + 2)\ (x - 3) = (x)(-3) = -3x$$

$$\text{Inner: } (x + 2)\ (x - 3) = (2)(x) = 2x$$

$$\text{Last: } (\text{x} + 2)(\text{x} - 3) = (2)(-3) = -6$$

Combine like Terms:

$$(x^2) + (-3x) + (2x) + (-6) = x^2 - x - 6$$

Review Video: Multiplying Terms Using the FOIL Method
Visit mometrix.com/academy and enter code: 854792

To divide polynomials, begin by arranging the terms of each polynomial in order of one variable. You may arrange in ascending or descending order, but make sure to be consistent with both polynomials. To get the first term of the quotient, divide the first term of the dividend by the first term of the divisor. Multiply the first term of the quotient by the entire divisor and subtract that product from the dividend. Repeat for the second and successive terms until you either get a remainder of zero or a remainder whose degree is less than the degree of the divisor. If the quotient has a remainder, write the answer as a mixed expression in the form: quotient $+ \frac{\text{remainder}}{\text{divisor}}$.

Rational expressions are fractions with polynomials in both the numerator and the denominator; the value of the polynomial in the denominator cannot be equal to zero. To add or subtract rational expressions, first find the common denominator, then rewrite each fraction as an equivalent fraction with the common denominator. Finally, add or subtract the numerators to get the numerator of the answer, and keep the common denominator as the denominator of the answer. When multiplying rational expressions factor each polynomial and cancel like factors (a factor which appears in both the numerator and the denominator). Then, multiply all remaining factors in the numerator to get the numerator of the product, and multiply the remaining factors in the denominator to get the denominator of the product. Remember – cancel entire factors, not individual terms. To divide rational expressions, take the reciprocal of the divisor (the rational expression you are dividing by) and multiply by the dividend.

Review Video: Simplifying Rational Polynomial Functions
Visit mometrix.com/academy and enter code: 351038

Below are patterns of some special products to remember: *perfect trinomial squares*, the *difference between two squares*, the *sum and difference of two cubes*, and *perfect cubes*.

- Perfect trinomial squares: $x^2 + 2xy + y^2 = (x + y)^2$ or $x^2 - 2xy + y^2 = (x - y)^2$
- Difference between two squares: $x^2 - y^2 = (x + y)(x - y)$
- Sum of two cubes: $x^3 + y^3 = (x + y)(x^2 - xy + y^2)$
- Note: the second factor is *not* the same as a perfect trinomial square, so do not try to factor it further.
- Difference between two cubes: $x^3 - y^3 = (x - y)(x^2 + xy + y^2)$
- Again, the second factor is *not* the same as a perfect trinomial square.
- Perfect cubes: $x^3 + 3x^2y + 3xy^2 + y^3 = (x + y)^3$ and $x^3 - 3x^2y + 3xy^2 - y^3 = (x - y)^3$

In order to **factor a polynomial**, first check for a common monomial factor. When the greatest common monomial factor has been factored out, look for patterns of special products: differences of two squares, the sum or difference of two cubes for binomial factors, or perfect trinomial squares for trinomial factors. If the factor is a trinomial but not a perfect trinomial square, look for a factorable form, such as $x^2 + (a + b)x + ab = (x + a)(x + b)$ or $(ac)x^2 + (ad + bc)x + bd = (ax + b)(cx + d)$. For factors with four terms, look for groups to factor. Once you have found the factors, write the original polynomial as the product of all the factors. Make sure all of the polynomial factors are prime. Monomial factors may be prime or composite. Check your work by multiplying the factors to make sure you get the original polynomial.

Solving Quadratic Equations

The **quadratic formula** is used to solve quadratic equations when other methods are more difficult. To use the quadratic formula to solve a quadratic equation, begin by rewriting the equation in standard form $ax^2 + bx + c = 0$, where a, b, and c are coefficients. Once you have identified the values of the coefficients, substitute those values into the quadratic formula $x = \frac{-b\pm\sqrt{b^2-4ac}}{2a}$. Evaluate the equation and simplify the expression. Again, check each root by substituting into the original equation. In the quadratic formula, the portion of the formula under the radical $(b^2 - 4ac)$ is called the **discriminant**. If the discriminant is zero, there is only one root: $-\frac{b}{2a}$. If the discriminant is positive, there are two different real roots. If the discriminant is negative, there are no real roots.

To solve a quadratic equation by factoring, begin by rewriting the equation in standard form, if necessary. Factor the side with the variable then set each of the factors equal to zero and solve the resulting linear equations. Check your answers by substituting the roots you found into the original equation. If, when writing the equation in standard form, you have an equation in the form $x^2 + c = 0$ or $x^2 - c = 0$, set $x^2 = -c$ or $x^2 = c$ and take the square root of c. If $c = 0$, the only real root is zero. If c is positive, there are two real roots—the positive and negative square root values. If c is negative, there are no real roots because you cannot take the square root of a negative number.

Review Video: Factoring Quadratic Equations
Visit mometrix.com/academy and enter code: 336566

To solve a quadratic equation by **completing the square**, rewrite the equation so that all terms containing the variable are on the left side of the equal sign, and all the constants are on the right side of the equal sign. Make sure the coefficient of the squared term is 1. If there is a coefficient with the squared term, divide each term on both sides of the equal side by that number. Next, work with the coefficient of the single-variable term. Square half of this coefficient and add that value to both sides. Now you can factor the left side (the side containing the variable) as the square of a binomial. $x^2 + 2ax + a^2 = C \Rightarrow (x + a)^2 = C$, where x is the variable, and a and C are constants. Take the square root of both sides and solve for the variable. Substitute the value of the variable in the original problem to check your work.

Quadratic Function

A *quadratic function* is a function in the form $y = ax^2 + bx + c$, where a does not equal 0. While a linear function forms a line, a quadratic function forms a **parabola**, which is a u-shaped figure that either opens upward or downward. A parabola that opens upward is said to be a **positive quadratic function** and a parabola that opens downward is said to be a **negative quadratic function**. The shape of a parabola can differ, depending on the values of a, b, and c. All parabolas contain a **vertex**, which is the highest possible point, the **maximum**, or the lowest possible point, the **minimum**. This is the point where the graph begins moving in the opposite direction. A quadratic function can have zero, one, or two solutions, and therefore, zero, one, or two x-intercepts. Recall that the x-intercepts are referred to as the zeros, or roots, of a function. A quadratic function will have only one y-intercept. Understanding the basic components of a quadratic function can give you an idea of the shape of its graph.

Example graph of a positive quadratic function:

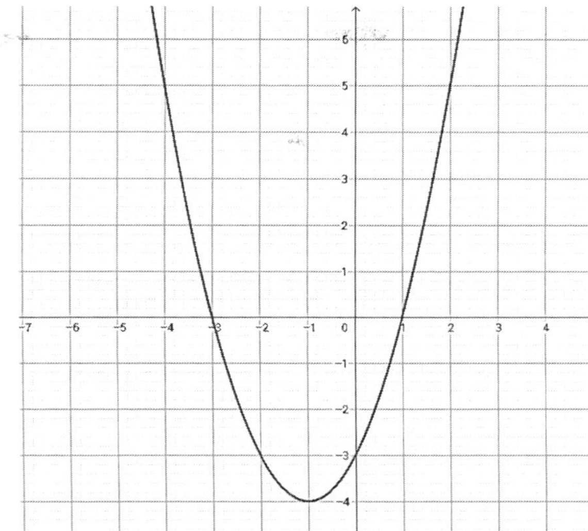

Simplifying Polynomial Expressions

A polynomial is a group of monomials added or subtracted together. Simplifying polynomials requires combining like terms. The like terms in a polynomial expression are those that have the same variable raised to the same power. It is often helpful to connect the like terms with arrows or lines in order to separate them from the other monomials. Once you have determined the like terms, you can rearrange the polynomial by placing them together. Remember to include the sign that is in front of each term. Once the like terms are placed together, you can apply each operation and simplify. When adding and subtracting polynomials, only add and subtract the **coefficient**, or the number part; the variable and exponent stay the same.

Position of Parabola

A **quadratic function** is written in the form $y = ax^2 + bx + c$. Changing the leading coefficient, *a,* in the equation changes the direction of the parabola. If the value of a is **positive**, the graph opens upward. The vertex of this parabola is the **minimum** value of the graph. If the value of a is **negative**, the graph opens downward. The vertex of this parabola is the **maximum** value of the graph. The leading coefficient, a, also affects the width of the parabola. The closer a is to 0, the wider the parabola will be. The values of b and c both affect the position of the parabola on the graph. The effect from changing b depends on the sign of a. If a is negative, increasing the value of b moves the parabola to the right and decreasing the value of b moves it to the left. If a is positive, changes to b have the opposite effect. The value of c in the quadratic equation represents the y-intercept and therefore, moves the parabola up and down the y-axis. The larger the c-value, the higher the parabola is on the graph.

Finding Roots

Find the roots of $y = x^2 + 6x - 16$ and explain why these values are important.

The **roots** of a quadratic equation are the solutions when $ax^2 + bx + c = 0$. To find the roots of a quadratic equation, first replace y with 0. If $0 = x^2 + 6x - 16$, then to find the values of x, you can factor the equation if possible. When factoring a quadratic equation where $a = 1$, find the factors of c that add up to b. That is the factors of -16 that add up to 6. The factors of -16 include, -4 and 4,

-8 and 2 and -2 and 8. The factors that add up to equal 6 are -2 and 8. Write these factors as the product of two binomials, $0 = (x - 2)(x + 8)$. You can verify that these are the correct factors by using FOIL to multiply them together. Finally, since these binomials multiply together to equal zero, set them each equal to zero and solve for x. This results in $x - 2 = 0$, which simplifies to $x = 2$ and $x + 8 = 0$, which simplifies to $x = -8$. Therefore, the roots of the equation are 2 and -8. These values are important because they tell you where the graph of the equation crosses the x-axis. The points of intersection are $(2, 0)$ and $(-8, 0)$.

Review Video: Finding the Missing Roots
Visit mometrix.com/academy and enter code: 198376

Solving Quadratic Equations

Methods

One way to find the solution or solutions of a quadratic equation is to use its **graph**. The solution(s) of a quadratic equation are the values of x when $y = 0$. On the graph, $y = 0$ is where the parabola crosses the x-axis, or the x-intercepts. This is also referred to as the **roots**, or zeros of a function. Given a graph, you can locate the x-intercepts to find the solutions. If there are no x-intercepts, the function has no solution. If the parabola crosses the x-axis at one point, there is one solution and if it crosses at two points, there are two solutions. Since the solutions exist where $y = 0$, you can also solve the equation by substituting 0 in for y. Then, try factoring the equation by finding the factors of ac that add up to equal b. You can use the guess and check method, the box method, or grouping. Once you find a pair that works, write them as the product of two binomials and set them equal to zero. Finally, solve for x to find the solutions. The last way to solve a quadratic equation is to use the **quadratic formula**. The quadratic formula is $x = \frac{-b\pm\sqrt{b^2-4ac}}{2a}$. Substitute the values of a, b, and c into the formula and solve for x. Remember that ± refers to two different solutions. Always check your solutions with the original equation to make sure they are valid.

Example

List the steps used in solving $y = 2x^2 + 8x + 4$.

First, substitute 0 in for y in the quadratic equation:

$$0 = 2x^2 + 8x + 4$$

Next, try to factor the quadratic equation. If $a \neq 1$, list the factors of ac, or 8:

$$(1, 8), (-1, -8), (2, 4), (-2, -4)$$

Look for the factors of ac that add up to b, or 8. Since none do, the equation cannot be factored with whole numbers. Substitute the values of a, b, and c into the quadratic formula, $x = \frac{-b\pm\sqrt{b^2-4ac}}{2a}$:

$$x = \frac{-8 \pm \sqrt{8^2 - 4(2)(4)}}{2(2)}$$

Use the order of operations to simplify:

$$x = \frac{-8 \pm \sqrt{64 - 32}}{4}$$

$$x = \frac{-8 \pm \sqrt{32}}{4}$$

Reduce and simplify:

$$x = \frac{-8 \pm \sqrt{(16)(2)}}{4}$$

$$x = \frac{-8 \pm 4\sqrt{2}}{4}$$

$$x = -2 \pm \sqrt{2}$$

$$x = -2 + \sqrt{2} \text{ and } x = -2 - \sqrt{2}$$

Check both solutions with the original equation to make sure they are valid.

Simplify the square roots and round to two decimal places.

$$x = -3.41 \text{ and } x = -0.586$$

Laws of Exponents

Multiply $(2x^4)^2(xy)^4 \cdot 4y^3$ using the **laws of exponents**.

According the order of operations, the first step in simplifying expressions is to evaluate within the parentheses. Moving from left to right, the first set of parentheses contains a power raised to a power. The rules of exponents state that when a power is raised to a power, you *multiply* the exponents. Since $4 \times 2 = 8$, $(2x^4)^2$ can be written as $4x^8$. The second set of parentheses raises a product to a power. The **rules of exponents** state that you raise every value within the parentheses to the given power. Therefore, $(xy)^4$ can be written as x^4y^4. Combining these terms with the last term gives you, $4x^8 \cdot x^4y^4 \cdot 4y^3$. In this expression, there are powers with the same base. The rules of exponents state that you *add* powers with the same base, while multiplying the coefficients. You can group the expression as $(4x^8 \cdot x^4) \cdot (y^4 \cdot 4y^3)$ to organize the values with the same base. Then, using this rule add the exponents. The result is $4x^{12} \cdot 4y^7$, or $16x^{12}y^7$.

Review Video: Laws of Exponents
Visit mometrix.com/academy and enter code: 532558

Using Given Roots to Find Quadratic Equation

Example
Find a quadratic equation whose real roots are $x = 2$ and $x = -1$.

One way to find the roots of a quadratic equation is to factor the equation and use the **zero product property**, setting each factor of the equation equal to zero to find the corresponding root. We can use this technique in reverse to find an equation given its roots. Each root corresponds to a linear equation which in turn corresponds to a factor of the quadratic equation.

For example, the root $x=2$ corresponds to the equation $x - 2 = 0$, and the root $x = -1$ corresponds to the equation $x + 1 = 0$.

These two equations correspond to the factors $(x - 2)$ and $(x+1)$, from which we can derive the equation $(x - 2)(x + 1) = 0$, or $x^2 - x - 2 = 0$.

Any integer multiple of this entire equation will also yield the same roots, as the integer will simply cancel out when the equation is factored. For example, $2x^2 - 2x - 4 = 0$ factors as

$2(x - 2)(x + 1) = 0$.

Simplifying Rational Expressions

To *simplify a rational expression*, factor the numerator and denominator completely. Factors that are the same and appear in the numerator and denominator have a ratio of 1. The denominator, $(1 - x^2)$, is a difference of squares. It can be factored as $(1 - x)(1 + x)$. The factor $1 - x$ and the numerator $x - 1$ are opposites and have a ratio of -1. Rewrite the numerator as $-1(1 - x)$. So, the rational expression can be simplified as follows:

$$\frac{x - 1}{1 - x^2} = \frac{-1(1 - x)}{(1 - x)(1 + x)} = \frac{-1}{1 + x}$$

(Note that since the original expression is defined for $x \neq \{-1,1\}$, the simplified expression has the same restrictions.)

Review Video: Reducing Rational Expressions
Visit mometrix.com/academy and enter code: 788868

Matrix Basics

A **matrix** (plural: matrices) is a rectangular array of numbers or variables, often called **elements**, which are arranged in columns and rows. A matrix is generally represented by a capital letter, with its elements represented by the corresponding lowercase letter with two subscripts indicating the row and column of the element. For example, n_{ab} represents the element in row a column b of matrix N.

$$N = \begin{bmatrix} n_{11} & n_{12} & n_{13} \\ n_{21} & n_{22} & n_{23} \end{bmatrix}$$

A matrix can be described in terms of the number of rows and columns it contains in the format $a \times b$, where a is the number of rows and b is the number of columns. The matrix shown above is a 2×3 matrix. Any $a \times b$ matrix where $a = b$ is a square matrix. A **vector** is a matrix that has exactly one column (**column vector**) or exactly one row (**row vector**).

The **main diagonal** of a matrix is the set of elements on the diagonal from the top left to the bottom right of a matrix. Because of the way it is defined, only square matrices will have a main diagonal. For the matrix shown below, the main diagonal consists of the elements $n_{11}, n_{22}, n_{33}, n_{44}$.

$$\begin{bmatrix} n_{11} & n_{12} & n_{13} & n_{14} \\ n_{21} & n_{22} & n_{23} & n_{24} \\ n_{31} & n_{32} & n_{33} & n_{34} \\ n_{41} & n_{42} & n_{43} & n_{44} \end{bmatrix}$$

A 3×4 matrix such as the one shown below would not have a main diagonal because there is no straight line of elements between the top left corner and the bottom right corner that joins the elements.

$$\begin{bmatrix} n_{11} & n_{12} & n_{13} & n_{14} \\ n_{21} & n_{22} & n_{23} & n_{24} \\ n_{31} & n_{32} & n_{33} & n_{34} \end{bmatrix}$$

A **diagonal matrix** is a square matrix that has a zero for every element in the matrix except the elements on the main diagonal. All the elements on the main diagonal must be nonzero numbers.

$$\begin{bmatrix} n_{11} & 0 & 0 & 0 \\ 0 & n_{22} & 0 & 0 \\ 0 & 0 & n_{33} & 0 \\ 0 & 0 & 0 & n_{44} \end{bmatrix}$$

If every element on the main diagonal of a diagonal matrix is equal to one, the matrix is called an **identity matrix**. The identity matrix is often represented by the letter *I*.

$$I = \begin{bmatrix} 1 & 0 & 0 & 0 \\ 0 & 1 & 0 & 0 \\ 0 & 0 & 1 & 0 \\ 0 & 0 & 0 & 1 \end{bmatrix}$$

A **zero matrix** is a matrix that has zero as the value for every element in the matrix.

$$\begin{bmatrix} 0 & 0 & 0 & 0 \\ 0 & 0 & 0 & 0 \\ 0 & 0 & 0 & 0 \\ 0 & 0 & 0 & 0 \end{bmatrix}$$

The zero matrix is the *identity for matrix addition*. Do not confuse the zero matrix with the identity matrix.

The **negative of a matrix** is also known as the additive inverse of a matrix. If matrix *N* is the given matrix, then matrix $-N$ is its negative. This means that every element n_{ab} is equal to $-n_{ab}$ in the negative. To find the negative of a given matrix, change the sign of every element in the matrix and keep all elements in their original corresponding positions in the matrix.

If two matrices have the same order and all corresponding elements in the two matrices are the same, then the two matrices are **equal matrices**.

A matrix N may be **transposed** to matrix N^T by changing all rows into columns and changing all columns into rows. The easiest way to accomplish this is to swap the positions of the row and column notations for each element. For example, suppose the element in the second row of the third column of matrix N is $n_{23} = 6$. In the transposed matrix N^T, the transposed element would be $n_{32} = 6$, and it would be placed in the third row of the second column.

$$N = \begin{bmatrix} 1 & 2 & 3 \\ 4 & 5 & 6 \end{bmatrix}; \; N^T = \begin{bmatrix} 1 & 4 \\ 2 & 5 \\ 3 & 6 \end{bmatrix}$$

To quickly transpose a matrix by hand, begin with the first column and rewrite a new matrix with those same elements in the same order in the first row. Write the elements from the second column of the original matrix in the second row of the transposed matrix. Continue this process until all columns have been completed. If the original matrix is identical to the transposed matrix, the matrices are symmetric.

The **determinant** of a matrix is a scalar value that is calculated by taking into account all the elements of a square matrix. A determinant only exists for square matrices. Finding the determinant of a 2×2 matrix is as simple as remembering a simple equation. For a 2×2 matrix $M = \begin{bmatrix} m_{11} & m_{12} \\ m_{21} & m_{22} \end{bmatrix}$, the determinant is obtained by the equation $|M| = m_{11}m_{22} - m_{12}m_{21}$. Anything larger than 2×2 requires multiple steps. Take matrix $N = \begin{bmatrix} a & b & c \\ d & e & f \\ g & h & j \end{bmatrix}$. The determinant of N is calculated as $|N| = a\begin{vmatrix} e & f \\ h & j \end{vmatrix} - b\begin{vmatrix} d & f \\ g & j \end{vmatrix} + c\begin{vmatrix} d & e \\ g & h \end{vmatrix}$ or $|N| = a(ej - fh) - b(dj - fg) + c(dh - eg)$.

There is a shortcut for 3×3 matrices: add the products of each unique set of elements diagonally left-to-right and subtract the products of each unique set of elements diagonally right-to-left. In matrix N, the left-to-right diagonal elements are (a, e, j), (b, f, g), and (c, d, h). The right-to-left diagonal elements are (a, f, h), (b, d, j), and (c, e, g). $\det(N) = aej + bfg + cdh - afh - bdj - ceg$.

Calculating the determinants of matrices larger than 3×3 is rarely, if ever, done by hand.

The **inverse** of a matrix M is the matrix that, when multiplied by matrix M, yields a product that is the identity matrix. Multiplication of matrices will be explained in greater detail shortly. Not all matrices have inverses. Only a square matrix whose determinant is not zero has an inverse. If a matrix has an inverse, that inverse is unique to that matrix. For any matrix M that has an inverse, the inverse is represented by the symbol M^{-1}. To calculate the inverse of a 2×2 square matrix, use the following pattern:

$$M = \begin{bmatrix} m_{11} & m_{12} \\ m_{21} & m_{22} \end{bmatrix}; \; M^{-1} = \begin{bmatrix} \frac{m_{22}}{|M|} & \frac{-m_{12}}{|M|} \\ \frac{-m_{21}}{|M|} & \frac{m_{11}}{|M|} \end{bmatrix}$$

Another way to find the inverse of a matrix by hand is use an augmented matrix and elementary row operations. An **augmented matrix** is formed by appending the entries from one matrix onto the end of another. For example, given a 2×2 invertible matrix $N = \begin{bmatrix} a & b \\ c & d \end{bmatrix}$, you can find the inverse N^{-1} by creating an augmented matrix by appending a 2×2 identity matrix: $\left[\begin{array}{cc|cc} a & b & 1 & 0 \\ c & d & 0 & 1 \end{array}\right]$.

To find the inverse of the original 2×2 matrix, perform elementary row operations to convert the original matrix on the left to an identity matrix: $\left[\begin{matrix}1 & 0\\0 & 1\end{matrix}\middle|\begin{matrix}e & f\\g & h\end{matrix}\right]$.

Elementary row operations include multiplying a row by a non-zero scalar, adding scalar multiples of two rows, or some combination of these. For instance, the first step might be to multiply the second row by $\frac{b}{d}$ and then subtract it from the first row to make its second column a zero. The end result is that the 2×2 section on the right will become the inverse of the original matrix: $N^{-1} = \begin{bmatrix} e & f \\ g & h \end{bmatrix}$.

Calculating the inverse of any matrix larger than 2×2 is cumbersome and using a graphing calculator is recommended.

Basic Operations with Matrices

There are two categories of basic operations with regard to matrices: operations between a matrix and a scalar, and operations between two matrices.

Scalar Operations

A scalar being added to a matrix is treated as though it were being added to each element of the matrix:

$$M + 4 = \begin{bmatrix} m_{11} + 4 & m_{12} + 4 \\ m_{21} + 4 & m_{22} + 4 \end{bmatrix}$$

The same is true for the other three operations.

Subtraction:

$$M - 4 = \begin{bmatrix} m_{11} - 4 & m_{12} - 4 \\ m_{21} - 4 & m_{22} - 4 \end{bmatrix}$$

Multiplication:

$$M \times 4 = \begin{bmatrix} m_{11} \times 4 & m_{12} \times 4 \\ m_{21} \times 4 & m_{22} \times 4 \end{bmatrix}$$

Division:

$$M \div 4 = \begin{bmatrix} m_{11} \div 4 & m_{12} \div 4 \\ m_{21} \div 4 & m_{22} \div 4 \end{bmatrix}$$

Matrix Addition and Subtraction

All four of the basic operations can be used with operations between matrices (although division is usually discarded in favor of multiplication by the inverse), but there are restrictions on the situations in which they can be used. Matrices that meet all the qualifications for a given operation are called **conformable matrices**. However, conformability is specific to the operation; two matrices that are conformable for addition are not necessarily conformable for multiplication.

For two matrices to be conformable for addition or subtraction, they must be of the same dimension; otherwise the operation is not defined. If matrix M is a 3×2 matrix and matrix N is a

2×3 matrix, the operations $M + N$ and $M - N$ are meaningless. If matrices M and N are the same size, the operation is as simple as adding or subtracting all of the corresponding elements:

$$\begin{bmatrix} m_{11} & m_{12} \\ m_{21} & m_{22} \end{bmatrix} + \begin{bmatrix} n_{11} & n_{12} \\ n_{21} & n_{22} \end{bmatrix} = \begin{bmatrix} m_{11} + n_{11} & m_{12} + n_{12} \\ m_{21} + n_{21} & m_{22} + n_{22} \end{bmatrix}$$

$$\begin{bmatrix} m_{11} & m_{12} \\ m_{21} & m_{22} \end{bmatrix} - \begin{bmatrix} n_{11} & n_{12} \\ n_{21} & n_{22} \end{bmatrix} = \begin{bmatrix} m_{11} - n_{11} & m_{12} - n_{12} \\ m_{21} - n_{21} & m_{22} - n_{22} \end{bmatrix}$$

The result of addition or subtraction is a matrix of the same dimension as the two original matrices involved in the operation.

Matrix Multiplication

The first thing it is necessary to understand about matrix multiplication is that it is not commutative. In scalar multiplication, the operation is commutative, meaning that $a \times b = b \times a$. For matrix multiplication, this is not the case: $A \times B \neq B \times A$. The terminology must be specific when describing matrix multiplication. The operation $A \times B$ can be described as A multiplied (or **post-multiplied**) by B, or B **pre-multiplied** by A.

For two matrices to be conformable for multiplication, they need not be of the same dimension, but specific dimensions must correspond. Taking the example of two matrices M and N to be multiplied $M \times N$, matrix M must have the same number of columns as matrix N has rows. Put another way, if matrix M has the dimensions $a \times b$ and matrix N has the dimensions $c \times d$, b must equal c if the two matrices are to be conformable for this multiplication. The matrix that results from the multiplication will have the dimensions $a \times d$. If a and d are both equal to 1, the product is simply a scalar. Square matrices of the same dimensions are always conformable for multiplication, and their product is always a matrix of the same size.

The simplest type of matrix multiplication is a 1×2 matrix (a row vector) times a 2×1 matrix (a column vector). These will multiply in the following way:

$$\begin{bmatrix} m_{11} & m_{12} \end{bmatrix} \times \begin{bmatrix} n_{11} \\ n_{21} \end{bmatrix} = m_{11}n_{11} + m_{12}n_{21}$$

The two matrices are conformable for multiplication because matrix M has the same number of columns as matrix N has rows. Because the other dimensions are both 1, the result is a scalar. Expanding our matrices to 1×3 and 3×1, the process is the same:

$$\begin{bmatrix} m_{11} & m_{12} & m_{13} \end{bmatrix} \times \begin{bmatrix} n_{11} \\ n_{21} \\ n_{31} \end{bmatrix} = m_{11}n_{11} + m_{12}n_{21} + m_{13}n_{31}$$

Once again, the result is a scalar. This type of basic matrix multiplication is the building block for the multiplication of larger matrices.

To multiply larger matrices, treat each **row from the first matrix** and each **column from the second matrix** as individual vectors and follow the pattern for multiplying vectors. The scalar value found from multiplying the first-row vector by the first column vector is placed in the first row, first column of the new matrix. The scalar value found from multiplying the second-row vector by the first column vector is placed in the second row, first column of the new matrix. Continue this pattern until each row of the first matrix has been multiplied by each column of the second vector.

Below is an example of the multiplication of a 3×2 matrix and a 2×3 matrix.

$$\begin{bmatrix} m_{11} & m_{12} \\ m_{21} & m_{22} \\ m_{31} & m_{32} \end{bmatrix} \times \begin{bmatrix} n_{11} & n_{12} & n_{13} \\ n_{21} & n_{22} & n_{23} \end{bmatrix} = \begin{bmatrix} m_{11}n_{11} + m_{12}n_{21} & m_{11}n_{12} + m_{12}n_{22} & m_{11}n_{13} + m_{12}n_{23} \\ m_{21}n_{11} + m_{22}n_{21} & m_{21}n_{12} + m_{22}n_{22} & m_{21}n_{13} + m_{22}n_{23} \\ m_{31}n_{11} + m_{32}n_{21} & m_{31}n_{12} + m_{32}n_{22} & m_{31}n_{13} + m_{32}n_{23} \end{bmatrix}$$

This process starts by taking the first column of the second matrix and running it through each row of the first matrix. Removing all but the first M row and first N column, we would see only the following:

$$\begin{bmatrix} m_{11} & m_{12} \end{bmatrix} \times \begin{bmatrix} n_{11} \\ n_{21} \end{bmatrix}$$

The first product would then be $m_{11}n_{11} + m_{12}n_{21}$. This process will be continued for each column of the N matrix to find the first full row of the product matrix, as shown below.

$$\begin{bmatrix} m_{11} & m_{12} \end{bmatrix} \times \begin{bmatrix} n_{11} \\ n_{21} \end{bmatrix} = \begin{bmatrix} m_{11}n_{11} + m_{12}n_{21} & m_{11}n_{12} + m_{12}n_{22} & m_{11}n_{13} + m_{12}n_{23} \end{bmatrix}$$

After completing the first row, the next step would be to simply move to the second row of the M matrix and repeat the process until all of the rows have been finished. The result is a 3×3 matrix.

$$\begin{bmatrix} m_{11} & m_{12} \\ m_{21} & m_{22} \\ m_{31} & m_{32} \end{bmatrix} \times \begin{bmatrix} n_{11} & n_{12} & n_{13} \\ n_{21} & n_{22} & n_{23} \end{bmatrix} = \begin{bmatrix} m_{11}n_{11} + m_{12}n_{21} & m_{11}n_{12} + m_{12}n_{22} & m_{11}n_{13} + m_{12}n_{23} \\ m_{21}n_{11} + m_{22}n_{21} & m_{21}n_{12} + m_{22}n_{22} & m_{21}n_{13} + m_{22}n_{23} \\ m_{31}n_{11} + m_{32}n_{21} & m_{31}n_{12} + m_{32}n_{22} & m_{31}n_{13} + m_{32}n_{23} \end{bmatrix}$$

If the operation were done in reverse ($N \times M$), the result would be a 2×2 matrix.

$$\begin{bmatrix} n_{11} & n_{12} & n_{13} \\ n_{21} & n_{22} & n_{23} \end{bmatrix} \times \begin{bmatrix} m_{11} & m_{12} \\ m_{21} & m_{22} \\ m_{31} & m_{32} \end{bmatrix} = \begin{bmatrix} m_{11}n_{11} + m_{21}n_{12} + m_{31}n_{13} & m_{12}n_{11} + m_{22}n_{12} + m_{32}n_{13} \\ m_{11}n_{21} + m_{21}n_{22} + m_{31}n_{23} & m_{12}n_{21} + m_{22}n_{22} + m_{32}n_{23} \end{bmatrix}$$

<u>Example</u>

A sporting-goods store sells baseballs, volleyballs, and basketballs.

Baseballs	\$3 each
Volleyballs	\$8 each
Basketballs	\$15 each

Here are the same store's sales numbers for one weekend:

	Baseballs	Volleyballs	Basketballs
Friday	5	4	4
Saturday	7	3	10
Sunday	4	3	6

Find the total sales for each day by multiplying matrices.

The first table can be represented by the following column-vector:

$$\begin{bmatrix} 3 \\ 8 \\ 15 \end{bmatrix}$$

And the second table can be represented by this matrix:

$$\begin{bmatrix} 5 & 4 & 4 \\ 7 & 3 & 10 \\ 4 & 3 & 6 \end{bmatrix}$$

Multiplying the second matrix by the first will result in a column vector showing the total sales for each day:

$$\begin{bmatrix} 5 & 4 & 4 \\ 7 & 3 & 10 \\ 4 & 3 & 6 \end{bmatrix} \times \begin{bmatrix} 3 \\ 8 \\ 15 \end{bmatrix} = \begin{bmatrix} 3 \times 5 + 8 \times 4 + 15 \times 4 \\ 3 \times 7 + 8 \times 3 + 15 \times 10 \\ 3 \times 4 + 8 \times 3 + 15 \times 6 \end{bmatrix} = \begin{bmatrix} 15 + 32 + 60 \\ 21 + 24 + 150 \\ 12 + 24 + 90 \end{bmatrix} = \begin{bmatrix} 107 \\ 195 \\ 126 \end{bmatrix}$$

From this, we can see that Friday's sales were \$107, Saturday's sales were \$195, and Sunday's sales were \$126.

Solving Systems of Equations

Matrices can be used to represent the coefficients of a system of linear equations and can be very useful in solving those systems. Take for instance three equations with three variables:

$$a_1x + b_1y + c_1z = d_1$$

$$a_2x + b_2y + c_2z = d_2$$

$$a_3x + b_3y + c_3z = d_3$$

where all a, b, c, and d are known constants.

To solve this system, define three matrices:

$$A = \begin{bmatrix} a_1 & b_1 & c_1 \\ a_2 & b_2 & c_2 \\ a_3 & b_3 & c_3 \end{bmatrix};\ D = \begin{bmatrix} d_1 \\ d_2 \\ d_3 \end{bmatrix};\ X = \begin{bmatrix} x \\ y \\ z \end{bmatrix}$$

The three equations in our system can be fully represented by a single matrix equation:

$$AX = D$$

We know that the identity matrix times X is equal to X, and we know that any matrix multiplied by its inverse is equal to the identity matrix.

$$A^{-1}AX = IX = X; \text{thus } X = A^{-1}D$$

Our goal then is to find the inverse of A, or A^{-1}. Once we have that, we can pre-multiply matrix D by A^{-1} (post-multiplying here is an undefined operation) to find matrix X.

Systems of equations can also be solved using the transformation of an augmented matrix in a process similar to that for finding a matrix inverse. Begin by arranging each equation of the system in the following format:

$$a_1x + b_1y + c_1z = d_1$$

$$a_2x + b_2y + c_2z = d_2$$

$$a_3x + b_3y + c_3z = d_3$$

Define matrices A and D and combine them into augmented matrix A_a:

$$A = \begin{bmatrix} a_1 & b_1 & c_1 \\ a_2 & b_2 & c_2 \\ a_3 & b_3 & c_3 \end{bmatrix};\ D = \begin{bmatrix} d_1 \\ d_2 \\ d_3 \end{bmatrix};A_a = \begin{bmatrix} a_1 & b_1 & c_1 & d_1 \\ a_2 & b_2 & c_2 & d_2 \\ a_3 & b_3 & c_3 & d_3 \end{bmatrix}$$

To solve the augmented matrix and the system of equations, use elementary row operations to form an identity matrix in the first 3×3 section. When this is complete, the values in the last column are the solutions to the system of equations:

$$\begin{bmatrix} 1 & 0 & 0 & x \\ 0 & 1 & 0 & y \\ 0 & 0 & 1 & z \end{bmatrix}$$

If an identity matrix is not possible, the system of equations has no unique solution. Sometimes only a partial solution will be possible. The following are partial solutions you may find:

$\begin{bmatrix} 1 & 0 & k_1 & x_0 \\ 0 & 1 & k_2 & y_0 \\ 0 & 0 & 0 & 0 \end{bmatrix}$ gives the non-unique solution $x = x_0 - k_1z;\ y = y_0 - k_2z$

$\begin{bmatrix} 1 & j_1 & k_1 & x_0 \\ 0 & 0 & 0 & 0 \\ 0 & 0 & 0 & 0 \end{bmatrix}$ gives the non-unique solution $x = x_0 - j_1y - k_1z$

This process can be used to solve systems of equations with any number of variables, but three is the upper limit for practical purposes. Anything more ought to be done with a graphing calculator.

Geometric Transformations

The four *geometric transformations* are **translations**, **reflections**, **rotations**, and **dilations**. When geometric transformations are expressed as matrices, the process of performing the transformations is simplified. For calculations of the geometric transformations of a planar figure, make a $2 \times n$ matrix, where n is the number of vertices in the planar figure. Each column represents the rectangular coordinates of one vertex of the figure, with the top row containing the values of the x-coordinates and the bottom row containing the values of the y-coordinates. For example, given a planar triangular figure with coordinates (x_1, y_1), (x_2, y_2), and (x_3, y_3), the corresponding matrix is $\begin{bmatrix} x_1 & x_2 & x_3 \\ y_1 & y_2 & y_3 \end{bmatrix}$. You can then perform the necessary transformations on this matrix to determine the coordinates of the resulting figure.

Translation

A **translation** moves a figure along the x-axis, the y-axis, or both axes without changing the size or shape of the figure. To calculate the new coordinates of a planar figure following a translation, set up a matrix of the coordinates and a matrix of the translation values and add the two matrices.

$$\begin{bmatrix} h & h & h \\ v & v & v \end{bmatrix} + \begin{bmatrix} x_1 & x_2 & x_3 \\ y_1 & y_2 & y_3 \end{bmatrix} = \begin{bmatrix} h+x_1 & h+x_2 & h+x_3 \\ v+y_1 & v+y_2 & v+y_3 \end{bmatrix}$$

where h is the number of units the figure is moved along the x-axis (horizontally) and v is the number of units the figure is moved along the y-axis (vertically).

Reflection

To find the **reflection** of a planar figure over the x-axis, set up a matrix of the coordinates of the vertices and pre-multiply the matrix by the 2×2 matrix $\begin{bmatrix} 1 & 0 \\ 0 & -1 \end{bmatrix}$ so that $\begin{bmatrix} 1 & 0 \\ 0 & -1 \end{bmatrix} \begin{bmatrix} x_1 & x_2 & x_3 \\ y_1 & y_2 & y_3 \end{bmatrix} = \begin{bmatrix} x_1 & x_2 & x_3 \\ -y_1 & -y_2 & -y_3 \end{bmatrix}$. To find the reflection of a planar figure over the y-axis, set up a matrix of the coordinates of the vertices and pre-multiply the matrix by the 2×2 matrix $\begin{bmatrix} -1 & 0 \\ 0 & 1 \end{bmatrix}$ so that $\begin{bmatrix} -1 & 0 \\ 0 & 1 \end{bmatrix} \begin{bmatrix} x_1 & x_2 & x_3 \\ y_1 & y_2 & y_3 \end{bmatrix} = \begin{bmatrix} -x_1 & -x_2 & -x_3 \\ y_1 & y_2 & y_3 \end{bmatrix}$. To find the reflection of a planar figure over the line $y = x$, set up a matrix of the coordinates of the vertices and pre-multiply the matrix by the 2×2 matrix $\begin{bmatrix} 0 & 1 \\ 1 & 0 \end{bmatrix}$ so that $\begin{bmatrix} 0 & 1 \\ 1 & 0 \end{bmatrix} \begin{bmatrix} x_1 & x_2 & x_3 \\ y_1 & y_2 & y_3 \end{bmatrix} = \begin{bmatrix} y_1 & y_2 & y_3 \\ x_1 & x_2 & x_3 \end{bmatrix}$. Remember that the order of multiplication is important when multiplying matrices. The commutative property does not apply.

Rotation

To find the coordinates of the figure formed by rotating a planar figure about the origin θ degrees in a counterclockwise direction, set up a matrix of the coordinates of the vertices and pre-multiply the matrix by the 2×2 matrix $\begin{bmatrix} \cos\theta & \sin\theta \\ -\sin\theta & \cos\theta \end{bmatrix}$. For example, if you want to rotate a figure 90° clockwise around the origin, you would have to convert the degree measure to 270° counterclockwise and solve the 2×2 matrix you have set as the pre-multiplier: $\begin{bmatrix} \cos 270° & \sin 270° \\ -\sin 270° & \cos 270° \end{bmatrix} = \begin{bmatrix} 0 & -1 \\ 1 & 0 \end{bmatrix}$. Use this as the pre-multiplier for the matrix $\begin{bmatrix} x_1 & x_2 & x_3 \\ y_1 & y_2 & y_3 \end{bmatrix}$ and solve to find the new coordinates.

Dilation

To find the **dilation** of a planar figure by a scale factor of k, set up a matrix of the coordinates of the vertices of the planar figure and pre-multiply the matrix by the 2×2 matrix $\begin{bmatrix} k & 0 \\ 0 & k \end{bmatrix}$ so that $\begin{bmatrix} k & 0 \\ 0 & k \end{bmatrix} \begin{bmatrix} x_1 & x_2 & x_3 \\ y_1 & y_2 & y_3 \end{bmatrix} = \begin{bmatrix} kx_1 & kx_2 & kx_3 \\ ky_1 & ky_2 & ky_3 \end{bmatrix}$. This is effectively the same as multiplying the matrix by the scalar k, but the matrix equation would still be necessary if the figure were being dilated by different factors in vertical and horizontal directions. The scale factor k will be greater than 1 if the figure is being enlarged, and between 0 and 1 if the figure is being shrunk. Again, remember that when multiplying matrices, the order of the matrices is important. The commutative property does not apply, and the matrix with the coordinates of the figure must be the second matrix.